200+ Ideas for Drama

200+ IDEAS FOR DRAMA

Anna Scher / Charles Verrall

HEINEMANN
Portsmouth, NH

HEINEMANN EDUCATIONAL BOOKS, INC.
361 Hanover Street   Portsmouth, NH 03801
Offices and agents throughout the world

Library of Congress Cataloging-in-Publication Data
Scher, Anna.
    200 + ideas for drama / Anna Scher, Charles Verrall.
        p.   cm.
    ISBN 0-435-08606-5
    1. Theater—Study and teaching.   I. Verrall, Charles.   II. Title:
    Two hundred plus ideas for drama.
    PN2075.S34   1992
    792'.07—dc20   91-29021
                                                CIP

Printed in the United States of America

92 93 94 95 96 9 8 7 6 5 4 3 2 1

Contents

Travelling Through the Tapestry

It has been a great pleasure and privilege to have been part of the lives of the thousands of children and young people that have passed through the doors of The Anna Scher Theatre (AST), which started life as a school's drama club in 1968.

AST has cast me in a variety of roles—Teacher; Writer; Broadcaster; Agent; Director; Producer; Social Worker; Friend; Fundraiser; Godparent; Honored Guest at weddings, christenings and bar mitzvahs; and even Mourner at funerals.

AST has spilt over into all areas of my life; and, I suppose, AST and AS are kind of interchangeable. In a way, I am a creative catalyst. I feel very fortunate to be doing work that I love and that is so fulfilling; it is a way of life that I wouldn't change for the world.

From Monday through Thursday we run our community theatre sessions. The professional groups meet on a Friday and Saturday. The Young Professionals, or YP's, are selected from the community groups and reviewed each term; the criteria for entry to the YP's are not only based on talent and castability but on The Three A's—attendance, attitude and application. Members need to *earn* their success; successful child actors, like successful child swimmers, need to work at it. Words like 'fame' and 'star' are not used. Heads are kept very firmly on shoulders. Having said that, the professional opportunities in theatre, film, television and radio have given our YP's an education—in the broadest sense of the word—second to none. AST has consistently been strong on the idea of the community and the professional walking hand in hand.

We work on a different Umbrella Theme each term aiming to develop talent and be a supplement to our members' education; those twin aims have been constant since the early days. The Umbrella Theme has provided a most useful way in which to discuss, improvise and make up plays; over the years Umbrella Themes have included such rich and varied subjects as King Arthur and the Knights of the Round Table, People in History, Poetry in Motion, Aesop's Fables, Heroes and Heroines, Mottoes, Issues, Theatre Through the Ages, Favourite Films, Greek Mythology, Shakespeare's Plays, Children's Classics; each session focuses on an aspect of the Umbrella Theme for full group discussion and improvisation.

Every class is topped and tailed with Enter–Exit Music, often classical favourites such as Vivaldi's Four Seasons, or Bizet's March of the Toreadors from *Carmen.* Another AST feature is the 'Winston' word, named after Winston Churchill, who learned a new word every day of his adult life.

As AST's members come in to register they look at the Notice Board and note the day's bill of fare—the EnterExit Music, the Umbrella Theme details, and the Winston word. My own personal favourite Winston word is *sisu,* a Finnish word meaning perseverance, backbone, endurance. We continually encourage our members to be aware, to be perceptive, to *notice.*

Then, *carpe diem!* Seize the day, as Walt Whitman says and we do, we do. Starting with a double body warm-up first a slow and stretchy one, followed by a fast and furious one, we continue with a voice warm-up preceeded by five positive pointers towards good communication—posture, projection, diction, eye contact, and a friendly tone of voice. Thoroughly warmed up in body and voice we're into the Umbrella Theme and it's think-on-your-feet-time; improvisation is the name of the game.

Improvisation has been our staple diet since day one. Improvisation is a marvelous vehicle for self-expression, observation and creativity. Improvisation provides an effective method for finding and developing a character. Improvisation can address issues such as racism, sexism and ageism head on. Improvisation provides a springboard for hundreds of ideas. These ideas have always been recorded not just for posterity's sake but for sharing with those working in the field here and now. Improvisation is thought-provoking, stimulating, entertaining and educative.

I like the session to end on a high note. So for the finale I might include a piece of poetry, a few choice *bon mots,* or perhaps a piece of pocket philosophy such as was passed on to me by a local actor, David King, some years back: all actors should have The Three Hums—humanity, humility and humour! Then on with the Enter–Exit Music as they travel through the tapestry.

AST, a staunch supporter of equality and civil rights, is well known for flying the flag for fairness, which for me is what feminism is about. As a teacher I do my best to impart and share knowledge so my pupils can be empowered to make careful choices and well-thought-through decisions and lead independent lives—that they themselves will be in control of in the future—their future.

'Simple is good' said Jim Henson, and I agree whole-heartedly. Keep it simple and keep it positive. Here are my own simple and positive five priorities that are worth putting time and effort into:

WORK, RELATIONSHIPS, HOME, ORGANISATION, FINANCE

I have found that being in control of these five priorities gives me the security and satisfaction I need in order to thrive rather than just survive. I want my pupils to thrive rather than just survive. I value my pupils and want them to value themselves as well as each other. I ask them what they want out of life. I ask them to listen to themselves, visualise what it is they want and focus on it. Work at it. Earn it.

I try to live—and teach—by my principles, principles like telling the truth; being open, honest, and receptive; keeping in touch with reality; sharing responsibilities; taking ownership for my words and deeds; equipping myself with life skills; learning from experience and mistakes. If I can instill some of these values into my pupils by building up their confidence and competence, by giving encouragement and praise, by using constructive criticism, by sharing fun and laughter, by teaching them to appreciate one another and respect another's point of view and by giving them space, then the legacy left will be a good one.

Above all, the Anna Scher Theatre celebrates individuality. Black, white, fat, thin, freckled, unfreckled, boy, girl, homosexual, heterosexual, Catholic, Jewish, atheist, agnostic—integration, tolerance and awareness seep through every session.

'We must learn to live together as brothers or perish together as fools.' These words of wisdom came from one of the twentieth century's greatest heroes, the civil rights leader, Dr. Martin Luther King, whose photograph adorns our foyer. He had a dream, and it was a good dream. Speaking as an Irish, Jewish integrationist I would say AST does everything in its power to, as the King Foundation would put it, live the dream.

Next to Dr. Martin Luther King's photograph in our foyer, writ clear and large in black and white, is AST's motto:

TALENT THRIVES ON TRAINING TOGETHER
—Anna Scher

The Invisible Thread

100 + Ideas for Drama was published in 1975. It was the product of seven years' experience in drama teaching and was intended to be a handbook for the busy drama teacher in need of an injection of new ideas. Rereading it now, one is surprised at how little it has dated and how little one would write differently today. One or two of the names of members of our theatre that we cited have become quite famous, many of them remain in touch and are good friends, which is a great reward. Most of the ideas in the book we would still use today, in one way or another.

100 + Ideas for Drama came to be in much demand. People wanted more of the same, and more of something more, as well. So *Another 100 + Ideas for Drama* appeared, with more ideas, and more about how to put them into use, to improvise more deeply, find a theme for several months' work, or mount a production.

After over twenty years of taking part in this strange business of drama—pretending to be what you're not and sometimes finding out what you are in the process—I've begun to understand a little more about what it is we do and why we do it.

We play. Children play and, if we are fortunate, we keep alive the child in us and are able to play, in some way, all our lives. So, we 'play' a musical instrument; a piece of drama is a 'play'; sportsmen and women are 'players'. Play is how children (and young animals) learn. And we are able, through developing forms of constructive play, to give it a greater significance.

Take three seemingly very different but, in my belief, closely linked kinds of activity: the arts, sport, and science.

Artists play in imaginary worlds. Their imaginary worlds

may closely simulate the real world or be distant from it. Consciously or unconsciously, they invent whatever rules they please to govern their worlds. Art is, primarily, the play of the emotions.

Sports players play in a model world. The field of play is a microcosm that derives from the realities of hunting, fighting, or chasing. Rules have been invented to govern each miniature world of sport, and the competitors obey them. Sport is, primarily, the play of the body.

Scientists play in the real world. In order to understand it they create mental and mathematical models of it. They seek to discover rules to describe it. Science is the play of the reasoning mind.

These three different forms of constructive play can be seen to be linked; they all arise out of the human creative urge, which drives us from our first childish stories and games and questions to *The Magic Flute,* the Marathon, and theorems of mathematics. But of the three, the process of artistic creation, because it is the most inward, is ultimately the most mysterious and beyond complete explanation.

Art is like the reflection of a dancer on a darkened window. We half see the dancer, we half see the room behind her, but she seems to be dancing in the shadowy landscape beyond.

So then, where in our psyche does this artistic creativity arise? Surely it is very close to the zone of dreams. Now the first thing to say about dreams is that they are not simply escapist or hallucinatory. In the words of the psychologist Anthony Storr they 'can equally well be regarded... as attempts to come to terms with reality, rather than to escape from it.' Dreams are one of the mechanisms that help us to make sense of the world. We all dream. We all must dream.

Fantasy is the waking cousin of dream. Drama is an actualisation of fantasy. With each piece of drama a new fantasy world is created. Fantasies, being under our conscious control, can easily be inhibited. Hence one of our aims is to free our students from any unnecessary degree of inhibition. We may, at the same time, be setting him or her a strict task, technically. The two do not necessarily run counter to one another. Paradoxically, concentrating on some technical aspect of the exercise can release inhibitions over the content of an improvisation.

Fantasy is spun from the stuff of dreams. Therefore, when we comment on our students' improvisations, we must tread softly, paraphrasing Yeats, for we tread on their dreams. Ask for more or better but, if it comes from the heart, do not reject what they give you. It is because we may expose so much of ourselves in improvisation that it is necessary to hide behind the masks of character. By maintaining the convention that it is a character speaking, rather than us ourselves, we are able to speak through that character and, maybe, lay bare our innermost feelings.

So: artistic creation, though it cannot perhaps be fully explained, is something that we are all capable of, just as we all dream. More than that, it's something that we have a strong urge to do. Look at the graffiti-covered walls of any inner-city housing project—it may be ugly, but it's definitely art. The desire for self-expression arises spontaneously and will find its means of satisfaction willy-nilly. There's a natural pleasure in creating, or witnessing creation. It releases our inner tensions; we learn from it—it is part of our emotional education; it helps us to find meaning in our lives. The ideas in this collection are, in large part, enabling devices for you to use to foster artistic creation in your pupils.

It is not that we do much to develop our students' imagination. It is more that we enable them to use the imagination that is already there. There is no mathematical limit to the number of ideas that one human mind can generate; the only limit is the time available in which to express them (bearing in mind that one also needs to eat, sleep, and do many other things). Further, as the scientist

Richard Feynman says, 'The imagination of man is only a small part of the imagination of nature.'

Imagination is an ocean: one only has to swim in it. No one lacks imagination, just as no one is unable to swim, but some may be prevented from swimming by fear of the water. Similarly, if one has been punished or suffered trauma in the past, he or she may be prevented from letting his or her imagination run free. People can't swim if they are carrying a heavy weight, and those carrying heavy mental burdens need to be relieved of them before they can embark. No one should be thrown in out of their depth; better that they should play in the shallows and, with a good teacher, gradually learn that the waves can be enjoyed rather than feared.

Something I sometimes say to a group of students if they can't think of an idea for a piece of work is, 'OK, don't think of one idea, think of ten ideas.' Then I'll add, 'Don't be afraid of being boring and unoriginal, and don't be afraid of being crazy.' Thus released from the obligation to think of one perfect idea, they will throw in ten 'junk' ideas, from which at least two or three good ones will emerge. Actually, of course, often all ten will be good ideas.

Artistic creativity depends on freedom of expression, subject, of course, to law and custom. One of our responsibilities is to try to maximise the freedom of our students by using our power (which derives from knowledge and respect rather than authority) to create an atmosphere of relaxed concentration in which fresh ideas can bubble to the surface, the diffident can be encouraged, the weak protected, and no one person will become dominant.

I'll always encourage students to 'think big' with an improvisation. Go for the strongest emotion—but that doesn't mean going 'over the top' and losing all subtlety. And 'think deep' as well—not just skimming the surface of a character, but getting deep inside its skin so that one's automatic responses are those of that character and, for those watching, it's as if one could remain in character all night long. It's like the cartoon character who runs off the edge of a cliff: as long as he doesn't look down, he can't fall.

Drama comes out of our imagination and goes into the imagination of the audience. I like to ask the question 'Where does a play happen?' Not on the stage; not in the pages of the script; not in the minds or bodies of the actors. No, the play takes place in the minds of the audience. It's the effect on them that's important; but we can only produce that effect if our minds are engaged too. Put at its lowest, a dramatic performance is a series of psychological tricks to persuade the audience, who willing suspend their disbelief, that a set of imaginary people exist, that their imaginary relationships are real, and that a set of imaginary events are really happening. Actors are skilled deceivers, but their deceptions can reveal the truth about ourselves.

Much is made of drama having emerged from ritual. The human need for ritual can easily be observed as it manifests itself, not only in rites of passage, such as weddings and funerals, but also in parades, on the sports field, at concerts, and in many more, often quite mundane situations—any place where something or someone needs to be designated as being special, or where group identity needs to be reinforced. Even in improvisation rituals develop, as if of their own volition. Different parts of the room acquire their own significance, sets are made up in a particular way, it becomes the custom to walk from behind a certain screen when starting a piece of work. These become valuable landmarks, standing out amongst the changing seas of the work itself. And then from time to time you can be revolutionary, and alter the landscape entirely...

A word about the actual content of drama: the philosopher Joseph Campbell has written about the similarities of myths from all over the ancient world. To him myths are how we find meaning and celebrate the rapture of existence. They are all part of the monomyth, the archetypal myth, which shadows the story of our life from birth to death—comedy and tragedy, plaited together into one single cord: the comedy of our little life, which ends in the tragedy of our little death, which, in turn, is only part of the comedy of universal life, wild and regardless.

Modern myths don't exist because now our life is fragmentary and changing, where then it had the constancy of tribal tradition. Theatre, as we know it, grew out of mythic ritual at the same historical moment as this fragmentation of our lives started to take place. But the old myth isn't dead. Its elements lie sleeping within us all, and cannot help but be awakened in our drama. In any piece of work you will find parallels with the myths and legends of old. Despite the richness of human imagination that we have talked about, it sometimes seems we cannot tell a new story, only an old story (the old story) in a new way. Thus our drama always leads us back towards primeval rapture.

We hope that you will find these ideas useful to encourage people, young and old, to make their voyage of discovery about themselves and the world.

—Charles Verrall

100 + Ideas for Drama

Introduction

WHY WE ARE WRITING THIS BOOK

We have been running the Anna Scher Children's Theatre since 1968, and in that time we have developed and used literally hundreds of different ideas in drama. We receive a large number of visitors from all parts of the world, as well as running Drama Workshop Courses for students, teachers, social workers, etc., and we are also sent hundreds of letters asking for advice and help. One of the things that all these people want is to build up a fund of practical ideas which they can use, be they a teacher faced with a new class, a social worker starting a neighbourhood drama group, or a student working in an improvisation group.

The aim of the book is to fill this need.

WHAT THIS BOOK IS

It is a recipe book containing hundreds of drama ideas. It is not our intention that the recipes should be followed slavishly; we hope that the book will be used as a source book in which material can be found which can be adapted and developed for use in any particular situation. To this end we have as far as possible presented ideas open-endedly, suggesting as many developments and variations as possible, so that each reader can use the ideas in his or her own way.

Again, in this book we do not lay down a suggested course or syllabus in drama; we hope that our ideas could be usefully incorporated in any teaching programme. Some of the ideas are of our own devising, others are old and well known; all of them have been tried and tested and found to work with a wide range of children and adults.

WHO THIS BOOK IS FOR

Teachers, students at Colleges of Education (not just those specializing in drama for secondary schools but also all those who will be working in primary schools, where most teachers take some drama); social workers; playgroup leaders; librarians; people involved in community projects; parents looking for things for their children, and their children's friends, to do in the holidays; students at drama schools and university drama courses; actors; fringe, underground and student theatre groups; and everyone interested in children's theatre or theatre generally.

We are not just thinking of drama taking place in schools: although we have generally used the words 'class' and 'teacher', the descriptions could equally well apply to other situations. So for 'class' you can read 'drama group', 'club', 'cub pack', 'adventure playground', 'amateur dramatic society' and so on. Likewise, we have generally used the word 'children' but many of the ideas can be just as successfully used with adults.

HOW THE BOOK IS LAID OUT

We have divided the book up into chapters, each chapter containing ideas of a particular type: 'Games', 'The Spoken Word', 'Warm-Ups, Mime and Movement', 'Character, Props and Costumes', 'Situation Drama and Improvised Plays', and 'Technique'. These are, of course, not watertight divisions, merely convenient ones. The contents of the chapters overlap a great deal, and it was in some cases difficult to decide which chapter a particular idea should go into.

We have not split up the chapters into age ranges, 'Drama for Juniors' or 'Drama for Teenagers', for example, because children vary so much that one cannot

lay down any hard and fast rules. While there are
obviously some ideas that are for adults and near adults
only, and others for infants only, a great deal depends on
the child's age, ability and stage of development, and
also on what experience they have had of drama. Some
groups of children simply have more grown-up tastes
than others. Many ideas can be used at a variety of
different age-levels, by altering the presentation in a way
appropriate to the age group you are working with.

In any class or other drama group there will be individuals working at different stages at the same time (e.g.
some children will be ready to do character work long
before others). This is no disadvantage. In our own
experience, we typically work with groups with age
range six to eleven, or eleven to eighteen — with some
children attending for the first time working in the same
group as others with several years experience of drama.
A spread of age, ability and experience in a group can be
an advantage rather than a handicap. Children learn from
each other.

Usually we don't mention the purpose of individual
exercises — in some cases the purpose is obvious — but in
other cases different teachers and classes will use the
ideas in varying ways and derive different benefits from
them. Our main aim in this book is to provide tools that
can be used, rather than to theorize on the structure that
can be built with them.

WHAT DO CHILDREN GAIN FROM DRAMA?

First and above all — enjoyment. Then comes a wide
range of other benefits: it provides an outlet for self-
expression and helps the development of imagination and
artistic awareness; it increases social awareness
(particularly through role play), mental awareness,
fluency of speech, self-knowledge, self-respect, self-

discipline and self-confidence. It gives children the opportunity to learn how to co-operate with others and helps
develop orderly thinking and the ability to organize. It
improves physical co-ordination and physical fitness. It
may also have a therapeutic effect, through helping
children to deal with their real life problems, or a
cathartic effect, by enabling them to act out violence and
frustration. It provides social and moral training, and
helps young people to mature emotionally, preparing
them for adult life.

Drama is a marvellous vehicle for general knowledge,
and in schools there are many ways in which it can be
linked with English, History, Art, Music, etc. It also
provides a good outlet for the ability of bright but non-
academically-minded children, and also gives opportunities to do well for children on whom society may
tend to force low expectations, for racial or other
reasons.

The benefits do not only accrue through children
participating actively in drama; they can also learn from
observing others, particularly if they are encouraged to
watch positively and critically by being asked to comment
and give praise afterwards.

PLAY, DRAMA AND THEATRE

Play, Drama and Theatre are linked, and each is a development of the other. There is a great deal to be gained
by children at each level. Each is valuable for its own
sake, but Play leads to Drama, and Drama leads to
Theatre.

At the 'Drama' stage, thoughts and feelings are
experienced and shared by members of a participating
group. In time we learn to communicate these to others,
so that at the 'Theatre' stage, because of the use of
technique, people not involved in the action — a whole

roomful of people — can share in the experience too.

DISCIPLINE

One of the questions we are most frequently asked is how do we maintain order, especially when taking large classes of eighty-plus, as we often do. We believe in *organized* drama — the first thing the children learn is to be a *good audience* — a disciplined framework gives children freedom to express themselves in a satisfying way.

Here are ten discipline 'tips' which we hope will be useful to student-teachers:

1 *Holding interest.* In order to hold a child's interest the lesson must be well prepared and interesting for the child. Try and look at it from the child's point of view, as well as your own.

2 *Mutual respect.* When you talk they listen to you, when they talk you listen to them — the whole class listens to them — it works both ways.

3 *Self confidence.* Usually, you're bigger than they are — who would challenge a giant? If you're not bigger than them, think of the zoo-keeper entering a cage with a lion in it. He behaves calmly and confidently — and the lion immediately co-operates. So don't think yourself into a weak position before you even start. Put yourself into a positive frame of mind. Have everything prepared and ready — then you can look forward to each lesson. Get them to sit down while you're standing — this gives you a strong psychological advantage. Start off firmly — after a while it is easy to relax a little — but it is very difficult to do the reverse, if you have been starting off too casually.

4 The word *'Freeze'* uttered crisply is valuable in drama, likewise *'Stop'* rather than 'stop talking'. 'Freeze' can be

used in a play context. 'When I say "freeze" everyone must stop absolutely still like a statue: it's as if I'd gone into a roomful of Madam Tussaud's waxworks. You mustn't move a muscle! Freeze!' It works.

5 The *tone* of your voice — low key is very effective. Constant shouting is *not*. Say a few words loudly to get people's attention and then gradually drop your voice to a pleasant, quiet, conversational level. The children will get used to you talking in a constantly quiet voice and having established this as the norm there will be little or no need to raise your voice.

6 Gimmicks like 'hands on heads', 'look at my finger', the drawing pin 'test' are useful with younger children if used occasionally. The drawing pin 'test' cannot really be carried out with any group more than once a term. Raise your hand high, holding in it one small brass drawing pin. 'Now we cannot begin until we have done the drawing pin "test". I want absolute quiet in this room; so quiet that when I drop the drawing pin I want to hear it as clear as can be.' Wait for quiet — and drop the pin!

7 Taking away a break is quite an effective sanction.

8 The teacher's *appearance* is important. The children care how you look and they react to the way you look.

9 Giving special *attention* to the difficult child often cures the difficulty. Give a dog a bad name — it's a very unfortunate child that is labelled all the way up the school. Boys and girls know when they have a bad name. Knowing the children really well as individuals and having continuous relationships with them is very important.

10 Concentration exercise. First define the meaning of the word *concentration* — 'keeping your mind on some-

thing'; to do a job well you must concentrate — *'If a job is worth doing it's worth doing well'*. Simple concentration exercises like closing the eyes and listening to the teacher's voice can have a very soothing effect.

The more *energy,* mental and physical, you can put into your work the more effective you will be, and you will get a better response from the children. If you are physically fit you are less likely to get tired and bad-tempered at the end of a long day.

Encouragement and rewards are much more effective than punishments, as well as being kinder; at the same time, when the need arises one must not be afraid to say 'No', decisively and firmly.

DRAMA IN DIFFICULT SITUATIONS

Many of you are, or soon will be, attempting to teach drama in tough schools or other difficult situations, particularly in educational priority areas in the big cities.

By a 'tough' school we mean one with high staff turnover, few experienced teachers, little contact between parents and staff, poor discipline, little encouragement given to the children at home, high rates of truancy and delinquency, bad housing conditions, and all the rest of it. Many of the children will view school as an unpleasant institution which they dislike having to attend. By the age of fourteen or fifteen, they are likely to be hostile, uncooperative or apathetic towards drama.

What is one to do in a first lesson with such a group?

To start with, you can only hope for fairly limited success. You are being asked to fight battles that may have been lost years before. If drama is a compulsory subject no teacher should feel they have failed if the

customers don't like it — why should young adults enjoy
doing what they are forced to do against their will,
however much it is supposed to be for their own good?
They think of themselves as being entirely grown up, even
if they aren't, and they don't like being treated or referred
to as 'children' or 'kids'.

One way of beginning with a new class is through
discussion, or Speakeasy, choosing a subject which they
are likely to have a strong interest in. This bypasses any
inhibitions they may have about actually getting up and
doing things. You will need to be a strong chairman,
keeping the discussion to the point and insisting on only
one person speaking at a time; they will accept this
necessary discipline as fair, as each of them will want
the others to listen while they have their own say. While
the discussion is going on you will be able to observe the
boys and girls and get to know them, and they will be
getting to know you.

Another way of starting off is through games, choosing
those which are appropriate to the age group you are
working with. Through games they will become used to
getting on their feet and moving around, without being
called upon to do anything the least bit arty or unmanly.
Also, they will accept the discipline that is necessary for
playing a game, again on the grounds of fairness. Possible
games are Dog and Bone, The Hunter and the Hunted, and
Statues, which introduces the vital work 'Freeze'.

Then you can start on simple improvised situation
drama using a simple format (not too many people),
themes close to everyday life, and situations about which
they will feel strongly, e.g.

a girl comes home two hours late from the disco and
finds her Mum waiting for her;
a boy must tell his friend that he has taken his

fashionable new jacket and lost it;
two girls find out by accident that they have been
going out with the same boy, leading to a jealous
argument.

You can give plenty of praise and encouragement,
while at the same time showing that you will be looking
for a high standard of work. (In a single sex school your
choice of situations will be restricted: one way round it
is to work with a neighbouring school of opposite sex,
if this can be arranged.)

Another important point is to apply a little group
psychology. In most classes there is one person with an
extroverted, dominant personality, a natural group
leader; you can spot him straightaway. Give him plenty
of attention and get him on your side; his attitude will
influence the others.

After this you must play it by ear. Don't let them get
bored. Be ready to change your plan. If you try an idea
and it doesn't work, drop it and try something else. If
in a first lesson you try ten ideas and only one of them
works, then count that as a success because now you
will have something to build on next time. Gradually
they will accept you, and even begin to enjoy themselves.

CHILDREN'S DEVELOPMENT IN DRAMA

If the first prerequisite for good drama is order, then
one of the first things that children must learn in drama
is to be a good audience. The division into performers
and audience is temporary; everyone spends some of
their time in each, and the audience is encouraged to
listen and watch intelligently. The children will learn from
each other, in the same way as they like to hear each
other's compositions in English, sharing ideas and helping
one another.

Two ways in which a child's development in drama can be hindered are:

1 By the teacher asking too little: children's work improves fastest when their teachers have high expectations of them. Far more children are potentially talented than is generally recognized — their ability just has to be discovered and encouraged at the right time. So a good working principle is to assume that *every* child has talent waiting to be found and encouraged.
2 By the teacher asking too much: there is no surer way of damaging a child's confidence than by asking him to do something which is too difficult or which he is not yet ready for. Young children, particularly, are not themselves the best judges of what they can handle.

So one should always be asking for a little bit more from a child, but not too much more, eventually stretching them fully; they will respond to being stretched — but never force them.

Clearly, in order to be able to judge what you should be asking of each individual child, you must observe them closely. What are they doing in the lesson? How are they reacting? Which one needs encouraging? Which has reached an important jumping-off point and is ready to move on?

Treat them as individuals; they are all different. Individual work is valuable for their personal development. Too many children are only treated as part of a crowd all their lives.

Keep up to date with the children's interests and fashions. This way you will understand the same language; you can do this without pretending to be one of them.

If you are working in a school get to know the boys and girls outside the school situation; this will help to build their confidence and trust in you, which takes time.

If you take them out, keep an Outings Book and make sure that everyone gets their turn, so that it is fair, and seen to be fair.

EDUCATIONAL DRAMA AND PERFORMANCE DRAMA

A dogma has grown up that the presence of any element of performance in drama is incompatible with educational value, and that the teaching of dramatic technique will stifle children's creativity. In our opinion, this view is mistaken.

In the past 'The School Play' was often produced by a teacher with no drama training and with children with no drama experience. In this situation the difficulties of getting children to learn their lines, deliver them audibly and remember their moves would force creative self-expression to take a back seat. However, this is not the result of attempting performance drama, it is the result of attempting performance drama without proper preparation.

The point is that the educational benefit of drama is not just limited to the exploration and expression of the child's own feelings and ideas by itself. No man is an island, and sooner or later the child needs to communicate those feelings and ideas with other people, and to receive similar communication from them. The more effectively this can be done, the more satisfactory the experience will be, and this is where the teaching of drama technique comes in: it is taught so that the children's desire to communicate will not be frustrated by their lack of the best means with which to do so.

So, points of technique can be introduced in a positive way, as the need arises in the children's own work, starting with simple ones such as: 'If you want people to hear you, you've got to speak loudly enough for them to do so', or 'If you start giggling in the middle of a piece of drama, it means you've stopped believing in what you're doing, and so will everybody else'. Technique in drama is not an end in itself, just the means to an end, as it is in any art, craft or skill, be it music, pottery or football.

There are so many conflicting theories of how drama should be taught — whether the teacher should take an active role, whether it should be 'child-centred' and so on — how is the individual teacher to choose between them? The only answer is to study them all and develop your own synthesis, not automatically adopting whatever is fashionable, or whatever is traditional, but by reading round the subject, and observing and absorbing other people's methods, to find out what best suits you and the children you are working with.

BELIEVABILITY

However much fantasy you use in drama, never lose touch with reality. The real world is not populated with woodcutters and swordfighters, so don't spend too much time in drama on chopping wood and fighting with swords.

To establish a base of realism right from the start, you must have situations which are real to the children — which they can identify with and believe in. Believability in any given situation is essential.

HIGH STANDARDS

It is important not to confuse an emphasis on a high standard of work with the fostering of an over-competitive attitude. There is a welcome tendency in education to favour co-operation rather than competition, but this should not lead to a decline in standards.

Children want to learn to do drama properly, just as they want to do proper experiments in science.

THE STRUCTURE OF A LESSON

Everyone will want to devise their own style and methods, but to give an idea of the pattern in which the ideas in this book have been developed: in a typical session of one and a half hours, we would plan to use about fifteen items, of which about 40 per cent would have the entire class working together, 40 per cent would be in groups of two or more, and 20 per cent would have children working individually. This is approximately the same for all age groups, with slightly more class and group work with younger children and slightly less with older ones. Music is used for about 30 per cent of items.

Have your lesson prepared well in advance. Make sure that the record player and other equipment is working properly, that the records are ready in correct order, and that anything else you will need is on hand. The person in charge of the session must not rely on anyone else to do this, he must do it himself.

Although your lesson will have been prepared, you must be ready to sense the changing mood of the class and vary your programme accordingly — skipping a couple of items, changing the tempo, staying with something that is getting interesting and developing it.

To hold the interest of the class you will need to keep the pace of the lesson going well and to maintain continuity — no long gaps while the room is being rearranged or you decide what to do next.

Staying with a single topic for a long time does not necessarily enable you to explore it any more deeply. Speed need not lead to superficiality — it makes it possible to obtain a more intense degree of concentration, which could not be maintained for a longer period of time.

Remember that you cannot expect improvisation to come out of thin air. People must have a framework to work within. When working on an improvisation idea for the first ime, you will need to give a fair amount of guidance and make plenty of suggestions. Then, with experience, the children will learn how to draw on their imagination and can gradually be given a more open brief.

STARTING A DRAMA CLUB

One of the ways to build up drama in a school is to invite children to join a drama club which they attend of their own volition. It is entirely optional, they will come because they want to come. This puts the teacher in a strong position. The interest is there, it is now up to you to sustain that interest.

So to begin with, just announce at School Assembly, or in your classes, that you are going to start a drama club in the lunch-hour and/or after school, and that all those interested will be most welcome to attend. You might add as a foretaste the kind of activities you will be doing — there'll be music and movement, games, mask work, plays — whet their appetites from the word go.

If you do not work in a school and want to start an independent drama club you will need to find suitable premises: a church hall or community hall that can be hired. Alternatively, you can work within an already existing organization such as a youth club. Posters (clearly stating time and place) can be displayed in adventure playgrounds, youth clubs or schools (with the Head's permission). Children don't always read posters so it is most important that you yourself are the advertisement for the drama club; if you start with a small nucleus of boys and girls you already know, word will soon spread among both parents and children and numbers will grow.

If you are not under the aegis of any official body you will have to make sure the premises you are using are considered suitable by the local authority, and you will also need to insure against injury that may be suffered by any child in your care.

Equipment

The following is a list of simple equipment which will be most useful for the drama club:

Basic equipment

Record player and records	Box of Hats
Costumes	Scarves
Stage blocks	Masks
Table, chairs	Wigs
Mirror	Bags
Notice board	

Props

Telephone	Pack of cards
Bell	Tea things — Tea-pot
Vase of flowers (plastic)	and mugs
Newspaper	Tray
Doll in shawl	Guns
Football rattle	Clock
Rubber gloves	Chalk
Knitting	Bus stop
Books	Pairs of glasses
	Iron

Most of these props will probably be brought in by the children themselves. Get some large cardboard boxes and cover them in attractive coloured paper, labelling

15

them 'Hats', 'Scarves', 'Masks', 'Wigs', 'Bags'. If you ask the children to search round for old hats, etc. at home, you will soon be inundated with them. Old mirrors, masks, and all kinds of other oddments can be found in street markets. If you have someone who is skilled at carpentry they can make a bus-stop, and also a bench, which is very useful. A television set, with the inside taken out to make it lighter, is useful for every home scene, but you can use a stage block to represent this equally well. A large tray is useful to hold your small props like the iron, knitting, vase of flowers, etc., and is convenient if you have to store everything away at the end of a session. A dress rail obtained from a shopfitters is invaluable for your costumes; better than a dressing-up box where the clothes can't all be seen at once and also tend to get crumpled. Costumes such as roomy dressing gowns, raincoats, housecoats, cloaks, nightgowns, baggy trousers and the like are much more adaptable than pretty summer dresses and tight fitting blouses and skirts. There will be plenty of applicants for Wardrobe Mistress! Also have someone in charge of props. It is important to stress from the beginning that the children should respect the equipment and put it back in its place after use.

RECORDS

Music can be used in a drama lesson to provide rhythm for movement work, to set a mood, and as an aid to concentration. The use of live music and records of orchestral music in these ways is generally accepted; pop records are often neglected because they are not considered 'cultural'.

In our own work we use a large library of pop records, mainly instrumental, as well as other types of music. There is a great wealth and variety of material available,

and the use of pop music, particularly at first, enables
you to avoid the resistance you may find children have
to working with forms of music with which they are less
familiar.

There is no need to buy records. It is easy to build up
a collection by getting the children to bring in any old
pop records they no longer want; you can keep the ones
that sound useful, and give away the rest, or else sell
them in aid of a drama fund or a charity.

Second-hand and ex-jukebox records are often for
sale very cheaply on street market stalls, in junk shops,
newsagents, etc. Many budget-priced labels produce LP's
of television and film themes: the advantage of these is
that you get plenty of different moods and rhythms on
one record. Film soundtrack LP's are often good, too, for
the same reason.

Artists to look out for on old 45's are: Duane Eddy,
Sandy Nelson, Kenny Ball, B. Bumble and the Stingers,
the John Barry 7, Whistling Jack Smith, Herb Alpert,
Isaac Hayes, Junior Walker, and of course any 'Band'
or 'Orchestra'. West Indian records are often very
suitable, as well.

Whenever a new instrumental or other suitable record
gets into the charts you can buy it, thus ensuring you
have some up-to-date sounds on hand!

1

Games

Here are some games that are linked with drama, chosen to benefit children through improved co-ordination, agility, experience of teamwork, self-reliance, improved fluency, and general knowledge.

Games like these can provide a light-hearted way in to drama for a new class, and they can also make a good way of relaxing and letting off steam at the end of a session.

1 PHYSICAL GAMES

Up Down Freeze Game

The boys and girls all run round the room in the same direction until the teacher calls 'Freeze', when they all stop absolutely still like statues. The object of the game is to keep as still as possible. Anyone who moves is out and goes back to his place. On 'Go' the class run round the room again until the teacher calls 'Up' and everyone stops still and puts their hands in the air. Again, anyone who moves is out. And so the game continues. If the teacher calls 'Down' everyone drops to the ground; 'Heads' means hands on heads; 'Shoulders'—hands on shoulders; 'Turn'—everyone turns and stands still (which means that on 'Go' they will now run round in the opposite direction); 'One Leg'— everyone has to stand still with one foot in mid air.

As the game progresses the judging has to get more and more stringent. Anyone moving the least fraction is out (though they are allowed to blink and breathe!). They are also out if they follow the wrong instruction, stop running, run in the wrong direction, react too slowly, talk, or laugh. Last survivor wins the gold medal!

Who is Missing?

This is a good observation game for younger children. They all run round the room several times. On 'Freeze — eyes closed', they stop still and close their eyes. Then they they are instructed to make themselves into a small ball on the ground, their eyes closed all the time. The teacher tiptoes towards one child and taps him on the back, motioning him to hide outside the door. The children, who still have their eyes closed, are told to stand: then they are told to run round again and can, of course, open their eyes. At 'Freeze' the teacher asks 'Who is missing?' And so the game continues.

Pip, Squeak and Wilfred

The children stand in a circle and are given the names Pip, Squeak, Wilfred, Pip, Squeak, Wilfred. . . . The teacher calls out 'Pip' and all the Pips run anti-clockwise round the outside of the circle and keep running round until the teacher blows the whistle which means 'Home'. On the whistle they must run round the circle to their places *without changing direction* — even if they're only just past their home position. The last person 'home' is out and sits cross-legged on the ground in his place, so that no one will trip over him. Anyone running in the wrong direction is out as well.

While the children are running round and round, the teacher can call 'Turn', whereupon everybody must turn and start running in the new direction. The teacher can repeat this several times before blowing the whistle.

When the numbers have thinned down a bit, the teacher can call 'Pip and Squeak together' or 'Pip and Wilfred together' or even, 'Pip, Squeak and Wilfred'. The last person left in is the winner.

The Mad Relay

The principle is the same as in an ordinary shuttle relay when each member of a team has to run from behind the starting line to the other end of the room and back again, passing on a baton to the next person. The difference in the Mad Relay is that instead of ordinary running, more unusual forms of locomotion must be used.

Various numbers can take part. Suppose there are two teams each having four children: the number ones hold one foot in their hands and hop on the other foot to the end of the room and back. As soon as number one returns, number two sets out, running backwards. When he gets back numbers three and four together form a wheelbarrow, one walking on his hands while his legs are carried by the other. Back to number one again who this time must be carried by number two. Then number three goes backwards, jumping in the air, clapping his hands above his head and hooting at the top of his voice, and finally number four does an ordinary run.

Two umpires, one for each team, can be selected to detect unfair play; they each wear a hat and if there is any cheating that team's umpire waves his hat in the air, and with no argument, the contestant concerned has to start out from 'home' all over again.

On completion, the winning team is the first to sit at the home base, cross-legged, in silence and with hands on heads.

Any number of variations on this can be invented: running on all fours, on your knees, on your bottom – anything you like.

Cat and Mouse

Say there are thirty in the class. Divide them into four groups of seven. Each group stands in a line, stretching both arms out with fingers touching to form a wall, so that you have four parallel lines of seven making four separate walls with alleyways between them. On 'Turn' from the teacher, everyone turns a quarter-turn in the same direction to make seven lines of four people, fingertip to fingertip, with a new set of alleyways in between.

The two remaining children that are not making up the walls are chosen to be the cat and the mouse. This is a game of chase and the object is for the cat to catch the mouse. The cat chases the mouse along the alleyways but to thwart his designs the teacher frequently calls 'Turn' whereupon everyone does a quarter-turn to form the other set of walls. Neither cat nor mouse is allowed to break through the walls but must go along the alleyways. As soon as the mouse is caught, the cat and mouse change places with two children from the walls who become the new cat and mouse. This is very popular, even with older children.

Dog and Bone

There are two teams with up to twelve players each. Both teams are numbered so that the two number ones are opponents, so are the number twos, threes, fours, etc.

The teams stand behind chalk lines about twenty feet apart and the 'bone' (in the shape of a durable hat) is placed in the middle, in a position indicated by a chalked circle.

The teacher calls 'Number one' and both number ones go for the 'bone'. If team A's number one can grab the 'bone' and carry it 'home' without team B's number one touching him, team A scores a point. If team B's number one touches him before he reaches home, then team B scores the point. However, if B's number one touches the other *before* he has picked up the 'bone', then team A takes the point. The game continues with the numbers being called in any order.

The game is best played at an attacking pace so if it becomes too defensive the teacher can do a countdown from ten to zero and if no attacking move has been made before 'zero' both opponents go back to their places and there is no score for that round.

After each round the hat must be put back in the circle immediately, ready for the next number to be called. Suitable for all ages.

Pass the Shoe

The children sit in a circle. As soon as the music starts a shoe is passed round from child to child — anyone who throws it is out. Suddenly the music stops and the child who has the shoe in his hand is out. The circle gets smaller as the children are eliminated. The last child not caught holding the shoe wins. Suitable for juniors.

O'Grady Says

Everyone finds a space and stands facing the teacher. The teacher calls out 'O'Grady says do this' and performs an action (raising hands above head, clapping, putting hands on shoulders, hands on hips, marching on the spot, etc.). 'O'Grady says do this', and the teacher does a new action which everyone copies. The object of the game is for everybody to follow the action immediately if O'Grady has said to do it, but if it's just 'Do this' and not 'O'Grady says do this', they must take no notice.

The game proceeds in a fast-moving way and quick thinking on the part of the class is essential. If an action is committed without O'Grady commanding it or if anyone fails to keep up with the game, then they are out. Last man in is the winner.

Musical Bumps, Musical Chairs and Statues

Musical Bumps. Play a popular record. Everyone finds a space and dances. When the music stops everyone goes down on the ground — last one down is out. The teacher stops the music at irregular intervals and the last person left in is the winner.

Statues works in a similar way only this time when the music stops everyone stops absolutely still like statues; anyone who moves is out. The judging becomes stricter as the game proceeds. Last one in is the winner.

Musical Chairs. Start with one less chair than the number of people playing. The chairs are placed together in two lines, back to back. When the music starts the children walk round the chairs: as soon as the music stops everyone sits on a chair except one. The one who doesn't manage to get a chair is out. One chair is taken away, the music starts up again and the game continues. Last man in is the winner.

A variation of this, particularly for older boys and girls, is to play the game in twos. The partners go round the chairs hand in hand and, when the music stops, sit on a chair with one sitting on the other's knee. This is great fun, especially with a mixed class at the end of term!

The Feeling Game

This game can be linked with the five senses. You can make a reference to Helen Keller, the blind and deaf American girl having to 'see' with her fingers. One person is blindfolded and turned round several times so that he loses his bearings in the room. He is then guided on a winding path up to someone and the object of the game is for him to recognize that person by using his sense of touch. Feel the size of the person, feel the hair, the shape of the head, the features, clothes — are they wearing a watch or any recognizable jewellery, etc? Who is it?

The Hunter and the Hunted

One person is nominated to be the hunter, another is the hunted. The hunter goes to one end of the room or hall and the hunted to the opposite end. Both shut their eyes. The object of this game is for the hunter to catch the hunted before he can reach 'home' at the other end of the room, but they must both keep their eyes closed so the only way for the hunter to 'capture' the hunted is by *listening* for his footsteps; therefore everyone in the room must be absolutely quiet. This is a very popular game with all ages; we have even played it with old age pensioners.

Adam and Eve

Everyone forms a circle and sits on the ground, making sure there are no gaps. Adam is chosen and blindfolded. Eve is chosen but not blindfolded. Adam and Eve must stay within the circle. The object of the game is for Adam to try to catch Eve. He calls out 'Where are you, Eve?' and she must reply immediately 'Here I am, Adam'. Adam goes towards her and she dodges him. He keeps calling 'Where are you, Eve?' and she has to keep on replying, straightaway 'Here I am, Adam'. Adam has to catch her within a time limit of thirty seconds.

2 MENTAL GAMES

The Hobbies Game

The boys and girls form a circle and each concentrates on the initials of their first name and surname. The object is to make up an imaginary hobby with the same set of initials

24

e.g. Martin Phillips   — Murmuring Poetry
　　 Ray Burdis   — Ringing Bells
　　 Dawn Gerron   — Drawing Giraffes
　　 Michael Scott   — Marvellous Singing
　　 Kim Taylforth   -- Kissing Teddybears
　　 John Williams   — Just Work
　　 Jennifer Brassett — Judging Boys
　　 Gary Kemp   — Gliding Kites

Then they can make up hobbies for each other's initials. Licence is essential.

Lists and Word Tennis

Lists. This can be competitive or otherwise. Each contestant has just one minute to name all the items he can think of from a given category, e.g. Fruit, Vegetables, Cities, Countries, Meals, Girls' Names, Boys' Names, Clothes, Parts of the Body, Cars. So, if the category were Meals, he would start off: 'Sausages and Mash, Fish and Chips, Steak Pie, Baked Beans on Toast . . .' and continue until he runs out of ideas or the minute is up.

Word Tennis. A development of Lists is Word Tennis. Two people face each other and both have to name in turn items from the given category. They go on until one of them cannot think of a new word within three seconds; he is out and someone else can then challenge the winner.

A harder version of Word Tennis is to take words from a given category — 'Countries', for example—and specify that the last letter of one word must be the first letter of the next, e.g. 'EnglanD', 'DenmarK', 'KenyA', 'AustraliA' . . . . This form of Word Tennis is not so fast-moving, so a longer time limit is called for.

Kim's Game or the Memory Test

Take fifteen items (any selection of props — a comb, doll,

25

telephone, flowers, etc.) and place them on a tray. The contestant has one whole minute to concentrate hard on the items — and then the tray is taken away. He is given another minute to see how many of the items he can recall.

The number of items used can vary according to the age of the child. We suggest fifteen items for children of eleven to thirteen; you can increase or decrease the number according to age and ability.

One Minute Please

In this game the competitor sits in the hot seat and talks for one whole minute on a given subject, which can be more or less anything (sausages, football, television, girls, boys, holidays, school, parents, food, parties, etc.).

The object is for the child to learn to speak fluently for one minute without drying up or wandering off the subject. This will provide an opportunity to comment on the importance of increasing your vocabulary, good presentation, etc.

For younger children you can make this 'Thirty Seconds Please'.

Greetings, Your Majesty

One child is selected to be 'It' and sits on a chair at one end of the room, blindfolded. Then the teacher points at someone who walks to the middle and in a disguised voice says 'Greetings, Your Majesty' or another set phrase. 'It' has to try and guess whose voice it is; he is given two chances. If he guesses correctly he remains 'It'. If 'It' doesn't guess who it is, then the child has done a good job at disguising his voice and he becomes 'It', and so on.

Who Am I?

The subject sits in front of the class; the object of the
game is for them to question him and guess what person
he is thinking of. The subject can only answer 'Yes' or
'No' and you can stipulate that there should be only
twenty questions. Because of this the class will not wish
to waste any questions.

Example:

Q. 'Are you alive today?' A. 'Yes.'

Q. 'Are you a woman?' A. 'No.'

Q. 'Are you well known to the public?' A. 'Yes.'

Q. 'Are your a politician?' A. 'No.'

Q. 'Are you over thirty?' A. 'Yes.'

Q. 'Are you English?' A. 'No.'

Q. 'Are you European?' A. 'No.'

Q. 'Are you American?' A. 'Yes.'

Q. 'Are you a film star?' A. 'No.'

Q. 'Do you appear on television?' A. 'Yes.'

Q. 'Are you a singer?' A. 'No.'

Q. 'Are you involved in any way in sport?' A. 'Yes.'

Q. 'Are you a tennis player?' A. 'No.'

Q. 'Are you a boxer?' A. 'Yes.'

Q. 'Are you black?' A. 'Yes.'

Q. 'Are you Muhammad Ali?' A. 'Yes.'

The audience can be broken down into teams and you
could see which team takes the least number of questions
to find the answer to 'Who am I?'

2

The Spoken Word

1 SPEAKEASY

This is a good introduction to discussions and because it is conducted in an orderly way, everyone gets a chance to have their say, be it short or long. (The title is taken from Jimmy Savile's BBC radio programme.)

Place a chair at one end of the room; this is the Speakeasy chair. Announce a speakeasy subject—for example, 'If I had £100'. Each person in turn comes out to the Speakeasy chair and starts 'If I had £100 I would . . .'

This naturally introduces the importance of projection and also good listening, so that the whole class can hear what each person has to say.

Here is a list of Speakeasy titles for all ages:

Hobbies and collections.
My mum.
My dad.
My family.
My teacher/describe a teacher.
If I had £100.
If I ruled the world.
If I were an M.P.
If I had one wish/three wishes
The gift I'd choose for . . . (you can choose a gift for someone in the class or outside e.g. 'The gift I'd choose for Tommy Pender is a football because he's always borrowing mine' or 'The gift I'd choose for the Prime Minister is some throat pastilles so he won't get a sore throat from all the speeches he makes.' It's important to explain the reason for each gift.)
The gift I'd like to receive.
If Jesus was born today, the gift I would give him.
The best present I received/gave.
Wedding presents.
Complaints about home/family.
Complaints about school.
My happiest moment.
My saddest moment.

My funniest moment.
Memorable moments.
Magic moments. (Have you had a magic moment that has stuck in your mind, like the time you found the teacher's purse when everyone was desperately looking for it, or the time you saw some kittens being born?)
My holiday.
If I didn't live where I do, where I'd like to live and why.
If I wasn't born human, the animal I'd be and why.
If I wasn't born me, the person I'd be and why.
⚹If my house was on fire, what I'd save and why. (Make it understood that all the human beings and animals have already been saved.)
The most beautiful thing in life.
The most ugly thing in life.
What makes me mad.
Myself.
A day from my diary.
The time I had to say goodbye to someone/something.
Reunions.
What I'll do when I grow up and why.
The job I'd like to have and why.
The job I'd hate to have and why.
How I see myself in ten years time.

The film/book I liked and why.
Description of a film.
Description of a book, or the book I am reading.
The programme/advertisement I like best/least on television and why.
Somebody nice that I like. (Straight description.)
The person I admire and why.
The person I'd like to meet and why.
Compliments. (A compliment is made to someone in the class: 'I'd like to compliment Tilly Vosburgh because she is always so sweet-natured a and helpful.' Tilly replies 'Thank you'. It doesn't have to be limited to people in the class.)
My favourite meal/my ideal menu.
The food I dislike and why.
In the box . . . . (Get the Speakeasy participant to close his eyes when he sits on the Speakeasy chair and imagine a box and its contents; after a short time ask what is in the box . . . .)
A letter to a friend.
⟍How did you have that accident? (This is an imaginary accident, not a real one, but the answers, though they may be funny, must strike at plausibility.)

About the dentist. (Describe your feelings about visiting the dentist and what you like and dislike about it.)

If I were marooned on a desert island, the person I'd like to be with and why.

Tell-a-joke.

The following Speakeasy Titles are suitable for older groups:

What I like about myself.

What I don't like about myself.

The qualities I haven't got.

Decisions. (Have you had any difficult decisions to make? Indecision is an unhappy state but did you make the right choice? Describe a decision.)

The crossroads of my life.

My most embarrasing moment.

The thing that hurt me.

Near misses.

If only . . . (The object of this quick Speakeasy is to start with the words 'If only . . .'. For example, 'If only I had a car, then I wouldn't have to walk to school'. 'If only I wasn't so bad-tempered, then I'd get on better with my sister.' They must state the consequence of their 'If only . . .'

Phobias.

My obituary.

The prize for . . . goes to . . . . (This can be either funny or straight. 'The prize for corny jokes goes to Keith Johnson. The prize for always being late goes to Ray Burdis.' It doesn't have to be limited to people in the class: 'The prize for not being amused goes to Queen Victoria.')

Love is . . . .

Puppy love. (The first time I fell in love.)

The sort of boy/girl I find attractive.

The girl/boy I'd like to marry. (The idea is not to name names but rather describe the qualities of the person you'd like to be your husband or wife.)

If I had a T-shirt with a message or slogan on it, what it would be and why.

2 DISCUSSION

The Speakeasy is a good introduction to discussion as it prepares the ground for treatment in depth of larger subjects. Signals like hands-up are useful because otherwise it is easy for the discussion to get out of control. A strong chairman, probably the teacher, is essential except in a very small group.

A variation of a discussion is 'Any Questions' in which, as in the BBC radio programme, there is a panel of about four people and questions are put by members of the class, asking the panel their views on matters of topical interest.

Here are some discussion themes:

Parents and family.
School (co-education or single sex, school uniform, etc.)
Your local environment.
Money.
Religion.
Morals.
Television and Radio.

Newspapers.
Topical and current affairs.
The monarchy.
Good and bad manners.
Prejudice.
Consumer questions.
Preferences in the content of drama lessons and new ideas.

3 STORIES, SOUNDS AND SPEAKING

Sound circle

The boys and girls form a circle and each in turn makes a sound from a given category. For example, you may ask for sound effects (a cork, creaking door, puffing up a tyre, an electric train, a racing car, escaping gas, factory hooter), or animal noises; a sentence in a dialect; names and emotions (saying your own name angrily, sadly, boredly, fearfully . . .); voice patterns (making a sound pattern out of your own name, or with the name of a city, like chanting Lon-don Lon-don to the tune of Big Ben); variety of sound (any sound which the human voice can make); speech inflexions (take a word or phrase like 'Yes', 'No' 'Thank you' or 'Hello, how are you?' Pass it round the sound circle and see how much variety there can be in modulation, pitch, tone and dialect); echoes

(one begins 'Are you feeling all right?', the second person
repeats the same phrase, imitating the voice, accent and
tone of the first as precisely as possible, the third person
chooses a new phrase, 'Phew, it's hot in here', said in
whatever way he wishes, which is in turn imitated by the
fourth. Go round twice so that everyone starts one phrase
and echoes one phrase).

Within the sound circle you can play guessing games
such as 'What's My Sound Effect?' and 'What's My
Dialect?'.

Stories-all-sorts

Making up a story as they go along is something many
children are very good at: improvising on the spot gets
round the 'writing it down' barrier.

Three props on a box. Select three props—say, a
telephone, an iron and a newspaper—and place them on
a box. Someone comes out and makes up a story
bringing in the telephone, the iron and the newspaper.

For *one-minute stories* three or more children sit in
front of the class and, on request, close their eyes. You
give them a theme — 'The Body' — and each has to name
one part of the body — the first child thinks perhaps of
the arm, the second thinks of the heart and the third of
the elbow. Then the first child is asked to tell a story
called 'The Arm', the second 'The Heart' and the third
'The Elbow'. The stories are to be about one minute long.
Other umbrella themes for one-minute stories include
'Food', 'Clothes', 'Other Countries', 'Animals'. In each
case the teacher asks the storytellers to close their eyes
and think of . . . 'a kind of food' . . . 'what food are you
thinking of?', etc.

Bell stories are a sharpening-up exercise for the more
advanced storyteller. He begins to tell a story but as soon
as the bell sounds he has to break off and start a new

story until the bell goes again. Each time the bell rings a new story is started, until the storyteller has started five or six stories. The teacher may ring the bell after two seconds, or he may decide to stay with one story for half a minute or more. *Bell letters* work on the same principle.

What does the music mean to you?

The class listens to a piece of music with eyes closed, and then one by one the children describe what they saw in their mind's eye while listening to the music. Any kind of music can be chosen.

Carry-on-story, etc.

The *carry-on-story* is what its name suggests. Four or five people take part each time. The teacher or first person starts off the story, talking for about half a minute and passing it on to the next person by the link work 'and . . .'. The last person finishes the story. The carry-on-story can also be started by the teacher announcing a title ('The Black Cat', 'Pancakes').

The *one-word-story* has two or more participants. They supply alternate words, going quickly backwards and forwards and making up a complete story. Listening and co-operation are very important. A one-word-story can either be told straight or acted out, as it is told, which is more difficult.

One-sentence-story takes place with a circle of people each supplying a single sentence in turn to form the story. Again, the listening is very important.

Finish-the-story is a variation of the carry-on-story. Two or three people go out of the room. They come back in one by one and the teacher or someone else starts off a story in the same way for each of them, which they have to finish in their own way. It's interesting to see how the stories may differ.

Other ways of doing stories are to give the storyteller a title, a first line, or a last line to use.

Letters, telegrams and cards

The idea of this is to improvise writing a letter you are going to send to a friend, your aunt, the teacher, or to apply for a job;

or to read aloud a letter you've just received — the teacher can specify that it must contain good news or bad news, or be a newsy family letter, or an official letter, etc.;

or the boys and girls form a circle and each improvise reading a telegram:

BOUNCING BABY BOY BOTH WELL SYD

FATHER ILL COME HOME IMMEDIATELY STOP
   MOTHER

BIRTHDAY GREETINGS LOVE HEATHER AND
   DAVE

or each can improvise a card: either a thank-you card, a picture post card, a Christmas card, a birthday card, a get well soon card, congratulations (on a wedding, birth of a baby, passing exams or driving test), or any other kind of card.

From morning till now

This is a detailed monologue in which each person describes what they have done that day from when they awoke in the morning to the present moment.

If desired, you can extend this by asking questions. What was the best thing that happened today? the worst? the most interesting? did they use their time well?

This is not the 'Truth Game'. It might be an idea to reassure everyone at the start that they are not going to be asked to reveal any secrets!

34

Interviews

To start with, the teacher can be the interviewer and each child in turn can be interviewed. It can be a straight interview or a simulation of an interview for a new school or for a job. This is good practice for the future. The importance of punctuality, tidiness and clear speech can be brought home here.

Standard questions include:

'What are your hobbies?'
'What do you like doing best at school?'
'Will you tell me about your brothers and sisters?'
'How many people are there in your school?'
'What books do you like reading?'
'Why do you want to come to this school?'/Why do you want this job?'

The interviewer and interviewee can exchange roles and after the interview they can comment constructively on how they think each other did.

Social procedures can be dealt with in the same way as interviews. For example, ordering a meal in a restaurant, booking a hotel room, making a complaint — and how best to get your way when you do so.

The Newscaster

This is quite a difficult piece of work as the Newcaster must not hesitate while reading the news, but must remain completely neutral and impassive — it's really an exercise in fluency and self-control.

The Newscaster sits at his desk and improvises the reading of three realistic news items (you can specify more). He must not pause or stumble — the aim is to be as articulate as possible.

On similar lines, you can ask for a radio or TV

commentary (specify which) on a sports event such as the Grand National or the Cup Final. For realism, care must be taken to be accurate with the technicalities of the particular sport; they should also perhaps be given licence to send it up.

Make friends, argue

Group the class into pairs at random and ask each pair to talk to each other, making friends; they do so until 'freeze'. Then you can possibly ask one pair to continue their conversation for everybody to listen to. Then everyone talks in their pairs again but this time their brief is to have an argument: after 'freeze' you can again spotlight one pair. Then everyone finds a new partner and continues to make friends − argue − make friends − argue.

This is a very good verbal warm-up.

The five senses

'Sight, sound, touch, taste and smell − we see with our eyes, we hear with our ears, we touch with our skin, we taste with the taste buds on our tongue and we smell with out nose . . . .' You can continue with a preamble on a blind man's use of the white stick, braille, etc., evoking sensitivity and awareness of the five senses.

Select five children: one is sight, one sound, one touch, one taste, and one smell. Ask each in turn to say:

Sight: What he'd love to see and what he'd hate to see.

Sound: What he'd love to hear and what he'd hate to hear.

Touch: What he'd love to touch and what he'd hate to touch.

Taste: What he'd love to taste and what he'd hate to taste.

Smell: What he'd love to smell and what he'd hate to smell.

4 WORD GAMES

Opposites Game

Select one child as 'It' and another (it can be two others) as the Questioner. The Questioner can ask any questions he chooses which have a yes/no answer and 'It' may only answer 'Yes' or 'No'. If the Questioner asks 'It' 'Are you a human being?', the answer is 'No' for in the Opposites Game you must give the *opposite* to the true answer.

e.g. Questions asked to John Blundell:

Q. 'Is your name John Blundell?' A. 'No.'
Q. 'Are you a girl?' A. 'Yes.'
Q. 'Did you brush your teeth with boot polish this morning?' A. 'Yes.'
Q. 'Have you got eight fingers?' A. 'No.'

If 'It' fails to give a correct opposite, or does not answer a question within five seconds, he is out. If he can survive for a minute, he wins.

If you want to make it even harder, another rule that 'It' may not laugh can be added.

Yes/No Game

The Questioner must be a skilled fast talker for the Yes/No Game. The contestant is led to the hot seat and is bombarded with a series of questions to which he must not answer 'Yes' or 'No' or nod or shake his head – but of course he must answer immediately. Needless to say, all questions are directed towards a yes/no answer like 'Do you go to school? Do you smoke? Did you watch tv last night? Are you married? Have you got brothers and sisters?'

If the contestant survives one minute of the ordeal, he is declared the winner.

Fortunately, unfortunately

The boys and girls form a circle. One starts off 'Fortunately I was on time for school today', the next continues 'But unfortunately the teacher told me off for not doing my homework', next 'But fortunately she soon forgot about me because at that moment the Headmaster came into the room', 'But unfortunately when he went out she took away my break', 'But fortunately it didn't really matter because just then a flying saucer flew past the window' . . . and so on.

Each alternate 'fortunately, unfortunately' must be consistent with the meaning of the story. No *non sequiturs*.

This can be developed into an elimination game. Any hesitation, repetition or *non sequitur* and you are out. To make it really hard, you can also forbid simple opposites (e.g. 'Unfortunately I lost my money', 'Fortunately I found it again').

The Minister's Cat

The boys and girls form a circle, either seated or standing. A rhythmical clap of four beats begins and the first person starts with the first letter of the alphabet: 'The minister's cat's an *angry* cat', clap, clap, clap, clap, and the next continues 'The minister's cat's an *ancient* cat', clap, clap, clap, clap, 'The minister's cat's an *artistic* cat', clap, clap, clap, clap, and on it goes. The first person unable to think of a new adjective or missing the beat drops out of the circle and so the next round begins, starting with the next letter of the alphabet, and the game gradually goes faster as it continues.

Sausage

The object of this game is for the contestant not to
laugh when answering 'Sausage' to each of the questions
asked. To put it in theatrical terms — there must be no
corpsing!

Appoint a child to sit on the hot seat:

Q. 'What's your name?' A. 'Sausage.'
Q. 'What's that in the middle of your face?'
   A. 'Sausage.'
Q. 'What is the Head of this school called?'
   A. 'Sausage.'
Q. 'Now, dear, look down at the floor — what are
   you wearing on your feet?' A. 'Sausage.'
Q. 'What did you have for breakfast?' A. 'Sausage.'
Q. 'Before you go to bed tonight, what will you
   brush your teeth with?' A. 'Sausage.'

If the appointed child survives ten questions with a
completely straight face, he's done very well!

Story charades

This is a variation of ordinary charades. One person tells
three different stories. In story number one he brings
in the first half of the word, in story number two the
second half of the word is brought in, and story number
three includes the complete word. The class endeavour
to guess the word at the end. No hands go up in the
middle of the story charades.

The Metaphors Game

For this you need a panel with about three members,
and a popular member of the class is chosen to be the
subject. The subject sits in front of the panel who
describe him by means of the metaphor: what animal

would the subject be if he were an animal? What colour would he be if he were a colour? What kind of food? What make of car? What record? What tv or film character? Article of clothing? What name, other than his own would he have? And so on.

3

Warm-ups, Mime and Movement

1 WARM-UPS

Each drama session begins with a warm-up.

The aim of this is to relax everybody, mentally and physically, and reduce any inhibitions they may have.

During the warm-up the class concentrates. A positive start helps everyone to get down to work in a business-like way.

Warm-up exercises

The children find a space, then stretch their arms out and swing them to make sure they won't hit each other. Either the teacher or a member of the class can lead the warm-up exercises.

Start warming up by shaking all over in time to some lively music (although music is not essential), rub the hands together and slap them all over the body. Continue with head movements, nodding up and down and turning from side to side, then rotate the head all the way round and all the way back, to relax the neck. Repeat. Shoulders next. Shrug shoulders up and down, then right shoulder, left shoulder alternately. Swing hips from side to side, rotate the pelvic girdle and stretch the trunk forwards, backwards and sideways.

Go right down to a squat position, with heels on the floor if possible, and up again. Repeat this several times. Stretch the arms as high as possible, growing at least two inches taller; jump up and down on the spot, leaping higher and higher, and then shake all over again. These simple warm-up exercises can be supplemented by floor

exercises: cycling with legs in the air, making scissors
movements and so on.

Curl and stretch — relaxing

The children start off by curling up in a tight little ball,
as small as possible, on the floor. To a background of
soothing music they gradually uncurl, get up and stretch
until their legs, backs and necks are stretched and their
arms, hands and fingertips completely extended upwards.
Then they start again from the curled position and work
upwards once more until their entire bodies are
completely stretched. This is repeated until the music
finishes, when the children stretch out on the floor. The
teacher tells them to flop completely, relaxing their
heads, bodies and limbs as if they were asleep. They can
be given the 'relaxation test' by lifting a hand or foot a
few inches to feel if it is tense or not; it should be
completely floppy. Don't drop their hand on the floor as,
if they are relaxing really well, it will hurt. Lay it down
gently.

Dance patterns and follow-my-leader

The class stands in a circle. The teacher goes to the
centre of the circle and starts a simple and repetitive
dance pattern to a strong rhythm (e.g. clicking
fingers followed by marching steps). The boys and
girls pick up the dance pattern until the teacher calls
'Freeze'; leaders from the class are then invited to start
off new dance patterns in turn, separating each by the
magic word 'Freeze'. Dance patterns can be done to
music with a strong beat, a drum or other percussion,
or to a clapping rhythm.

The dance pattern can also be done follow-my-leader
style round the room and on 'Freeze' the leader changes
the dance pattern.

42

Runabout

Everyone finds a space and when the teacher says
'Action' they run round the room without bumping into
each other, dodging in and out. At 'Freeze' they stop
absolutely still. The exercise is repeated, but this time
on 'Action' they run backwards, again without bumping
into each other. Several repeats forwards and backwards
will provide a good warm-up to a session, for any age-
group.

The rope-hauling mime

This is a warm-up in which the group haul on imaginary
ropes in strong dance rhythm, with or without music.

Pull the rope down from the ship's mast, tugging on
it repeatedly. Then heave the rope from the side; lasso
it, whirling it round your head and throwing it into the
distance. Then haul it back in, feeling the strain in your
hands, your face and your body while you are pulling it
in. Tie it up in a knot. Then wind it rhythmically round
your elbow. Then have a tug-of-war in pairs, one partner
staggering forward as the other pulls the rope backward.
Finally, pull the ropes down from the mast and heave
from the side again.

In a class situation the teacher leads the children in
the movements and calls out the changes. Tell the class
to feel the rope's strength and texture in their hands
while they do the mime.

Instruments of the orchestra

Start by inviting the children to name as many instruments of the orchestra as they can think of. This is an
opportunity to bring in general knowledge about the
families of the orchestra—string, woodwind, brass and
percussion—the conductor and his baton, famous
composers and what they wrote, etc.

Then, to any suitable orchestral or band music, let them mime each instrument in detail, e.g. when playing the piano, make sure they don't forget the pedal, and the left hand turning the page of the music. The teacher calls out each instrument to be mimed in turn: violin, flute, trombone, guitar, xylophone, cymbals, drums, and so on, not forgetting the conductor and singers, if appropriate.

Alternatively, you can divide the group up into sections, each section playing a given instrument and following the part of that instrument in the music.

Drums mime

This is another musical idea for younger children, in which they sit or stand in front of an entire imaginary drumkit, including bass drum and cymbal, and, accompanied by a suitable record, play in jazz or pop-drummer style, putting in such flashy details as throwing the stick under the leg and into the air and catching it. From time to time throughout the piece of music, the teacher can call out 'Spotlight on Martin Kemp', for example, whereupon Martin takes his solo, playing with great energy and concentration while the other drummers drop on one knee and extend one hand towards the soloist to give a spotlighting effect. At the end of the solo the call is 'And . . . everybody' and all the players pick up their drumming again.

Mambo Mamba and other dances

Mambo Mamba. This is good fun. The mambo is the dance, the mamba is the snake. The children are going to make a mamba out of the mambo. What you do is a mambo-type dance with the teacher leading to start with, picking two or three more children to join in on each circuit, making a snakelike pattern across the floor.

At the last step of each phrase the head is jerked forward and the bottom pushed back and the feet lift slightly off the floor. Simultaneously, you make a fairly high-pitched 'Ooh' sound. Listen to 'Florida Fantasy' from the *Midnight Cowboy* LP and you'll get the idea. For all ages.

We don't propose to go into dance in great detail but would like to suggest its value in warm-ups. Apart from the Mambo, the Charleston and Cha-Cha-Cha are equally good starting-off points for a drama session, and to be topical you could include Irish jigs and reels on St Patrick's Day (17th March), or the Highland Fling on St Andrew's Day (30th November), and various other national and folk dances. Dances from different historical periods, e.g. Elizabethan, are another field that can be explored.

Snowball

This makes a session end on a high note for any age group. Select a good dancing record from the top twenty (the children will often bring in their own). Someone starts dancing with a partner and then on cue (you can use a football rattle, a whistle or a bell, or simply call out 'Change'), they double up, each picking a new partner and continue dancing till the next change. Eventually you call out 'Everybody dancing' so there will be no wallflowers.

2 MOVEMENT

Marching, skipping and other ways of moving round the room

Marching. This is very simple and a guaranteed winner with younger children. Pick a leader who begins a rousing march round the acting area in time to appropriate music. On each circuit he picks two or three more

45

children to march round behind him in follow-my-leader style until eventually all the children are marching round one behind the other, swinging their arms, heads high or high-stepping like drum-majorettes.

The leader can march and countermarch them in S-shaped patterns all over the room until the music finishes.

Skipping. This is as simple as marching. One child starts off, picks a partner, and together they skip round the room. At the call of 'Change' the partners split up and each finds another partner to go on with. 'Change' again and all four choose new partners and so on until there are eight couples skipping round, or, in a large room, sixteen. Then the call is 'And back to your places', and someone else starts it off again, building up once more, until the end of the record. You will need music with a syncopated, skipping rhythm.

Other ways of moving round the room. Number the children 'one, two, three and four, one, two, three and four . . .' and tell all the 'ones' to go round the room in a specified way and then back to their places; the 'twos' continue with a different movement, followed by the 'threes' and then the 'fours'. There are many ways of moving round the room; here are some of them:

Silly walks; hopping; jumping; athlete's walk; walking backwards; moon-walking; running in slow motion; footballers training; skating; crawling; cartwheels; limps; clown's caper; creeping; tap-dancing; on tiptoe; heel walking; high kicking; as an old man; like a person in a hurry; as a Dalek; carrying a heavy bag; happily; miserably; proudly; lazily; drunkenly; ambling; like a mouse, an elephant, a horse, circus horses; through autumn leaves; and barefoot across shingle.

This can be done with all ages, using movements appropriate to each age group. Chirpy, energetic music is best.

Running

The children find a space and, to the accompaniment of fast music, start running on the spot with everyone putting lots of energy into it: then, while still running on the spot, they reach out to grab something — but it's always just out of reach. Next, they are running away, being chased in a nightmare, but their legs are carrying them no further than that same spot. Still they keep on running on the spot but now they are each an exhausted long distance runner; then, with a great spurt of energy they run with knees up, training for fitness. End with a triumphant lap of honour waving to the crowd. Khachaturian's 'Sabre Dance' is good for this.

Swimming

Invite the children to suggest all the swimming strokes; breast stroke, overarm, butterfly, back stroke, dog paddle. In time with music the children mime each stroke in turn as instructed by the teacher, starting by working on the spot and then changing to everyone going round the room in the same direction.

Ball games

The boys and girls find a space and begin by juggling with an imaginary ball, keeping their eyes on it. Then the ball becomes a beach ball which they bounce high and low; it becomes a big, heavy ball for bowling at a bowling alley; it is used for shooting in netball and then for bowling in cricket; then they play catch in pairs and play ball against the wall by themselves, or play basket-ball — or they can mime whatever ball game they like.

Other sports can be mimed to music by the teacher simply calling out the name of the sport — tennis, cricket, football, etc. The miming of the sports can be carried out in slow-motion as in an action replay, as well.

Boxing with an imaginary person

This is mainly for the boys. They find a space and box with an imaginary person, paying attention to strong punching movements, foot work, head and body reactions and knockdowns. They start as a group and on the teacher's request go back to their places. Individuals are called out to demonstrate their skills. They finish as a group again.

Kung Fu and James Bond type fighting, again with an imaginary person, is as cathartic and energetic as the boxing.

Theme music from film and television thrillers will give you the right atmosphere.

The Chase

In this, the secret agent shadows the villain, or the killer stalks his victim, through a dramatic landscape represented by stage blocks, screens, ramps, and over-turned chairs and tables; creeping round corners, leaping over walls, diving for cover, and so on, their tracks criss-crossing the acting area, the pursued always keeps one jump ahead of the pursuer.

For maximum effect, the participants must give each other room to work in: the idea is not to simply have one person chasing another around the room, so the pursuer must not get too close to the pursued.

Stylized movements — pirouettes, karate chops, Kung Fu, somersaults, stunt-man stage falls, can be brought in to give the chase extra excitement.

One possible dénouement is to have the victim reach

a telephone and start to summon help on it, only to be
gunned down, stabbed or strangled by his or her
pursuer, ending with a bloodcurdling scream.

Guns, dark glasses and sinister-looking hats are useful
props for this. Thriller/suspense type music and shadowy
lighting help to set the scene.

The Hands Dance

This is a very simple idea for younger children. The
children make their hands dance, expressing the feeling
of the music by making improvised abstract movements
in the air. After a while, more specific actions can be
introduced, e.g. representing a butterfly by linking the
thumbs and fluttering the fingers, or waving goodbye,
or moving the hands together as if in prayer, or sewing,
conducting, or playing the piano.

The Legs Dance

This is the same as the Hands Dance, but using legs
instead of hands, so there is not such a great variety of
possible movements. To start with, the class lie flat on
their backs with their legs in the air and move them in
a slow, single rhythm, and then in a fast, double rhythm,
bicycling and making scissors movements both forwards
and sideways. This can be repeated several times, slow
and fast. Then they can do their own improvised movements, in time with slow, rhythmic music.

Mirror-images

This can be done by all ages. The class divides into pairs
and, kneeling down facing one another, make movements
in time with the music, one being the leader and the other
following the same movements exactly, like a reflection
in a mirror, i.e. moving the left hand to correspond with
the other person's right and so on. Either improvised

abstract patterns can be used or else the intricate movements of brushing the teeth and combing the hair;
washing; for boys, shaving; and, for girls, doing their
make-up. The whole exercise can be repeated with the
leader and the reflection exchanging roles.

Machines

One member of the group starts making a repetitive
machine-like action, strong and stiff, over and over
again. He can stand on one spot and move his arms
round jerkily, or perhaps take three steps forward
and three steps back, or lie on the ground lifting alternate
feet in the air, or make any other movement that comes
into his head, in time with the music.

Others are picked to join in, one by one, adding their
mechanical actions to the machine that is being built up,
using different levels: standing, sitting, kneeling or lying
down, continuing until the teacher, or leader calls
'Freeze', and immediately restarting on 'Action'. The idea
is for the children to join in where they will fit in best
with the parts of the machine that are already there.
After the music stops, the teacher calls 'Freeze' and
instructs the machine to continue on 'Action', but
making machine-like noises.

Later on, you can adjust the machine to operate in
slow-motion with half-speed sounds and actions, and
then in rapid-motion with double speed and sound, again
using the words 'Freeze' and 'Action'.

With a large group you can build up two or three
machines at the same time, instead of one enormous
machine. Jerky, West Indian rhythms are ideal for this.

Space Creatures

Divide the children into groups of sixes and sevens. How

would they imagine a space creature? Each group makes a composite space creature with their bodies, not forgetting suitable facial expressions. They can either be mobile or stationary. Then follows a space creature parade, with the stationary ones in the middle, and the mobile ones moving round them, to eerie, science-fiction music, like that from the film *2001*, or weird sound effects effects such as those produced by the Moog synthesizer.

The Sculptor and the Statue

Everyone finds a partner and they sit on the ground together. For young children, you can explain the difference between a sculptor and a sculpture. Without talking, each sculptor must mould his partner into a sculpture. It can be grotesque or beautiful. As an example, the teacher can pick someone to be his own sculpture, shaping the head, moulding the face, eyes open or closed, fixing the expression, positioning arms, legs and body. When the music begins the children set to work on their own sculptures. After a couple of minutes, the teacher fades out the music and asks the sculptors to go back to their places in the audience. The statues remain where they are. Fade in the music again as the sculptors from their seats observe all the statues. Fade out the music and invite comments, or ask for titles for the statues. Tell the statues to go round the room in their shapes and characters, first slowly and then quickly — fade in the music for this.

Then the children can change partners, the sculptors becoming sculptures and vice versa.

A variation of this is 'The Spooky Garden', in which the sculptors make really grotesque statues and then two or three children wander among them, exploring 'the spooky garden'.

Another variation is 'What's my statue?', when,

51

again working in twos, one partner makes a statue of
the other as an occupation, e.g. pop singer, teacher,
dentist, and invites the class to guess 'What's my statue?'

Background music such as Peer Gynt 'Hall of the
Mountain King' (Grieg) is very effective; also electronic
music.

A more advanced idea, in which people work
individually, is 'Titles and Statues'. Each person
announces his title, which may be abstract, topical,
humorous or a well-known person, whatever they like,
and then forms himself into the shape of the sculpture
with that title. If mood music is used it is interesting to
see how it affects the character of the statues produced.

A similar idea is 'The Artist and the Painting'. One
artist is appointed to make a picture with a group of four
or five. He announces the title and then steps into the
picture himself.

A further development of this is for the artist to make
the picture and then to tell the story that the picture
illustrates.

Snake and Snake-Charmer

The children find a partner and sit on the ground. One is
the snake the other the snake-charmer. The snake-
charmers sit cross-legged, playing their flutes to coax
their snakes to dance. The snakes, making themselves as
small as possible, cup their hands in front of them to
represent the head of the snake and make snake-like
wriggling movements, twisting and turning to the music.
After a while the snakes and snake-charmers exchange
roles.

Indian music with sitars or flutes, can be used for this.

A dance drama: Under the Sea

Get the children to name as many creatures that live

under the sea as possible: fish, crabs, octopuses, sea anemones, etc.

From this you can develop a fantasy piece with King Neptune standing on a stage block in the centre of the arena. Around Neptune lie the underwater creatures, sleeping to begin with: a group of fish in one corner, four or six sea anemones in pairs with arms and legs entwined, nearby a couple of upturned crabs, two beautiful mermaids and half a dozen or so fat octopuses. Some dreamy music starts, Neptune comes down from his abode and wakes up the creatures in turn. On awakening they start to move: the fish darting to and fro, high and low amongst the other sea creatures; the sea anemones, all arms and legs, swaying from side to side and round and round; the upturned crabs wriggling their arms and legs; the two beautiful mermaids comb-ing their long tresses in mirror-images; and the fat octopuses clumping around in their corner. Neptune can perhaps wave a trident or a scarf over the water creatures to awaken them. As the music finishes, the water creatures return to their starting positions and adopt the same sleeping poses as before, while Neptune goes back and stands high on his rock.

There are several other dance dramas that can be adapted using suitable music, such as the story of Samson and Delilah set to 'The Good, the Bad and the Ugly'; a tribal dance set to one of the sections of the 'Missa Luba'; dolls (teddy bear, jack-in-the-box, clockwork soldiers, clowns, etc.) coming to life in the attic, set to 'Puppet on a String'. Then there are many songs with a story that immediately lends itself to mime; for example 'Little White Bull; 'Goodness Gracious Me'; 'Seven Little Girls Sitting in the Back Seat'; 'Cinderella Rockefella'; 'Tubby the Tuba'; 'The Sorcerers Apprentice'.

Good atmospheric music, like Grieg's 'In the Hall of the Mountain King' and Handel's 'Arrival of the Queen of Sheba', is bound to conjure up ideas for the children to make up their own dance dramas.

More experienced boys and girls can bring in their own music and work out mime and improvisation ideas based upon it.

The Man-eating Plant

Dance dramas can be done to a combination of story and music as well as to music alone; for example, 'The Man-Eating Plant'. Everyone sits on the floor and the story begins, to the accompaniment of dramatic music.

'You are a traveller in a far-off land, the weather is very hot and you have been walking since seven o'clock in the morning. Now it is lunchtime and you lie down exhausted in the shade of a big plant with large green leaves . . . you are eating the sandwiches you have brought with you . . . you finish off the last bite of the last sandwich . . . and screw up the paper into a ball and put it back tidily in your knapsack . . . and now you begin to feel really sleepy . . . and you lean back against the stem of the plant with your eyes half closed . . . and then, out of the corner of your eye, you notice that, although there is no wind, the branches of the plant are slowly waving in the air and coming nearer and nearer to you . . . and, too late, you realize it's a man-eating plant, and it's got you in its grasp . . . and you struggle against it . . . trying to fight off the branches . . . and you're getting weaker and weaker . . . but then the plant seems to give up the struggle, and its branches retreat . . . that was a close shave . . . but it's coming back again . . . and this time it finishes you off.'

While the story is being told the class improvise the movements suggested by it.

54

Greeting each other in a new way

The Eskimos rub noses together. The English shake hands. The Russians kiss on either cheek. Frenchmen kiss a lady's hand.

The children go into pairs and, to lively music, find a new way of greeting each other — perhaps they might even start a new fashion! When they've worked out their greeting action (it could be pulling each other's hair followed by two jumps, or it could be clapping hands on shoulders and doing a leapfrog), they go back to their places ready to show the teacher and class each greeting in turn. This can be done by all ages.

The Touch Game ──────────────────────── partners

In total silence, the class walk slowly around the room with their eyes closed. As soon as anyone senses some-one near them, they move out of that person's way without bumping into each other.

Then the teacher, who is the only one with his eyes open, asks everyone to reach out and find a partner. This they do; anyone who hasn't found a partner raises his hand and the teacher brings them into pairs. They do not open their eyes. The teacher tells them to feel each other's hands, the texture, the shape, the nails — are they sharp? Is it a hot hand? Is it a cold hand? Is it clammy? Shake hands. Clap each other's hands. Make friends with each others hands. Argue. Again make friends and argue with the hands. And . . . open your eyes! Everyone will enjoy this game — provided they don'it cheat by opening their eyes in the middle.

The teacher can link this with the five senses and how important the sense of touch is to the blind.

A similar exercise can be done using backs instead of hands.

3 MIME

Miming actions

Explain that mime is drama with actions but without
words, therefore the actions must be made very clearly;
so clearly, in fact, that if someone is miming sewing with
a needle and thread you want to, in effect, be able to see
that needle and thread!

The following actions can be mimed by all the class —
knitting, sewing, writing, playing the piano, lighting a
cigarette and smoking it, typing (putting the paper in
first), make-up including varnishing nails, or shaving,
peeling onions, sharpening a pencil, sugaring and stirring
tea, stroking a cat, polishing shoes, brushing teeth,
painting a picture, sweeping the floor, polishing the floor,
painting a door, cleaning the windows . . . .

This can be developed into more detailed mime such
as different ways of combing your hair: fussy and
nervous, backcombing, vain, bored, it's tangled, finding
dandruff on your shoulder . . .

The miming of eating different foods is fun: a banana,
chicken leg, apple, soup, spaghetti, orange, steak, boiled
egg, ice cream . . . and eating in different ways — slowly,
greedily, nervously, fussily, with the mouth open, made
to eat something you don't like, hurriedly, it's too hot,
chewing, something gets stuck in your throat, you're
preoccupied, reading the paper at the same time . . . .

The key point is concentration. For example, suppose
the class are miming painting a picture. Tell them to
visualize the half-finished picture in front of them: a
portrait, a landscape, or an abstract; ask them one by
one to describe their painting. If they are writing, what
are they writing? A letter, school work, a story? What
does it say? Are they writing with a pen or a pencil? And
so on.

You can go on to more detailed mime, including preparing a scrambled egg or omelette, making the tea, making a daisy chain.

Touch mime

This is a more complicated form of the miming actions idea and needs the right atmosphere to evoke the sensitivity required.

How does it feel?

Pat a dog; pull it back by its collar; it jumps up at you.

Pick up a heavy rock; throw it in a pool; wipe the grit off your hands.

Touch a polished oak table.

Put on a warm fur coat.

Walk barefoot down a stony beach; the water is freezing cold; now the sun comes out – enjoy it.

Pick up an apple; toss it in the air and catch it; feel the skin of the apple; smell its scent; take a bite and taste it.

You are asking the class not only to mime the actions, but also to recreate in their minds the sensations produced by them. This idea develops sensitivity and awareness.

Guess-the-mime (What's my job? etc.)

One person starts by announcing 'What's my job?' and begins to mime his job – a chef, teacher, mechanic, or whatever. On finishing the mime he asks again 'What's my job?' and the class guesses. If the mime is really good, they will get it right. (No hands go up in the middle of the mime – not until 'What's my job?' is said for the second time.) Then someone else has a turn; it could be the person who has guessed the previous job correctly.

Variations of this include 'What's my animal?', 'What's my sport?', 'What's my musical instrument?', and 'What's my circus character?'.

Mime charades is a more complicated guess-the-mime. The principle is the same as in ordinary charades but no words are spoken, of course. Words like 'window', 'monkey', 'football', 'carpet', and 'sandwich' are easily illustrated in a mime charade.

Take 'monkey': Act One (one finger raised in the air): Monk; a monk praying, the rosary, etc. Act Two (two fingers): Key; a key is taken from a pocket, turned in a lock and the door opened. Act Three (three fingers): Monkey; A monkey scampers around the room, swinging its arms, scratching itself and so on. Then the rest of the class have to guess the word.

Once a class have plenty of experience of mime, guess-the-mime as a group exercise is very enjoyable. The class divide into groups of about six and each mime a story from a given field, such as the Bible, Mythology or History. The audience guess-the-mime.

The Indefinite Prop and the Imaginary Prop

Take a prop — for example a carpet-beater — and place it in the middle of the floor. You want the children to use this as any object other than a carpet-beater. Each in turn uses the indefinite prop in a specific way — it could be a lollipop, a tennis racket, a frying pan, a mirror, a shovel, a sword and so on. The idea is firstly for them to use their imagination to think up more and more unlikely uses for the indefinite prop, and secondly for them to do a well-presented mime to illustrate what they have thought of. This can be done with any age-group.

The imaginary prop is similar to this except that you don't use an actual prop at all. The teacher can begin by eating an imaginary apple and then passing it to the person next to him. It now becomes a ball and is bounced on the floor before being passed along to the next person — now it is a hamster, which is being stroked — the person after that sees it as a flower . . . . As the imaginary prop is passed on, it is important to pay attention to the detail of the mime in order to make it real for everybody.

Animal walks

Number the children one, two, three and four, one, two, three and four . . . . Put on some music and tell the 'ones' to be giraffes going round the room and returning to their places, 'twos' monkeys, 'threes' mice, 'fours' elephants — back to the 'ones' again and select new animal walks — or even birds and fish.

'My animal is . . .' is a development of this where each child individually chooses an animal and after announcing what it is, does a mime of the animal, without music; they can make the animal's sounds as well. This is not a guessing game; the idea is for everyone to imagine what it is like to be that particular kind of animal.

Reactions (football, etc.)

The children are spectators at a football match, either watching the game live at the stadium or on television (say which). The local team are playing against Leeds United. You ask for their mimed reactions as the match proceeds: 'We've scored; they've scored; we've got a goal but the ref. says it's offside; a foul by us; a foul by them; a penalty for us; a penalty for them; someone's thrown a bottle on to the pitch; one of our players is badly hurt; the ball's gone into the crowd and they won't give it back.'

From the football pitch back to the class. Ask them to sit in different ways concentrating on facial expressions as well as whole body reactions. 'You are dejected; you are embarrassed; excited; bored; comfortable . . . .'

Other reactions of various kinds can be suggested by
the teacher uttering short descriptive phrases: 'A bird
falls from a wall, it is very bady hurt' — you feel pity;
'The postman brings a large parcel addressed to you' —
surprise; 'From an upstairs window you see the boy next
door throwing stones at your dog' — anger; 'You are at
home alone at night and you hear a strange noise coming
from upstairs' — fear, etc.

You can ask older age-groups to sit in different ways,
concentrating on whole body reactions as well as facial
expressions. Again, you will tell them the nature of each
reaction involved, but you will leave it to each individual
to create the reason for it in his own mind: 'You are
feeling confident; you are embarrassed; excited; bored;
in love . . . .'

The Goalkeeper

This is a good character mime which can be done
individually or with a whole group.

The goalkeeper is standing in his goal and he mimes
his reactions to the progress of the game. He is bored
because play is all at the other end of the pitch. His team
has scored a goal. Someone throws something from the
crowd. Ready for a corner kick, he shouts (in mime) at
the defenders. He makes a save. He goes for a high ball
but is fouled in mid-air. The opponents score a goal. He
shouts (in mime) to blame a defender. He picks up the
ball from the back of the net.

Mime sketch: the four secretaries

Four attractive secretaries are sitting in front of their
typewriters, typing busily. A plate glass window
separates them from the street outside. A 'pick-up'
of dubious character prowls outside the plate glass

window, raps on the glass and tries to get each girl
in turn to come outside. We see the reactions of each
girl as our man in the street tries his luck. He may be
successful or he may not!

4

Characters, Props and Costumes

1 CHARACTERS

From the beginning, children enjoy 'being' other people —
dressing up as mums and dads, old ladies, teachers,
soldiers, tramps.

Character work such as that described here extends
their experience of this. As they go into character work
more deeply, their awareness of other people's individual
personalities will increase and they will observe people's
behaviour more carefully, leading to greater understanding.

Waxworks

This is a good introduction to character work for juniors,
and it can be done with older children as well. Everyone
finds a space. 'Who has been to Madame Tussaud's?
There are lots of different waxworks there, kings, queens
and famous people, all absolutely still.

'Now, in a moment, when I say the word 'Waxworks',
you are all going to become waxworks, and the first kind
of waxwork you are going to be is a teacher. So, without
saying anything, let's see everyone starting to be a
teacher, doing what a teacher does . . . and . . .
Waxworks!' Everyone freezes in the position of a teacher,
writing on the blackboard, ticking off a class, helping
someone with their work. You can walk among the waxworks, commenting on the concentration and degree of
realism. 'And now, in a minute, Susan's waxwork is going
to come to life, so sit down, on the floor, the rest of you
and . . . Action' and Susan's waxwork comes to life:

'Stop that talking at once! There's too much noise in this room . . .' and so on.

Then the children can make waxworks of other sorts: a mother or father (not necessarily their own mother or father), a person at work, a criminal, a clown, a monster, a crank . . . each time, one or more of the characters can be brought to life on 'Action' and go back to being a waxwork again on 'Freeze'.

One-line characters

This is another way into character work. Take a group of about six or seven children and ask them all to be a mum or a dad — and ask them for one phrase or sentence illustrating what that person would say and do (i.e. one line to establish the character). Then, still in the same characters, ask one of them to give one line which that person would say when angry; another to be happy; another sad, and so on.

Take another group of children and change the character to a teacher, or a doctor, a lorry driver, a salesgirl in a boutique, or a market stall-holder. There are many characters they can do; after starting with the more familiar mum and dad type characters, develop to less straightforward ones: tv compere, businessman, comedian, a crank, man in man's shop, football spectator, professional sportsman, politician, scientist, pop singer, film star, wife whose husband has left her/or vice versa, bus conductor, waitress, priest, etc., concentrating on believability rather than caricature.

One-line characters can be extended so that you hear more than one line of what the character says and does. If desired, 'Action' and 'Cut' can be used as a starting and stopping device.

A variation of this is to take a group of seven boys and girls and let each represent one of the seven deadly sins (pride, sloth, envy, covetousness, lust, anger, gluttony). Again, start with them as one-line characters, extending further later on.

Characters and emotions, etc.

For this, slips of paper must be prepared; written on them are adjectives describing emotions or other characteristics, e.g. kind, cruel, aggressive, sensitive, inquisitive.

As in one-line characters, a group of six or seven children are chosen, and each draws a slip from out of the hat and has to be a character that could be described by the word on the slip of paper. For example, if they have drawn 'kind', they become a kind person. To start with they work as in one-line characters, just giving one sentence or phrase of what that person might do and say. Later, you can extend it, through the use of 'Action' and 'Cut', to longer pieces.

After a while, you can choose two suitably matched characters from the group and give them about five minutes to prepare a short duologue using those characters in, say, a home setting, or at a table in a café, or on a park bench, or you can give them a free choice.

Later on, another development is to divide the class into pairs and let each person choose a slip of paper with an adjective on it. Each pair has to prepare a duologue on any theme they choose using characters described by the words on the slips of paper.

More words that can be used are: proud, greedy, shy, nervous, stupid, friendly, careless, clumsy, mad, old, peculiar, bad-tempered, worried, angry, happy, conceited, ignorant, sexy, overworked, depressed, enthusiastic, intelligent, sad.

If you put the words on slips of paper, there is no risk that anyone will feel that an adjective has been assigned for personal reasons.

Characters from costumes

Ideas for characters can be suggested by clothes as well. If costume is available, juniors can be asked to dress up, which is always fun, and then improvise a character suggested by their costumes — the person who wears those clothes in real life. The work can be organized in the same way as 'one-line characters' and 'characters and emotions'.

With a more experienced group, you can allocate them items of clothing at random. Ask them to develop characters based on that costume and to prepare a piece of work, either working singly or in pairs, or as a group in a specified location, e.g. home, restaurant, bus stop, airport lounge.

General characters

We now come to the stage where the class are interested in developing characters of their own devising.

The character must be regarded as a three-dimensional, flesh and blood, real-life person — one must get to know what it feels like to be that person.

It is here that careful preparation and thought is necessary. Each person must research his character. What is his name? How old is he? Where does he live? The details are all important.

One way of organizing this work is to have a 'Character of the Week' spot, followed up by constructive comments from teacher and class.

The characters can be seen in monologue in various settings, e.g. giving their thoughts aloud on a park bench, in half-a-duologue (i.e. conversation with an imaginary other person), or they can be prepared in pairs, in order to work in duologue form. Costume can be used.

If necessary, you can offer them suggestions on which to build a character: a teacher or Head (always very popular); a clairvoyant; a barrow boy or old Woman from the market; a spoilt child; the Maestro; the vicar; a young child; Mad Harry; Oscar Goldwater, the Film Producer; a hypochondriac, a pop star; a small-time crook; a schizophrenic . . . .

Later, you can bring three or four of the established characters together in a specified location like a restaurant, or a doctor's waiting room.

People Meet People

This is a piece of work in which we can explore a character really deeply, with the whole class working together.

'People Meet People' is an imaginary television programme. There is a chairman, a guest and a studio audience. To start with, the chairman can be the teacher, the guest will be the character we are going to find out about, and the studio audience will be the members of the class. The idea of the programme is that a varied selection of people are invited to be guests week by week, and the studio audience can ask them any questions they like, about themselves, their life, and their opinions.

So a typical programme might begin with the chairman talking to an imaginary camera:

Ch: 'Good Afternoon, and welcome to People Meet People, the programme in which we get the chance to meet, and talk to, people from all walks of life. This week our studio audience is made up of children from the Mozart Road Secondary School, and our first guest is Mrs Lily Skinner, known to her friends as Lil, who has lived in the same district as the children live in for over eighty years. Lil, to start off the questions, may I ask just how old you are?'

Lil: 'Eighty-five last birthday, love.'

The first few questions come from the Chairman, then it is thrown open to the audience.

Q. (from the audience): 'Do you think the world's a better place today than when you were a child?'

Lil: 'No, dear, I don't. We knew how to enjoy ourselves in those days. People today with all their cars and their colour tellies; they don't get no plaesure out of it. Not like we used to.'

Q: 'Do you have any children and grandchildren?'

Lil: 'I've got three boys but one of them was killed in the war. I've got grandchildren and great-grandchildren now.'

Q: 'What do you like to have for breakfast in the morning?'

And so it continues, for as long as you like. Each guest is a character that someone has prepared.

In order for this to work there must be complete belief in the situation from everybody, and it is necessary for the audience to listen very carefully so that they can follow up the answers to earlier questions.

Instead of using the format of a tv programme, the same sort of thing can be done using the characters as visitors to the school, and the class and teacher as themselves.

2 PROPS

The Telephone

A telephone is a most useful prop — an absolute must for the basic equipment of a drama class. A battery-operated electric bell (purchased from any hardware store) is also needed.

Answering the phone

The telephone is placed on a box in the middle of the room with a chair next to it. The teacher rings the bell and beckons someone to answer the phone. They can talk to the 'person' on the line about anything, but to start with the teacher can brief them specifically beforehand. For example, they can be told that when answering the phone they will receive good news, or bad news, or receive a surprise, or have a gossipy conversation. After each call the teacher rings the bell and someone else comes out to answer the phone.

Later on, the exercise can be for the person to say only 'yes' or 'no', or talk in gibberish . . . or the call can be one that makes you happy, sad, angry, bored, afraid, annoyed . . . or the call can be from someone you love, or maybe from someone you love but they don't know it.

One must always be aware of the 'person' on the line. It is important to *listen* to that 'person' as well as speak to them.

This can be done with all ages.

Making a call

Each person in turn makes a call, remembering to be accurate with details like the number of digits he dials. Again, the class can make up their own personal calls or you can give them a specific brief such as ringing up someone to make a complaint, or to break off a boy-girl relationship, or with a particular beginning like 'Is Mr Johnson there?', or a given ending, or phoning the police, the butcher, the doctor, the dentist, a friend, or a repair man. If ringing one of these people, each caller must be sure to give his name and address, unless it is a person who would recognize him by his voice.

An effective piece of situation drama using the telephone is 'The Prowler in the Next Room.'

You tell the subject:

'You are on your own in the house and to your horror you hear someone prowling in the next room. Very gingerly, you make a telephone call for help to the police or someone else. The prowler must not hear you.'

Perhaps he will accidentally knock over a lighter or other prop, thus building up the suspense even more.

The Telephone Game

Ask the class to think of a word each, the first one that comes into their heads. It could be Scheherezade, outside, chicken, thimble, fingers, think, yellow. Ask each of them to say the word they're thinking of; then ask some of them to make a phone call bringing the word they have chosen in to the conversation. Naturally, you will choose the difficult words, and there must be complete concentration – no giggling.

Telephone conversation and dialects

Telephone conversations provide a handy and informal way of doing work on dialects.

The telephone bell rings and members of the group answer the telephone, in turn, each time having a conversation using a different accent or dialect.

As soon as one conversation ends, the bell rings again. Once a dialect has been used once, it cannot be used again. Go round the group until you run out of dialects.

Dialects and accents that can be used include: Posh English, Cockney, Scottish, Welsh, Irish, Lancashire, Yorkshire, Birmingham, West Country, American (several kinds), West Indian, Indian, African, Australian, French, German, Italian, Russian, Japanese.

The Frustrated Secretary

This is a fun piece of sketch drama in which you have a secretary with three phones on her table. Phone A starts ringing. She answers it. There is a Very Angry Person on the line. She tries valiantly to pacify him. Phone B starts to ring. She picks it up with her free hand, pleading with

the Very Angry Person to hold the line for one minute.
Phone B is another Very Angry Person and desperately
she tries her best with him. Then back to A again, who
apparently is in a fury by now, and thus she goes back
and forth from A to B working up a great frustration.
The climax of this sketch drama is when phone C rings.
The frustrated secretary lets out an almighty scream, or
breaks down and sobs, or ends it in any way she chooses.

Crossed Lines

Three telephones are needed for this. If you don't have
three, they can be mimed.

Anne rings Kim, telling her about the latest film on
at the Odeon, her new bargain tights, her latest boyfriend, and other girlie gossip. Someone breaks into
their conversation on a crossed line. Leave it to Kim and
Anne to deal with him in whatever way they like. They
could be very annoyed, insisting the intruder get off the
line straightaway, or they could play it for fun. It's two
against one — the intruder responds as best he can.

Pick a Bag

It's useful to have a box of bags in your basic equipment.
A shopping bag, evening bag, satchel, brief-case, hand
bag, shoulder bag, even a suitcase.

In the same way as in one-line characters, ask members
of the class to pick a bag and take their character from
the kind of bag it is. For example, if it's a shopping bag
it could be a hard-working housewife for ever worried
about rising prices; a brief-case might suggest a spruce
business man from the City, and so on.

First see the characters individually, and then couple
them in suitable pairs at a specified location, like at the
bus stop.

Pick a Pair of Glasses

Like bags, spectacles are useful props for the basic equipment of a drama class. There are many kinds: swept up at the sides; black, square and studious; dark glasses; water goggles; rimless spectacles; National Health style; gold rimmed; tinted lenses.

'Pick a Pair of Glasses' is an idea carried out on the same lines as 'Pick a Bag', taking your character from the type of glasses, e.g. an unfashionable National Health pair might conjure up a weakling character, a natural butt for the school bullies. Some fashionable sunglasses might suggest a sexy lady sunning herself on a Costa Brava beach, surrounded by admirers.

After seeing each of the characters on their own, you can couple pairs of them in a convenient setting, such as sharing the same table in a crowded restaurant.

Pick a Prop

A member of the group selects a prop from the props table and improvises a situation centred round the prop. For example, the prop chosen could be a mirror. A girl might improvise a situation in which she critically contemplates her face. What can she do about those freckles? Why are her eyes not bigger? People say she's got a nice smile, though . . . .

Other 'Pick a Prop' monologue situations can be centred round a whistle, a violin, a football rattle, a string of beads, a doll (it can represent a baby), knitting, and many more.

The indefinite prop and the imaginary prop (see page 58) are linked with this piece of work.

The Seat

Seat Perching. A chair is placed in the middle of the room and children in turn find a new way of perching themselves on it: it could be kneeling on it, or doing a head

stand on it, or sitting cross-legged, or they can turn the
seat upside down and perch on it that way round. Once
one way has been attempted the next person must find
a new way. The teacher should stand in easy reach of the
seat in case of minor tumbles.

If the class is small enough, another way that Seat
Perching can be done is for everybody to find a place with
their chairs and then to perch on it in their own ways and
freeze; then for each of them to find a second position
and freeze, and then a third. You can do the same thing,
but without the seat, using the four basic levels: first
lying, then sitting, then kneeling, then standing, and
making the positions as dramatic and acrobatic as possible.

Seat Perching in Pairs can be done with two people
to each seat.

The Different Kinds of Seat. A chair is placed in the
middle of the room. The teacher says 'It's a burning
hot seat' and picks a child who is to sit on it.

The child walks out from his place; it looks like a
perfectly ordinary chair, and he is going to sit down
on it, and . . . 'Yow!', he stumbles back to his place,
rubbing his burnt behind.

This is an exercise in believability and the teacher can
say whether he thinks the child's reaction is true or
false: the child sustains his reaction from the burning hot
seat all the way back to his own place.

Next, the seat can have an imaginary drawing pin on
it, or wet paint, it can be a throne, a seat with glue on it,
a slippery seat, a seat with itching powder on it, a smelly
seat, one with a comfortable cushion, a seat next to
someone you don't like, next to someone you love, a
seat in a church, a seat with someone already sitting on
it, and so on.

This is very popular with juniors but can be done by
all ages if pitched at a suitable level.

Free Improvisation

The idea of this is for the teacher, using stage blocks and whatever other equipment is to hand, to quickly lay out a simple arrangement of them in the acting area. Then, in ones or twos, members of the class have to do an improvisation using this as their set.

As he is setting up, the teacher may say 'I want you to look carefully at this set, and think to yourselves, what can this represent? It can be anything you like; indoors, outdoors, at home, at work. In a minute we're going to see, first in ones and then in twos, what you think might happen in this setting.'

The more interpretations that can be put on the set, the better. Suppose you have laid out a bench, and a stage block next to it with two open boxes on their sides on top of this. Someone might see this as a park with an abstract sculpture in it, with a boy meeting a girl on the bench. Alternatively, the boxes could be rabbit hutches, and a child could discover his rabbit had run away, or they could be filing shelves in an office, or a cupboard at home.

3 COSTUMES

Masks

Masks and Movement. When donning a mask, the body must take on the character of the mask in a deliberate way. For instance, if the mask is a sad clown, the body becomes a droll, drooping, listless figure. If it's a devil's mask, the body becomes spiky, dynamic and frightening.

Everyone dons a mask and examines his appearance in a mirror. Divide the class into two halves. The first half put on their masks and move round the room, expressing their characters in a bold, uninhibited way. Music is useful to set the mood for this. The other half watches.

Then they change over. Individuals who have developed
the deliberate and dramatic movements can be picked out
again for everyone to watch. This can be done with all
ages.

Specific masked dance dramas can be set to suitable
music. For example, '*The Happy Clown and the Sad
Clown*'.

Enter the Sad Clown, all languid and droopy, shaking
his head miserably — nobody laughs at his jokes. He is
joined by the Happy Clown, with light, frisky movements, clapping his hands — everyone laughs at *his* jokes.

The Happy Clown spots the Sad Clown and good-
naturedly capers across to him, shaking him warmly by
the hand. The Sad Clown limply shakes his hand and
mournfully shakes his head from side to side. The Happy
Clown realizes that something is wrong and mimes
'What's up?'. The Sad Clown shakes his head again.
Nobody laughs at his jokes. The Happy Clown puts an
arm round the Sad Clown and, trying to cheer him up,
tells him a few jokes (in mime), throwing his head back
and laughing and slapping his new friend jovially on the
shoulder. But, alas, to no avail; the Sad Clown continues
to shake his head mournfully. The Happy Clown tries to
teach the Sad Clown to do a mock bow: the Sad Clown
tries but it is a pale imitation. Nothing works. In the end
they part company, the Happy Clown capering back to
the circus. The Sad Clown stands alone, utterly down-
cast.

Many masks can be worked into dance dramas,
depending on what's in your stock. Carnival masks can
be bought; otherwise they can be made out of papier
mâché, and painted; flat masks can be made by cutting
out colour photographs from magazines and mounting
them on stiff paper, cutting out eye holes and attaching
elastic or ribbons.

Mask characters

Someone selects a mask character — a space creature,
an old woman, a baby, a squirrel, Mickey Mouse — and
examines himself in the mirror, exploring the effect of
various mimes and movements. When wearing a full
mask, one's voice cannot be heard properly, so two
people work together; one wears the mask and the other
is his voice, staying at the side out of sight.

Suppose we have a space creature: he glides into view
and speaks in an unearthly monotone: 'I have arrived from
Planet 142 857. Planet Earth is to be investigated. I see
living creatures.' Moving all the time in a space-creature-
like way, he goes up to one of them, a fair-haired girl
wearing a blue dress. 'Here is one of them. It has yellow
fur on its head, and a blue skin on its body. It is a good
specimen. I shall take it on board the spaceship for our
zoo', and so it goes on.

It is important that the Mask and the Voice should
work together, the movements harmonizing with the
words as they improvise.

Mask characters can also be portrayed using two masks
and two voices working together, in pairings like the
baby and the ghost, Frankenstein and Blondie, two
piglets, the old woman and the devil, the beautiful lady
and the spy, etc., depending of course on your selection
of masks. It is interesting how such seemingly diverse
characters can fit together well.

Pick a Hat

It doesn't take long to build up a collection of hats of
different kinds — a policeman's helmet, a baby's bonnet,
a balaclava, a workman's cap, a chef's hat, a fez, a
bowler, a jockey's cap, a crown, a woolly cap, a trilby, a
flowered hat, a broad-brimmed summer hat, a sombrero,
a bathing cap, a beret . . ..

Take a group of about six and ask them all to pick a
hat, look at it and put it on. They are going to become
the person that wears that kind of hat, and we are going
to see and hear a little of what that person might say and
do. In other words, with one line they are going to
establish the character of the person who would wear that
hat. This can develop from hearing one line to hearing a
lot more of each character. Then you can put two suitable characters together to work as a pair — they are to
meet each other in the street, or whatever.

Pick a Hat can also be done by asking for a different
dialect to fit each hat, or using different emotions — the
angry hats, when everyone in the line of hats is angry,
the proud hats, when each person takes on a proud
character, and so on.

The same idea can be used with *wigs,* if you have them.
Also, a slightly different variation is *scarves* (see page 77),
or you could give them a choice: Pick a Hat, Wig or
Scarf.

These ideas can be used with all ages, provided you
pitch them at the right level.

Two Hats, Two Characters

This is a more advanced idea which demands quick
thinking and concentration.

From the box of hats someone selects two with which
he improvises a situation using the hats to represent two
different people. For example, he might pick a cub
scout's cap and a smart hat with a spray of cherries on it.
When he is wearing the cub's cap he will be a cub scout
and when he is wearing the smart hat with cherries on it
he will be a Posh Lady. He dons the cub scout's cap and
turns to the right to the imaginery Posh Lady, saying
'Excuse me, Miss, have you got any jobs that need
doing?' He then quickly takes off the cub scout's cap

and puts on the smart hat with cherries on it, becoming
the Posh Lady, and turning left to the imaginary cub
scout, says 'Well, let me see, I suppose you could take the
dog for a walk.' Then quickly off with the smart hat
and on with the cub scout's cap: 'Do you mean the big
alsatian you've got chained up in the yard?' . . . etc.

It is important in Two Hats, Two Characters to use
two different voices for the two different characters and
to keep the eye level realistic, not talking to someone
as if they were either ten feet tall or two inches small.
Total concentration and belief in the situation are needed
to change from one character to the other quickly.

The same exercise can be done with wigs.

The Helmet that Won't Fasten

This is a piece of sketch material, done as a monologue,
about a crash helmet that won't fasten.

The boy has always been told by his mum that he must
wear a crash helmet when going out on his motor bike —
he knows it makes sense. The boy has to pick up his girl
friend at Waterloo Station at three o'clock. It is now
half past two. He lives half an hour away from the
station. He'll just about make it — except that he's not
going to be able to fasten his helmet. That is the brief
given to the boy.

He puts on his helmet — but the buckle won't do up.
He takes it off, examines the clasp. There doesn't seem
to be anything wrong with it. He puts it on again. Still
it won't tie. He tries several times, struggling with the
buckle. The thing simply will not fasten. He becomes
more desperate. Leave it to the boy to end it as he
pleases.

Scarves

From a collection of scarves (headscarves, neck scarves,

football scarves, chiffon scarves, saris, etc.) a group of
about six people pick one each. Each wears his scarf in
a different way — it could be worn simply as a headscarf,
as a hippie bandana, as a neckerchief, as a bandage nursing
a broken knee, as a sling, in charlady style, in pirate style,
like a belt, as a shawl — and, in the same manner as in
Pick a Hat, from the style he has chosen, he finds a
character to fit the way the scarf is worn, starting with
one line to establish the character and developing it later
on.

The Gloves that Have a Life of Their Own

Take a pair of gloves (they could be an old pair of
washing-up gloves or mittens, or boxing gloves) and
place them in the middle of the floor. 'These gloves are
magic gloves; when someone puts them on the magic
begins — the gloves have a life of their own; they take
over and control the movements of your hands.'

Someone comes out to put on the gloves. 'I'd better
start on the washing up', but as soon as he puts the
gloves on they take over, perhaps by pulling his arms
up into the air and down to the ground, twisting and
turning him round, making him punch at thin air,
sending him tumbling all over the floor, clutching towards
his neck to throttle him. Either he can escape from the
gloves' power by flinging them off, or else at the word
'Freeze' their magic wears off and he stops still.

This is a very popular idea. If you have a number of
pairs of gloves you can use that number of children all
wearing gloves at the same time. With older boys and
girls the magic needn't have the violent physical effect
you usually get with young ones. The effects can be more
subtle — it's up to their imagination.

The Shoes that Have a Life of Their Own works in
the same way as the gloves.

5

Situation Drama and Improvised Plays

The situation drama ideas set out in this chapter are, on the whole, designed to be carried out by a small group of two to four children, on their own, directed by the teacher, and without preparation. These ideas are suitable for children with some experience in basic drama, who show a readiness to move on.

In nearly all the ideas there is a strong element of conflict, and this is vital for dramatic purposes; from the educational point of view, this helps children learn to understand and deal with conflict situations.

In situation drama, the smaller the group the easier it is to work with: when starting off, a pair of children is ideal. This is because, for satisfactory drama, each member of the group must be aware of all the others. With five or six inexperienced children, this is rather too demanding, and the result tends to be confusing and chaotic. Also, look at real life. What size are the groups that form in the street, at home, in the school playground? How many people can sit round a meal table before two separate conversations develop?

The direction given before a piece of work in improvised situation drama is all important. State who the characters involved are, and give a brief description of the situation, seen from the characters' point of view. To stimulate the children's imagination, you can list some of the possible ways the scene may develop. A lot depends on how experienced the children are. The less experienced they are, the more guidance they will need, but whatever stage they are at, the brief you give them must be clear and positive.

Comments and criticisms afterwards are very important; they will improve the work, as well as developing the children's critical faculties. Invite the rest of the class to comment, always encouraging constructive comments rather than destructive ones. Find out what members of the group liked about the piece and why they liked it. Encourage children to praise each other; this fosters a friendly atmosphere in the class so that people will become less inhibited in what they do in front of the others. Make your own comments; it is best to be concise and limit yourself to the two or three most important points. Try to give praise if you can. Criticism can be depersonalized by referring to a general point of technique: 'Most of us couldn't see Tilly's face when she was opening the parcel, because Michael was masking her. So remember, when you're working with an audience, don't mask each other.' In this way, points of stage technique can be brought in as and when the work demands it.

A question that is often asked is 'Should the teacher intervene if a piece of work in improvisation seems to be going on too long and getting nowhere?' Clearly, this is a matter for individual judgement as to whether the work will benefit from your intervention; 'Try to find an ending' or 'Twenty seconds to finish' will usually serve to bring about a satisfactory conclusion without anyone feeling that they have been stopped in full flight.

Some teachers prefer to do situation drama by dividing the whole class up into groups of three, or whatever, and having them all do their improvisations at the same time, the idea being that the children will work more uninhibitedly with fewer people watching them, and also to use time more efficiently by having more children work at the same time. The drawbacks of this method are that it tends to produce a high noise level, which reduces concentration, and there is little opportunity for the invaluable comments and feedback from the teacher and the rest of the class.

Here is a selection of situation drama ideas for two or more people, most of them written as they might be introduced to a class by the teacher.

1 PLOTS

The Borrowed Dress

'Kay and Angela are two sisters. Kay, you have borrowed Angela's dress without asking her permission and, Angela, you go to the wardrobe because you want to wear this dress tonight for a party, and you find it with a horrible stain down the front. You realize that Kay must have borrowed it without telling you, and you are absolutely furious. It's six o'clock and you're going out at half past six. There's no time to take it to the dry cleaners or do anything that will clean it up. So you take the dress and storm in to Kay with it, and there's Kay coolly filing her nails on an emery board, and you really have it out with her . . . you can end it in whatever way you like.'

The Burnt Trousers is a corresponding idea for two boys. This time, one brother's new pair of trousers have been borrowed by the other, and they have been burned.

The Babysitter

'Sue, you are a young mother with a beautiful baby girl, Tracy. Phil, you are the boy next door and can earn fifty pence for yourself by babysitting for Sue. One Saturday evening, while you are babysitting for her, the phone rings and Terry, who lives across the road, invites you over to listen to his new stereo. It'll only be for

a minute, the baby'll be all right, you reckon. You go
over to Terry's place. The scene starts when Sue returns
to the house. Sue enters calling "Phil, I'm back! Phil!
Phil?" It soon dawns on you, Sue, that Phil has left the
baby by herself! You pick Tracy up in your arms, very
worried, but she's all right. Your anger with Phil starts
to grow and then he returns . . . and you can take it on
from there. So we start with Sue coming in, expecting to
find Phil and Tracy together . . . .'

The Lost Five-pound Note

'I want a mum and her son. Susan Onigbanjo, will you
be the mum? And John Williams, will you be Susan's son?
Now, John, you're a very good boy who does all the
shopping for your mum every week. This Friday, as usual,
you go to the supermarket and get all the shopping for
the week — baked beans, tomato soup, bread, biscuits,
washing powder, etc. — but when you come to pay for
it with the five-pound note mum's given you, the money
has gone, it is not in your pocket. We start off with John
coming home to mum *without* the shopping. And mum
says something like "Hello, John! Where's the shopping,
then?" John breaks the news. Take it on from there and end
it in any way you like.'

The Lost Gem Stone

'Martha and Vicky, you are two sisters and you get on
very well together, share each other's clothes and all that
kind of thing. Vicky, you lend your lovely pearl ring to
Martha for the Valentine's Disco. Martha, you had a
lovely time and danced all night with Steve. It was a
fabulous evening. You came home very happy. You looked
at the ring. The pearl had gone! It must have fallen out
when you were dancing with Steve. So we start when
Martha approaches Vicky and has to explain what's

happened. Vicky, you might react angrily or you might be sympathetic.'

The Lost Football

'Let's have two brothers, Steve and Graham Fletcher. You are both football fanatics. Graham, you have borrowed Steve's football to play in the street; but you were robbed of it by the Maxwell Street mob: it was six against one; you didn't have a chance. We start with Graham entering and explaining to Steve what happened. Steve, you react as you think you would. You might be mad at Graham, you might be sympathetic – it's up to you . . . .'

The Dyed Red Hair

'Pauline, you're a young housewife who has been feeling very restless lately. You need a change! They say a change is as good as a rest. You decide to dye your mousy hair red. Now, let's see you sitting in front of the telly with your new red look, wondering what your husband, John, will say when he comes home. We start when John comes in from work, and reacts as he feels . . . .'

The Pet that Died

'Bernadette, I want you to be Dexter's mum. Dexter, you play your own age. Dexter comes back from school at four-fifteen and today mum has some very sad news for him – his lovely black dog, Samson, has been run over by a car early this afternoon and is . . . dead. Mum has to tell Dexter. She knows it will break his heart because Dexter loved that dog. The first thing Dexter always does when he comes home from school is to call "Samson! Samson!" and the two of them play together. Now, Dexter, today you come in as usual at four-fifteen and say "Hello Mum! Samson! Samson! Where are you, Samson?" . . . So let's take it from there.'

Latch Key Kids

'I want a brother and a sister — let's have a real-life brother and sister: Frankie and Gloria Leon. Let's say that your mum works till seven o'clock in the evening, so there is no one at home to let you in after school — therefore, Frankie, being the elder of the two, is in charge of the key, which he always wears on a string round his neck. Now, on this particular day you both hurry home from school and you're very anxious to get indoors as quickly as possible as your favourite science-fiction tv programme starts immediately after school. You arrive, panting, at the doorstep — and, Frankie, you go to take the key from round your neck — but the key is missing — it is not there. What happens then between the pair of you is, of course, up to you. Are you going to miss your favourite programme? Are you going to be locked out till your mum comes home? Can you get in through a window? Has the key dropped off somewhere between school and home? Let's take it from when you arrive at the doorstep, out of breath, having run all the way from school.'

RSPCA

'Chris, you are walking home from school, whistling away to yourself, when you see a man brutally kicking a dog. You are shocked and immediately call out to him to stop. The man doesn't stop and, Chris, you know you must do something. You'd call the police and report the man to the RSPCA — but there are no policemen around. You try and persuade the man to stop. Callum, will you be the man and, Dexter, will you be the poor unfortunate dog? Can you whine, Dexter? Right! So let's see, first of all,

the man getting angry with the dog, and then, after a few
moments, along will come Chris . . . .'
    You can have an imaginary dog, instead of having a
child representing it.

Two Girls, Same Boyfriend

'Nula and Linda, you are sisters. We start off with Nula
on the phone to her boyfriend, Mario. Mario, you are
not seen or heard at this stage. While Nula is murmuring
sweet nothings to Mario, Linda comes in, pauses, and
stands at the back of the room, listening in on the conversation. You hear the name Mario being mentioned
several times in a rather tender way. And Mario is not a
very common name. When Nula puts the phone down,
Linda has it out with her. It transpires that you have the
same boyfriend — Mario has been two-timing the pair
of you. And so you sisters have a good old sisterly row.
The scene reaches a climax when Mario arrives,
brandishing a new girl on his arm (that is you, Sandra)
and asks if the two sisters would like to go bowling and
make up a foursome.
    So we start with Nula on the phone . . . .'

Wrong Change

'I want a busy, no-nonsense mum. You, Taiwo, Mrs
Ajenusi! Let's say you've got five kids, that is five
mouths to feed plus, of course, a hungry, hard-
working husband, and yourself. So when you do the
shopping you've got to count the pennies very carefully;
it's very difficult to make ends meet. Now, on this
particular day you've just popped out to the supermarket
to buy some washing powder, some baked beans and
two packets of fish fingers. You pay the girl on the till
(Joanne, will you be the girl on the till?) a five-pound
note and the girl gives you the change, but it's only the

change from a pound. Mrs Ajenusi, you look at the
change, saying something like "Hey, I gave you a five-
pound note and you've only given me the change for a
pound". Joanne, you deny this. You are sure it was one
pound that Mrs Ajenusi gave you. Now maybe she's made
a mistake, or maybe she's trying to cheat Mrs Ajenusi.
And what an argument the two of you have. End it in
whatever way you like.'

The Motorists

'Phil and Terry, you are two motorists. Can you each use
a red, oblong stage block to represent your car? You are
driving along when the cars crash. Terry runs into the
back of Phil. Both drivers get out to inspect the damage.
Phil accuses Terry of being the guilty party and vice
versa. End it as you please.'

The Saleslady and the Customer

'Katherine, you are a very persuasive saleslady. You get
a commission on every garment you can sell — and the
commission soon adds up to a very tidy sum; without
it, your wages are very low. Jenny is a customer who is
looking for a dress, but is not quite sure what she wants.
Jenny comes in to Katherine's shop, and Katherine has
to try and sell something to her, being as persuasive as
possible. It's up to you both whether a purchase is made
or not.'

This situation can be adapted to a saleslady or salesman
in any kind of shop.

The Malingerer

'Hayley, you are a sensible and conscientious mum. Your
son is, you, Tommy Pender! Tommy, Hayley is your
mum and you, I'm afraid, are a bit of a trickster and this
particular morning you don't feel like going to school so

you try to persuade Mum that you're not well — though
there is nothing whatsoever the matter with you. You
start by saying you have a slight headache — but that
doesn't seem to wash with Mum. Your headache gets
worse, you feel really sick! You make a great show of the
agony you are suffering! Perhaps Mum then suggests
calling the Doctor? I'll leave it to you to see how it ends.
Maybe Hayley sees through Tommy and packs him off to
school — maybe Tommy puts on a convincing case and
gets away with a day off school!'

Argument Over TV Channels

'Beverley and Clovis, you are brother and sister and the
pair of you are telly addicts. Now, Beverley's favourite
programme is Top of the Pops while Clovis always wants
to watch football. On this particular evening, Top of the
Pops and Football Special coincide on opposite channels.
Beverley stubbornly insists on watching Top of the Pops.
Clovis argues back with equal fervour for Football
Special. You fight it out between you! But fight with
words, not fists! Let's see who wins!'

The Crook and the Girl in the Jewellers'

'Maggie, you work in a very expensive jewellers' in the
West End of London. Now, normally you are not alone
in the shop but on this particular day the other girl is
off sick and the manager has just been called away by a
phone call. It is eleven o'clock and you are not at all
busy, in fact the shop is empty, when a young man —
Shefki — enters carrying a small, black brief-case. The
young man is a crook, although Maggie does not yet
know this. The young man asks the girl if he can see
'Tray F' from the window display. Maggie goes and gets
Tray F but when she turns round Shefki has locked the
door, pulled the blind, and is pointing a small automatic

100+ Ideas for Drama

towards her. He tells her to give him the keys to the safe.
But, bravely, Maggie refuses. Shefki threatens her and
what happens then is completely up to you.

Trying to Borrow Money from a Stranger

'They say the quickest way to lose a friend is to lend
him money. Do you agree?'
   'Kiaran, you are at the bus stop when you discover, to
your horror, that you've lost your purse. You search your
bag frantically but your purse has definitely gone. Now
you are in a predicament because here you are in London
— it's four o'clock — and you've got to get all the way
to Reading by early evening. You need at least a couple
of pounds for fares. Also waiting at the bus stop is a
middle-aged lady. You explain to her what has happened
and ask if you can borrow two pounds from her. Elizabeth,
will you be the lady and I'll leave it to you to decide
whether you believe Kiaran or not and whether you'll
lend her — or give her — the money.'

Many Years Ago . . .

'Let's have two old people sitting on a park bench —
Martin Phillips and Beverley Martin. You are both over
seventy years of age. You sit there reading your newspapers and gradually engage each other in conversation.
Something one of you says makes you gradually realize
that you knew one another over fifty years ago. Suddenly
you recognize one another. This delights the pair of you
and you take a nostalgic trip down memory lane. You
reminisce about the people you once knew and what
became of them, the places you knew, the fashions, the
manners, the two world wars, the Royal Family, you
talk about young people today — whatever. End it as
you please.'

You can either specify that the old people are living today and looking back fifty years in the past, or that they are people of their own generation seen fifty years in the future.

Pride Goes Before a Fall

'There are some parents who believe that their child is God's gift to the world and find it very hard to take any adverse criticism whatsoever about their beloved offspring. Such a parent is you, Angela — let's call you Mrs Scott. Your daughter, Rachel, is an absolute menace in her class and everyone knows it except you, Mrs Scott. You are the last to know. Rachel's teacher, Miss Burdis (all right, Bernadette?) calls to see you to have a talk and, in the most tactful way possible, to give you the full facts about your daughter, Rachel — her bad behaviour, her mean and spiteful acts towards the other children, how spoilt and selfish she is — but Mrs Scott cannot believe her ears at what Miss Burdis has to say. As far as she, Mrs Scott, is concerned, the sun shines out of Rachel's very eyes. But Miss Burdis goes on to give a blow by blow account of Rachel's antics. She's very worried about it; it's disrupting the entire class. Rachel then returns from her friend's house and sees her mother and teacher both looking very uncomfortable. End how you like. Who would like to be Rachel? All right, you Kim Doyle. So Angela is Kim's mum, and Kim is Angela's spoilt little girl. Let's start with Miss Burdis ringing on the doorbell.'

The Broken Glasses

'Let's have two friends — Michael Murphy and Paul Parsons. One of you is wearing a new pair of glasses, so can Paul go and get a pair of glasses from the props box. Both of you boys are watching television and Michael asks Paul if he can try on his new glasses. Paul reluctantly agrees. You don't like letting other people put on your glasses, especially as they're a new pair. Michael tries them on and fools around in them and suddenly he drops them on the floor, and they break! Paul is horrified — and terrified of what his mum will say because these new glasses cost a few pounds and she'll go mad that they're broken on the very first day! Paul, you are really broken-hearted and scared about Mum, and furious with Michael. Michael, you are very sorry — but there's no good in just being sorry in this world. What can you do? Let's take it from the beginning — both boys are watching telly and Michael asks Paul if he can try on his new glasses.'

To Leave School or Not to Leave School

'Phil, you are sixteen years of age and are suffering from an attack of schoolitis. Academically, you are very bright and Mum wants you to stay on at school another two years to do your A-levels. You want to leave now, get a job and earn some money. We see both sides of the coin: you feel you've outgrown school and you're impatient to get started in the world outside as soon as possible, while from your mum's point of view — she wants her son to get those qualifications in order to get a better job later on. She can't see why you should want to leave. I want a good, strong, articulate mum-character: you, Kate Saunders, you be Phil's mum.

'So we start when Phil comes in from school, and tells his mum he's fed up with the place and wants to leave.'

The New Girl in the Office

'You are experiencing new things for the first time quite a lot in your lives. For instance, one of you may have eaten a new kind of food for the first time recently. Or

you may have started a new job for the first time. It can
feel a little strange but it can also be tremendously
exciting. Penny, you are the new girl in the office. You've
just started the job this very morning and you are feeling
keyed-up and full of anticipation. John is your Boss —
he is tall, dark, handsome, and quite young — and
married. You are sitting at your desk typing away when
the Boss enters the room and gives you some important
invoices that must be done urgently. He notices how very
attractive you are and asks you how you're getting on
with the new job, leading to a more personal conversation. You, Penny, are quite relieved to find that your
Boss is friendly and human, and flattered by his attention.
But in the next few minutes he is asking you out to
dinner. Well, how do you cope with that, Penny? He's
a married man. Let's take it from where we see Penny
typing efficiently and John, the Boss, enters with the
invoices.'

Six Months Apart

'Trevor and Tina, you are standing at the bus stop — but
you don't see one another — you, Trevor, are looking
one way and you, Tina, are facing the other way. In due
course you turn round and recognize each other straight
away. You are meeting quite by accident; you haven't
seen one another for six months. Now, what happened
six months ago is up to you. You may have been boyfriend and girlfriend and had a row, one of you might
have gone away on a long holiday or had an accident
and been in hospital . . . . Here we see you both after the
six-month interval — and what happens next?'

The Boss and the Employee

'Peter, you are the Boss. Let's say you are manager of the
Princess Chocolate Factory. Phil, you are one of Mr Daly's

employees. Peter, this is your office, carpet on the floor,
three telephones — you're a bit of a big fish in a small
pond. You send for Phil: maybe you are going to give
him the sack; maybe you're going to promote him;
maybe you have a complaint — or a compliment — Phil
doesn't know — it's up to the Boss! We start with Phil
knocking on the door, not sure what to expect.'

Smoking (1)

'Martin Kemp, you are sitting alone in the cloakroom;
you have slipped out of Mr Webb's Maths class, and here
we find you having a quick smoke. You are nervously
puffing the cigarette, when suddenly Mr Webb enters!
Terry Bush, will you be Mr Webb? And obviously,
Terry, you are not pleased to see Martin in this situation.
Smoking is against the rules.'

Smoking (2)

'Jenny, you are at home watching telly and you decide to
have a secret smoke. Your mum's left her cigarettes lying
on the table and you take one of them. Nobody'll know,
you're alone in the house, or so you think. You've just
settled down to a cigarette when to your dismay your
mum returns (bingo ended early because of a power
failure). Mum (will you be the mum, Maria?) is astonished
to see her daughter smoking for the very first time. You
are surprised and angry and upset. Maybe when you calm
down you can offer your daughter some constructive
advice. So we start with Jenny sitting watching telly . . .
let's see you.'

Smoking (3)

'Kate, you are a chain-smoker complete with a smoker's
cough. You tried to kick the habit several times but have
never managed to give them up. You know it's ruining

your health. You known all about cancer risks, how it diminishes your life span, makes you unfit, etc. So be it. You carry on smoking. Sally, you are Kate's daughter and you love your mother very much. You see what smoking is doing to her and you're very worried about the consequences. We see you both in the living room, Kate having a last cigarette before going to bed: Sally decides to have a heart to heart chat with Mum — you desperately want her to stop . . . before it's too late.'

The Parting

'Gillian, you are a widow. Let's say your husband died of heart trouble two years ago. He has left you with a too-boisterous son who you cannot control — nor can his school teachers do anything with him. Perry, will you be the son who nobody can do anything with? You're always getting into trouble at school and you get fed up being stuck at home with Mum.

Gillian, as a last resort, you have decided to send Perry to boarding school. Let's see your last few minutes together before the taxi comes to take Perry to the station. It is the very first time mother and son will have been parted. When the taxi man knocks at the door Perry will have to go, and that'll be the end of the scene.

Another Kind of Parting

'John Blundell, you are a soldier, very happily in love with and engaged to Caroline North. All was bliss until this morning when you received orders posting you overseas immediately. You are to be stationed in Northern Ireland for six months, which seems an eternity to you young lovers. We see the pair of you at Euston Station five minutes before the train leaves . . . .'

Popping the Question

'There comes a time in almost every young man's life
when he finds a girl he loves and he asks her to marry
him. Now, choosing the right time and place for this
is very important; after all, you're asking the girl to
spend the rest of her life with you.

Terry Bush, you've been going out with Kim Taylfortt
for nine months now and the time has come, you feel,
to name the day, to propose — to pop the question.
Here you both are in Clissold Park, Islington. It is a
lovely Spring day. The time is right and so is the place
Kim, I shall leave it to you as to whether you accept or
reject. So, without in any way sending it up, you're
sitting in the park, talking to one another, and Terry
starts getting round to the subject . . . .'

Break-Up of a Marriage

'Paul and Veronique, you have been married for seven
years and you, Veronique, want a divorce. It's not
simply the seven-year itch but something rather more
serious — you are expecting another man's child. That
man lives next door; Ray Burdis, will you be the other
man? You and Veronique are very much in love, and
have been for the past year. Paul does not suspect.'

Ray: 'What about my wife, then?'

'Let's say you're unmarried. We start off with Paul
and Veronique watching television and, Veronique,
you broach the subject of your pregnancy with caution.
Paul, not surprisingly, may take it very badly. An
argument develops. And in the middle of it Ray comes in
through the back door . . . .'

Prejudice

'Linda: you're going out with Elvis. Linda is white and
Elvis is black. After they've kissed goodnight at the

doorstep, Linda comes inside and sees Mum (you, Caroline) looking very displeased. Caroline, you object to Linda going out with Elvis just because he is black, because you are colour-prejudiced. Mother and daughter confront one another and an argument blazes up. First let's see it this way round. And then from the other way round with Elvis going home to Dad (you, Herbert), and Dad starts on Elvis about Linda — because she is white.'

The Facts of Life

'Bridget: you're a mum and your little girl — May — is no longer a little girl but is fast growing up. You've heard that there will be Sex Education lessons at school next term but you decide to teach your daughter the facts of life yourself. The two of you are sitting cosily together in the living room, Mum knitting and May reading a comic, and the time is right to tackle the subject . . . .'

This can also be done with father and son, mother and son, and father and daughter.

Mum and Mum-to-Be

'Sonia, let's say that you have a three-month-old baby girl. Fern is your friend who lives in the flat next door, and she is going to have a baby herself quite soon. Fern drops in for a cup of coffee, and after a while conversation turns to what it is like looking after a small baby. Let's start with Fern ringing on the doorbell . . . .'

Hitch-hike

'Kim, I want you to be a hitch-hiker. We see you on the A23, hitching from London to Brighton. Now, you know how potentially dangerous it is to hitch a lift on your own. But, I'm afraid to say, you are heedless of your parents' and teachers' advice and warnings. So, here you are, hitch-hiking from London to Brighton. An articulated lorry approaches — Ozzie, would you quickly assemble the Cab of the lorry using the red stage blocks, please, and Gary, will you be the lorry driver who picks up the hitch-hiker. I'll leave it to you to see what happens, if anything — you might have an argument; there might be an accident; the lorry driver might try and get fresh with her; or you might just have a pleasant conversation — it's up to you.'

Something Only Your Best Friend Can Tell You

'Kim and Alison, you are best friends. Kim, although you like Alison very much, there is just one thing that you do *not* like about her . . . maybe it's something personal like Alison suffering from BO . . . maybe Alison is very bitchy towards other people . . . maybe she steals. Whatever it may be is up to you, Kim, but one day, when you are sitting together, you decide it's time that you told Alison the truth about herself. Alison, you react in whatever way you like: you might be furious or humble, or you might retaliate by telling Kim a home-truth too.'

Telling Your Problems to a Stranger

'You've heard the proverb "A trouble shared is a trouble halved"? Well, have you ever been in a situation where you had a problem that you couldn't share, even with your most sympathetic friend — yet you would feel more at ease talking it through with a stranger?'

'Stephanie, you are on a train journey. You've got a problem: it can be a boy friend problem, a domestic problem, a problem at school or at work, whatever you like. You haven't been able to discuss it with anyone. There is someone with a sympathetic face sitting opposite you in the compartment. Sometimes it's easier to talk to a stranger than to a friend. You tell your problem to the stranger. Dawn, you are the stranger . . . .'

Bus Stop (1)

'There are two gossips at the bus stop: let's have Denise
Cook and Hayley Glassberg. You've been waiting for
half an hour for that 73 bus! So you're not exactly in
the best of moods — far from it. We hear you moaning
away to each other about the terrible bus service and
especially about how infrequent the 73 bus is. At last,
in the distance, Denise spots it coming. At last! The 73
bus arrives and you're both just about to climb on when
an inspector appears and orders the bus back to the
garage. Well, that's the last straw. The pair of you are
fuming. You've been waiting half an hour and after
all that, when the bus finally does arrive, it's sent back
to the garage! It's a disgrace! So the pair of you turn on
the bus inspector and put the blame on him. The
inspector — that's you, Chris Leonard — has got to stand
up for himself and do his best to explain the delay —
there's a shortage of staff, and the buses get held up in
traffic jams, and so on . . . and good luck to you, Chris,
with these two very angry ladies. So we start with the
two of you waiting at the bus stop.'

Bus Stop (2)

'Two women standing side by side at the bus stop — you,
Marijke, and you, Kay. You don't know one another.
You have been some time at the bus stop — waiting for
the 38 bus. At last it arrives. The bus conductor (Tommy,
the bus conductor, please) calls out "One, and one only!"
Marijke goes to climb on the bus and Kay immediately
says something like "Here! I was here first" and pushes
her way on in front of Marijke. Marijke objects, insisting
she was first in the queue. You argue it out between you
but in the end the bus conductor gets fed up with the
pair of you, rings the bell, and off goes the bus. Then

you've both missed the boat . . . or rather the bus! End
it how you like.'

The Man from the Council

'Let's have a family, let's call it the Adams family. Peter,
you be Dad, Gillian is Mum, and let's have Callum and
Naomi as two of their four children. The other two are
playing outside. You are all living in a three-roomed flat
in very uncomfortable and overcrowded conditions. The
heating system is inadequate and there is a lot of damp
throughout the flat which you can't seem to get rid of.
You've been on the Housing List for six years now and
are forever hoping you will get one of these new flats
the Council are building on the Elgar Estate. On this
particular evening there is a knock at the door and it is
the Man from the Council — Mr Williams (Herbert,
will you be the Man from the Council?). Mr Adams
invites Mr Williams in and Mr Williams takes out the
housing application forms and discusses the situation
with the family. Now, Mr Williams may be sympathetic,
or maybe he is non-committal, or maybe he is totally
pessimistic. What chance have the Adams family of
getting one of those new flats on the Elgar Estate? Are
they destined to stay where they are? They've got to
try and persuade Mr Williams to help them. So let's
start with the family at home, and after a few moments
there comes a knock at the door . . . .'

Teacher Investigating Classroom Row

'Now, for this piece of work I am going to play the part
of a teacher — not myself, but a different teacher, let's
call her Mrs Selkirk — and all of you are going to be a
class. I'm going to pounce on two of you as being the
ringleaders in a row that took place in the classroom;
you both react as if it was a real classroom row . . . then

anyone who knows anything further, if they feel they
can contribute to the investigation, can put up their
hand, just as they would in real life.

'Lesley Theobald and Carol Byrne, come up to my
desk at once! Now, I want the truth, the absolute
truth . . . do either of you girls know anything about
May Leon crying and running out of school after break?'

'No, Miss,' murmur Lesley and Carol.

'We're all going to stay here until we find out what did
happen, so are you quite sure you don't know anything
about it?'

'I don't know nothing, Miss,' says Carol.

'Lesley?'

'May stole my purse, Miss.'

'What makes you say that, Lesley?'

'It was gone, Miss, when I went to the cloakroom at
break.'

'And what makes you accuse May Leon of stealing it?
Did you see her take it?'

'No, Miss! But she had twenty pence in her hand at
break and she had no money on her way to school this
morning.'

Jennifer Brassett's hand goes up: 'Please, Miss, I know
something about it.'

'Yes, Jennifer?' . . .

The investigation continues and more people can be
brought in, with the entire class improvising together.
Later, the teacher character can be played by one of the
children.

2 PLAYLETS

Here is a simple format for improvised playlets, in
which the director describes the characterization, basic
plot, and structure of the playlet which is then enacted
straightaway.

The playlets consist of three or four short acts divided by incidental music. The music begins and is faded out while the title is announced; then the playlet begins; music is faded in and out between each act. After the last act the participants come to the front and one after another, in character, give their thoughts aloud about the situation, as in a vox pop (see p. 128). Music again at the end.

Some examples of playlets
(i) The Dog that Must be Put Down
There are three characters: Mum, Dad and Child. There is an imaginary dog. The action takes place in their living room.

Act One. Mum and Child. Mum tells the child that the dog is ill; it must be put down because it is suffering. The child is upset.

Act Two. Child and Imaginary Dog. The child says goodbye to the dog.

Act Three. Dad and Child at bedtime. Dad tries to cheer the child up. The child goes to bed, still unhappy.

Act Four. Mum and Dad. They discuss how the child has taken the dog being put down and the effect it will have on him, and what they will do about it.

Vox Pop. The thoughts aloud of the three characters.

(ii) The Bad School Report
There are four characters: Teacher, Mum, Dad and Child. The action takes place in the living room.

Act One. Teacher and Mum. Teacher calls on Mum with the child's School Report. It is a very bad report. Teacher discusses it with Mum. Mum is very disturbed; she goes to get Dad. Teacher stays.

Act Two. Teacher and Child. Child arrives home and is aghast to see the teacher there. Teacher is grim-faced and they talk about the bad school report.

Act Three. Later. Dad and Child. Dad enters in a furious temper. He has it out with the child about his bad work and behaviour. Child is sent to do his homework.

Act Four. Mum and Dad. They discuss their child's bad school report. Why has it happened?

Vox Pop. The thoughts aloud of the four characters.

Pitched at the right level, this can be done with either Junior or Secondary age-groups.

(iii) The Divorce

There are three characters: Mum, Dad and Child. The action takes place in the living room.

Act One. Mother and Child. Mum explains to Child that she and Dad haven't been getting on very well lately. In short, they are going to have a divorce. The child reacts strongly. What's going to happen to them all? Mum exits to kitchen to make tea.

Act Two. Dad and Child. Dad comes in to find the child crying and comforts him. He tries to explain the situation as best he can. Child is still very upset and goes out.

Act Three. Mum and Dad. Yet another row. This time they bring into the argument the effect of the divorce on the child.

Vox Pop. The thoughts aloud of the three characters.

3 LOCATIONS

Instead of giving the children an outline of a plot to trigger off a piece of work in situation drama, you can instead specify a location to provide the guidelines for the piece. For example:

The Lift

Draw a chalked rectangle (about six feet by four feet)

on the ground to represent the lift. Two or three children enter the lift together. Their destination is the top floor of the block of flats. One presses the button and the lift starts — but suddenly, on a given signal, the lift gets stuck. Let the situation develop naturally; after a while you can make another signal (shaking a rattle or ringing a bell) which means that the lift has started again — and will bring them back to safety once more.

Outside the Headmaster's Office

'Hussein, you are sitting outside the Headmaster's Office, waiting to see him. Maybe you've been sent to him for bad behaviour, maybe it's about your work, maybe he's going to congratulate you for something, maybe you don't know why you're there. Anyway, you're sitting there when along comes Raymond, who's also been sent to the Headmaster. Let's see what happens outside the Headmaster's office. End it in whatever way you like.'

Other suitable locations

In the back row at school.
At an adventure playground.
The Doctor's or Dentist's waiting room.
At the tube station.
In the Customs. (Customs Officer and Traveller attempting to smuggle watches.)
At the police station. (Desk Sergeant, Detective, Man 'helping police with their inquiries'.)
In the hairdressing salon.
The prison cell. (Possibly planning their next job?)
In a convent.
In bed. (The last two minutes before falling asleep.)
Another planet. (The spacemen clamber down from their spaceship on to the surface of a newly dis-

covered planet and meet intelligent creatures living
on it, for the first time.)
Outside your home, cleaning the car. (Two neighbours.)
The transport cafe. (Proprietor, Lorry Driver, Hell's
Angels.)
The jewellers'. (An engaged couple.)
In Heaven.
At the magistrate's court.

4 OTHER SITUATION DRAMA IDEAS
Excuses

'Charles, will you be the teacher and sit up at the top
of the room with your table and chair? You start giving
the class a lesson on matrices or French verbs or the
Russian Revolution, or whatever you like. Beverley,
you are late for school and you gingerly come into the
class and, perhaps, try and quietly make for your seat,
hoping not to be seen. But the teacher sees you and
demands a reason for your lateness. Beverley, you make
up an excuse. The teacher listens to Beverley's excuse
and deals with it as he thinks he should.'

'After Beverley we'll have others, each coming in, in
turn, and giving a different excuse for being late. Be
original if you can, but always be credible. You're a bit
scared of this teacher, and you want him to believe you,
so don't make the excuses too fantastic. Start off,
Charles, please, and let's have Beverley in position ready
to come in and give the first excuse.'

Gossips

'Let's have a shop. And there is a shopkeeper (you,
Sharon) and a customer (Pauline). Every Friday you
both have a good old gossip over the counter when
Pauline comes in to do her week-end shopping. This
particular Friday is no exception: you both have a fine

gossip about the neighbours, the cost of living, the milk-man, the telly, the kids — you name it! It's up to you.'
     This gossip idea can be done in a variety of ways:
     Two housewives gossiping over a cuppa.
     Two schoolgirl gossips.
     Two people working on a factory assembly line.

The Pick-Up

'Theresa, you are on your own, at Highbury and Islington underground station, one night. There is not a soul other than yourself on the platform. Along comes Shefki. He gives you the once over, reckons on you . . . decides he definitely fancies you. Shefki, you try to pick up Theresa. Now, Theresa, you've been told by your mum a hundred times if you've been told once — never talk to strangers. But maybe Shefki can produce a line of chat that makes him irresistible. Let's see, Shefki, if you succeed in picking up the lovely Theresa.
     'The pick-up can also take place at the bus stop or at the cinema or at a dance. Roles can be reversed with the girl picking up the boy.'

Letting Someone into your Confidence

'Anita, you and Lucy are friends and one of the lovely things about friendship is the sharing of all sorts of things: fun and games, clothes, ideas, holidays, secrets and confidences. On this day, Anita has a particular confidence that she wants to share with Lucy. It is up to you what the subject of the confidence is. You are both sitting on the grass in your garden, soaking up the sun on a lovely summer's day, when Anita lets her friend into her confidence.'

The Political Speaker

'We're going to do a scene that takes place at Speakers' Corner in Hyde Park. Have you every been there?

104

Religious and political speakers stand on their soap boxes airing their opinions, and many of them are very colourful personalities. If you haven't yet been to Speakers' Corner it is worth a visit.

'Davidson, you are a political speaker — and a very lively one! I'll leave the choice of subject to you — you may be putting over your view on Northern Ireland, the Arabs and the Israelis, Women's Liberation, the Government, political parties . . . whatever you like. You are interrupted intermittently by hecklers (from the rest of the class). Make sure, hecklers, that you don't get out of control because for the purposes of theatre even if the situation gets a bit wild it must not get chaotic. So, hecklers, work with one another, not against one another. Self-discipline is important, in a crowd scene particularly. All right, Davidson, get on your soap box, and the rest of the class gather round him and listen.'

Miss World

For this piece of work there is a compere and a number of contestants: Miss Australia, Miss Nigeria, Miss Peru, etc. As each contestant's name is called, she walks forward, to the accompaniment of suitable music, and is given a thirty-second interview by the compere about her hobbies, ambitions, what she will do with the prize money if she wins, and so on. Then the result is announced and the winner is crowned while the losers bravely try to hide their disappointment. The situation can be sent up slightly, but without playing for laughs.

The same thing can be done with the sexes reversed, making it a Mr World contest.

Technical dialogue

A type of work that stretches verbal fluency is situation drama in a setting that requires the use of technical dialogue, e.g. a surgical operation, the control cabin of an airliner, a space vehicle. The more authentic vocabulary that can be brought in the better; if it is not authentic, then it must have the right style and sound to it. For science fiction, strings of letters and numbers are useful: 'The LRQs are on. CYP is negative, zero zero zero three. AGS thirty-five degrees. Firing retros. Three. Two. One. Zero.'

Free improvisation given partial information

As young people become more experienced, they will be able to create improvisation given less and less information to work on. You may give them a location, a single statement about a character, an item of costume, a hat, a prop, or any combination of these. Choose a couple of people to use these stimuli to create a piece of drama, without preparation, coming to a definite ending within a rough time-limit of two minutes.

For example: 'This table is in a cafe. Gary, sitting at the the table, is twenty-three and has just come out of the Army. Pauline, coming into the cafe, is wearing this pink hat.' Or 'June is waiting at the bus stop. She is a night-duty telephonist, going home. Shefki is also standing there, wearing this pair of dark glasses.'

A variation of this is *The Park Bench.* Two people, 1 and 2, sit on a park bench. They have a conversation. 1 gets up and goes. 3 comes along and sits down. 2 and 3 have a conversation. 2 gets up and goes. 4 comes along and sits down. 3 and 4 have a conversation, and so on indefinitely. Characterization, whether the characters know each other, and the content of the conversation are all left entirely open.

Real-life events

The re-enactment of real-life situations drawn from

newspaper and television stories can make for interesting
work. As well as providing good dramatic material, it
can lead children to examine their own and other
people's feelings more closely, and increase their sense
of awareness.

If you choose situations based on the children's own
experience at home, school, etc., great care must be
taken not to intrude on anyone's privacy, nor to reopen
any recently healed wounds. Also, remember that fairness demands that all sides of an argument should be
equally well represented.

Carry on the story in drama

Another way of doing situation drama is by telling the
beginning of a story to the class, casting it as you go
along, and then leaving it halfway through for the group
to improvise an ending. You will need to lay out a
simple set, suitable for the story, beforehand.

For example: 'Zanna, would you come and sit on this
chair. I'm going to tell a story, and I want you and a
couple of other people to improvise the ending. Right?'

'It was an unusual case. The girl had been picked up
by the police at two in the morning, wandering the
streets. She couldn't have been more than fourteen. No
money; nothing to identify her. She was wearing an
expensive coat, though. The odd thing was that she
wouldn't say a word to anyone. The ward-sister
[beckoning Rita into the scene] has tried everything,
but she could get no response. The girl had eaten her
breakfast though – as if she was starving. The psychiatrist
at the hospital was Dr Payne [beckoning Elvis Payne to
a table on the other side of the room], maybe he'd be
able to help. She looked such an odd little thing, sitting
there with a blank expression on her face. Probably just
ran away from home, thought the sister, and too scared

to say anything. Dr Payne could be relied upon to put some fancy explanation on it, though. Better call him in, anyway . . . .'

And the improvisation takes up the story from there and it ends in any way they want.

Change in a character

Characters change in reaction to the people they're with. An example of a piece of work that can be used to illustrate this:

'You, Catherine, are going away on holiday with the school. You are sitting in the train with your mum, Lilian, who has come into the compartment to say goodbye to you, and we hear your conversation. After a while, in comes Geraldine, a friend of yours from school, and the three of you talk together. Then the whistle blows for the train to go and Mum gets out, leaving the two girls by themselves; you can end in whatever way you want. Now, Lilian, you're in a real state about your daughter, because it's the first time she's been away from home and you hope she'll be all right. You hope there will be some nice girls with her. Catherine wishes her mum wouldn't fuss so, and treat her like a kid; still, it should be a laugh on holiday with Geraldine, maybe they'll meet some boys. Geraldine's mum didn't bring her to the station, she left her to find her own way. She's brought a packet of fags for the journey.'

Large groups

Situation drama with large groups is difficult. It demands awareness and concentration from all the participants. You need to choose situations where in real life a large group of people interact together for a common purpose, without splitting up into smaller groups.

Each of these pieces can be introduced by describing the situation and allocating characters, as required. There is no preparation time; what happens in the improvisation is up to the group.

Examples of group situations:

At School: Reactions to hearing your exam marks. (One of the class, as a teacher, reads out the exam marks for the group, ranging from very low to very high, and gives appropriate comments. The class react, without over-reacting, to hearing their own and each other's marks.)

The English Conversation Class: (Teacher, who must be strong. Pupils come from many different countries and although they don't speak very good English it is their only medium of communication. They are all ages; some are students, others are international businessmen. Some are very serious and conscientious. One or two are more interested in the girls than learning English. One turns up late.)

Television Programme: *The Football Panel 'What's Wrong with the Game?'* (Chairman, who must be very strong. Well-respected international player, near to retirement. Hot-headed young star. Referee. Mad Scottish Football Manager. Self-made millionaire, now chairman of Football Club. Sports journalist. Supporters, old and young, including a couple who have been fined for hooliganism. Ticket tout in dark glasses. Supporter's wife. Old-time footballer who played for five pounds a week.)

Case meeting about a boy who's got into trouble with the police. (Head of Social Team, who acts as chairman. Social Worker. The boy's teacher. Leader of his Youth Club. Educational Psychologist. The boy's parents can be brought in later, and then the boy himself.)

Group Therapy. (Psychiatrist. Members of the group

meet once a week. They are well enough to be out of hospital but have problems: Anxiety. Phobias. Alcoholism. Recovery from drug addiction. Young person not getting on with his or her parents. Husband not getting on with wife or vice versa. Shyness. Depression. The idea of the meeting is to discuss each other's problems and help each other.)

5 MONOLOGUES

Thoughts aloud

'Sarmila, would you sit on the ground in the middle of the floor, with your legs out in front of you. Would Claire find a space and do the same, and Broderick, and Haniff, and Rose. You are all in the bath! Not, I hasten to add, in the same bathroom, but each in your own, private bathroom. Let's see you scrubbing your back . . . and washing yourself all over. Let's hear you singing in the bath!'

'Now, some people get their best ideas while in the bath, you know. I want to hear your thoughts, aloud, in the bath. Maybe you think about your ambitions, or your wildest dreams, or maybe your thoughts are more down to earth — your science homework, what to get for your mum's birthday, what's on telly tonight. Your thoughts could be about school, home, family, boyfriends or girlfriends — whatever. Let's hear some of your thoughts in the bath, aloud, one by one. Sarmila? Action . . . .'

Thoughts aloud can also take place in the doctor's or dentist's waiting room, at the bus stop, or at the back of a classroom.

TV Channels

'I am going to be watching three different programmes on television. Each time I ring the bell that means I've changed channels. First, I might be watching a newscaster, then change to a play (it might be comedy, tragedy, kitchen-sink, or whatever), and then I change channels again: this time it's a pop programme.'

'Mario, will you go into the middle and be three different characters in turn — the choice is yours — changing roles each time I ring the bell and switch channels. Select any incidental props and costume now if you need them. At the sound of the bell you switch characters *immediately*, so keep your wits about you as this requires one hundred per cent concentration and quick thinking.'

A variation of TV channels is *Adverts*, with three TV Commercials as content.

The Mirror

'Everyone sometimes looks at themselves in the mirror, taking a long level look, while critically contemplating their physical appearance — your eyes are a bit piggy, your hair is greasy, your skin's got one or two nasty spots, but you've got quite a nice smile, though, you wish you were slimmer — those hips! Mind you, your legs aren't so bad . . . '

'Kim, take the mirror and honestly criticize yourself, or else you can send it up, exaggerating your beauty! After Kim, let's have John Blundell. Do remember, even if you are sending it up, to still play it for real and not for laughs.'

Half a Duologue, or Talking to an Imaginary Person

In this piece of work the individual taking part talks to an imaginary other person, behaving normally, as if the imaginary person is really there. It's important that they should listen to what the other person is saying, and react to what he does.

For example: 'Johanah Sheikh. Sit in the chair in the middle: I want you to talk to an imaginary teacher — not me, but an imaginary teacher. I'll give you the cue "Johanah Sheikh! Stand up!". And you improvise from there. Watch your eye-level — don't make the teacher twelve feet tall or two feet small. Keep a realistic eye-level so we can believe in the situation. Right! "Johanah Sheikh! Stand up!" '

Other imaginary people to talk to:

Boyfriend or girlfriend, flattering you.
Boyfriend or girlfriend, ending the relationship.
Very depressed person.
Old-age pensioner.
New-born baby (you are its mother).
Crowd (you are a political speaker).
A current pop star (specify who it is).
Foreigner (who speaks very little English).
Someone who's borrowed something from you
    without asking.
Friend who is dying.

6 IMPROVISED PLAYS

About four or five children is a good, manageable size for a group to prepare and perform an improvised play. It gets a bit chaotic if the group is any bigger, unless the children are very experienced, and this leads to disappointment.

At first it is best to appoint a director, who should have a strong personality. Although all the children contribute to the content of the play, the director has the last say, and is responsible for the over-all shape of the play.

Before the children set off to prepare plays, you will

have advised them on how to construct one: the
characters must be believable and the play must have a
good, strong plot; it must have a beginning, a middle
and a good, definite ending; also, stress the importance of
having the right length for the story, neither too long nor
too short — avoiding 'milking' the situation.

The amount of preparation time needed for improvised
plays is usually about ten minutes for Juniors (up to
eleven) and about fifteen minutes for Secondary (eleven
and over) and older. The more open the brief they have
been given, the longer they will need. They can be given
a title for the play, or a first line or last line, or a theme.
Later on, they can be given more time for thought by
appointing directors at the end of a lesson, and giving
them a title to work on for next time. Soon they will
want to write and direct plays entirely of their own
devising.

On average, about seven to ten minutes should be
sufficient time to allow for a simple improvised play,
including setting up, performance and time for constructive comments and criticisms. As in situation drama,
comments can be made by yourself and the rest of the
audience, but a nice idea is to choose about four members
of the class as a panel of 'experts', specially appointed
to comment on the play or plays of the day. Some
children like to be given points out of ten, and this can
be done by the panel.

In comments, one point to concentrate on at the
start is the importance of the action being continuous.
If two sets are required, they can be placed side by side,
instead of altering the set in the middle of the play.
Similarly, all announcements should be made together at
the beginning rather than having one of the actors come
out of character to announce: 'Scene Two. Next
morning. In the shed.'

Direction

When the teacher, or anyone else, is directing a play for improvisation that has already been thought out, it is important to present it to the cast in an orderly way or else they will become confused.

A typical sequence is:

1 Basic idea of the plot, expressed in one or two sentences.
2 Casting. Who the characters are and how they're related.
3 Set. How it will be laid out and what it represents.
4 Description of the action and outline of what the characters will say, dividing it up into sections. Make sure everyone knows their starting points, emphasize the key points in the action and concentrate throughout on what the characters are thinking and feeling.
5 Questions.
6 Suggestions.
7 Changes resulting from suggestions.
8 Run-though of any important or difficult sections.
9 Questions again.
10 Costume and props.
11 Music and lighting (if applicable).

The following play titles are suitable for all ages:

The Letter
Good News
Get Your Hair Cut
The Doctor and the Patient
Frou Frou, the Wonder Dog,
   or The Dog that can do
   Amazing Tricks
Crime
The Eavesdropper

The Baby
The Girl with Green Hair
Kidnapped
Gangsters
Marooned on a Desert Island
The Green Paper Bag
In the Middle of the Night
A Fairy Tale
Family Matters

The Secret Formula
The Box of Chemicals
The Key
The Door Marked 'Private'
Fire
The Hijacker
In the Aeroplane
The Time Machine
The Secret
Grandad
Beauty and the Beast
The Dream
The Man from the Council
Mother and Son
Father and Son
The Boy (or Girl) Who
    Wouldn't Speak
Old Uncle Bayram
The Thieves
Danger at the Zoo
The American Girl
Robbery with Violence
The Stranger at the Door
The Doctor
The Forbidden Planet
The Bomb That Wasn't
The Birthday Surprise
The Conflict
Robots
Bad News
The Bully at the Bus Stop
Shock
Gunman City
The Visitor who Came to Tea
Rat Poison

In the Year 2000
Planet X
Accident
The Black Box
The Special Dress
Incident at the Bus Stop
The Nagging Mother
The Monster
Ebenezer Scrooge
The Hat
Dial M for Murder
Two Workmen
The Haunted House
Whodunnit?
World War II
The Gipsy Fortune-Teller
The Nightmare
Grandma
Spoilt Children
The Truants
Teacher's Pet
Mother and Daughter
Father and Daughter
I Can Read Your Thoughts
Pauline and the Pop Star
Divorce
The Invisible Man
Baby-Snatcher
Poison Gas
The Man-Eating Plant
Grandad's Will
Please Don't Tease
Round the Flats
The Telephone

Additional play titles particularly suitable for younger children:

The Lost Ring
Can I Have a Pet?
What a Surprise
The Wicked Witch
The Boy (or Girl) with the Funny Nose (or Ears, etc.)

The Broken Window
Three Wishes
The Lost Kitten
Father Christmas

Additional play titles particularly suitable for older boys and girls:

Happiness
Jealousy
Pregnancy
Prowess
The Bringer of Bad News
Cheating at Cards
Hands
No Smoking
Have you Had It Yet?
The Hippie Commune
Behind the Scenes at the Wedding
The Prisoners of War
In the Mental Hospital
The Return of Al Capone
Learning to Fly
Why I Ran Away from Home
The Prisoner
In the Heat of the Night
Love and Money
The Wrong Number Was Right
The Worst Thing in the World

Before and After
The Wig
The Telegram
Cattiness
Expulsion from School
At the Office
Suddenly ...
Smoking
The Protection Racket
The Facts of Life
Blood on a Wednesday
We Rule This School
Witchcraft
Suspended from School
How to be a Lady
Acting Flash
The Most Important Thing in Life
The Death of the President
She Loves Me, She Loves Me Not
Everybody Loves Saturday Night
Runaway Lovers

Plays given the last line:

Welcome Home.
I don't care.

Don't talk to her like that.
Now look what you've made

Help! Help! Help!
We can't get out.
No. No. No.
You stupid idiot.
Too late.
Don't cry, love.
You must be out of your
    mind.
Now we'll have to start
    all over again.
I wish we could do this every
    day.
The answer is yes.
The answer is no.
This is the end.
I'll tell Miss on you.

me do.
You've only got yourself
    to blame.
No, it can't be.
We found out too late.
I didn't mean it, honest I
    didn't.
Why me?
It's not my fault.
Please don't tell anyone.
How can I ever thank you
    enough.
Well, thank God for that.
You're fired!
Oh my God he's (or she's)
    dead.

Plays given the first line:

Are you new here?
What's the matter with you?
Ow! The dog is biting my leg.
Sssh! She's coming.
Are you mad?
Where's the baby gone?
Hey mum, look what the
    cat brought in!
Have you got the right
    time?

Hello, what's your name?
Listen, I've got a great idea.
Come here immediately!
My purse is missing!
I wouldn't do that if I were you.
Blimey! look what we've got here.
Turn down that record-player,
    will you?
Your breakfast's getting cold.
I'm feeling fed up.

Themes for plays:

Love.
Plays with titles from current popular song titles.
Plays with proverbs as titles. (All that glitters is not
    gold. Still waters run deep. What the eye doesn't
    see, the heart doesn't grieve over. Two's company,
    three's a crowd.)

117

A play in which three words drawn from a hat are to
 be used (e.g. Key. Lift. Button. Glass. Sellotape.
 Poster. Vacuum Cleaner. Cake. Heart. Onion. Chalk.
 Cheese. Light. Grass. Bed. Farm. Nails. Angel. Pin.
 Hairbrush. Dandelion. Medicine. Vase. Shoes. Toilet.
 Paper. Wig. Boots. Pig.).
Plays with plots based on current newspaper stories.
Plays which must be set in the future, or which must be
 set in the past.
Plays in which a given prop must be used (e.g. a tankard,
 a pack of cards).
Plays with a supernatural theme.
Topical plays (e.g. Valentine's Day. St. Patrick's Day.
 Hallowe'en. April Fool's Day. Christmas. Guy
 Fawkes.).
Social themes (e.g. A play about a girl who finds herself
 pregnant: her reactions and those of her boy friend,
 other friends, parents, doctor, etc.).
Themes based on work in school outside drama.

6

Technique

As we said in the Introduction, regarding the distinction between drama and theatre, in drama an enriched experience is shared by members of the participating group; in theatre, through the use of technique, people not involved in the action can share the experience too. Because of the desire of most children to communicate with others in this way, for them drama develops inevitably towards theatre. Theatre is an art and, as in all art forms, there are skills to be learned — the skills of theatre technique.

Theatre technique should not be treated as an isolated subject but can be brought incidentally and unobtrusively into most classes, as the need for it arises.

If this is not done, children will be held back from realizing their potential. They will have something they want to communicate, but they will be deprived of the most effective way of doing so. Too little will have been asked of them.

To some, performance is a dirty word. It is certainly not beneficial if it is attempted without having the necessary strong foundations in play and drama. If this is done, too much will have been asked of the children rather than too little. Through trying and failing, their confidence may be destroyed, or they may be reduced to the level of parrots, mouthing lines learned by heart for an audience without regard to what they mean. That may be performance of a kind, but nothing worthwhile will be communicated.

Here, then, are a selection of drama ideas that have a strong technical content.

CONCENTRATION

Mind Concentration. This can be done at the start of a
drama session or at any other time when it is necessary
to restore a calm atmosphere. The class form a circle and,
on the teacher's instruction, all close their eyes. The
teacher, in a clear, quiet, deliberate voice, begins 'The
word concentration means "keeping your mind on something" and if you concentrate on what you're doing,
whether it's drama or football or school work, you're
going to do it that much better than if you've got half
your mind on it and the other half on what's on telly
tonight.' Pause while everyone concentrates. 'Now,
listen to all the sounds outside this room.' Pause. 'And
now listen to all the sounds inside the room.' Pause.
'Open your eyes.'
Active Concentration. The circle breaks up and each
person finds a partner. Get them to talk *at each other*.
They must concentrate on two things: one, what they
are saying to their partner; two, what their partner is
saying to them. Every now and then freeze them and test
at random: 'Penny, what was John talking about? John,
what was Penny talking about?' Change partners and
continue this active concentration exercise but this time
they sing at each other, say, 'Doh a Deer' and 'Frere
Jacques' or songs of their own choice. Ask one couple to
sing by themselves; they must not break concentration
by laughing and both must sing their different songs
simultaneously and in full throat.
Clapping Concentration Exercise. Divide the class into
pairs and each pair into A and B. They have to devise
a distinct rhythmical clapping pattern between them.
Then all the A's go to one side of the room and the B's
to the other side, sitting with their backs to each other.
The teacher selects someone from the A side to begin

clapping his rhythm. As soon as his partner from the B side recognizes his clapping pattern he joins in. Repeat several times, starting alternately with side A and side B. *Tongue Twisters* require concentration, as well as being a speech exercise. Start with an easy one, 'furious thrushes', repeated several times. Then progress through 'Peter Piper picked a peck of pickled peppers' and 'She sells sea shells on the sea shore' to 'The sixth sick sheik's sixth sheep's sick' which, according to *The Guinness Book of Records*, is the hardest tongue twister in the English language. If they can manage that at fair speed, then their concentration is very good indeed.

PROJECTION

The aim in projection is not just to speak loudly enough to enable everyone in the room to hear you, but also to speak clearly and distinctly. One person goes to one end of the room and another to the furthermost point opposite. Concentrating on voice projection without in any way straining the voice, they speak in turn to one another. They can be asked to have a conversation with one another on any given subject, or to play Word Tennis (see page 25), which is alternately calling out words from a given category (e.g. meals, flowers, products advertised on television).

The 'carry-on-story' and 'one-word-story' ideas (see page 33) can both be used for voice projection exercises too. If four people are taking part, each can go to a different corner of the room, and each person must be clearly audible to the other three.

METHOD

The title is from the American idea of method acting, i.e. losing yourself completely in the part. In *Method* we are working along similar lines, but in this case by becoming inanimate objects. For example, you may say to the class 'Everybody find a space . . . . Be a knife'. Everyone will get into knife-like positions, with hands together in the air, or sticking out like the blades of a penknife, or lying down on the ground, all with knife-like expressions on their faces. They will, as it were, be feeling what it is like to be a knife. Encourage them to use their own idea of a knife, and not to copy each other. Strike as total credibility.

Other inanimate objects that can be suggested are: a pair of scissors, the sun, a star, a scarf, a dress on a hanger, a pencil, a shoe, a bag, a table, a puppet, a banana, a cake, a ship, a kite, a potato, a flame, a ball, a clock, a jug, a tree, a box, spectacles, flowers, a bottle, the numbers 0–9, the letters of the alphabet.

The idea is to foster total belief in what you are doing. This does not only serve to make for credible performances, it is necessary for worthwhile drama of any sort.

This can be done with all ages from infants to adults. Younger children will take to it very readily.

VOICE MODULATION

Make a sound on a monotone. Get the class to sound a monotone and explore using different pitches. The voice modulates when talking — it varies in tone, volume and pitch. Do the following voice modulation exercises, bringing home the use of inflexion (e.g. the voice going up when asking a question), facial expression and emotion.

Take the sentence 'I can't see you tonight' (or 'Please don't do that to me', 'What about by brother?', 'I don't want to go home', or whatever) and ask a small group of about six people each to take a turn at saying it in different ways, starting off straight with no particular expression, then asking a question, answering a question, being angry, bored, frightened, proud, jeering, surprised, shy, outraged, shouting it as loud as possible (but without straining), whispering (but still projecting), sleepy (while suppressing a yawn), crying (but still the words must be clear), laughing, conspiratorially, in opera style, in pop style.

Take some gibberish, such as 'Gabbitas Motor Thing' or 'Carrie Alley Dot', and ask people individually to use the nonsense words to ask a question and to give the answer. 'Gabbitas Motor Thing? Gabbitas Motor Thing.' The class *listens* and will notice the different modulations in question and answer. The same varied emotions as before can be applied to the gibberish (angry, bored, etc.), but always sincerely. They must really mean it.

INFLEXIONS

Use simple words like 'yes', 'no' and 'oh' to explore the use of varying inflexions, either working individually or as a whole group; e.g. in twos, improvise a piece using only the words 'yes', 'no' and 'oh', letting the inflexions and the actions express the meaning. Or have one person on the telephone holding a conversation with an imaginary person at the other end of the line using only 'yes', 'no' and 'oh' with different inflexions. Inflexions of anger, delight, boredom, fear, surprise, etc. can be brought in. Divide the class into pairs and ask them to talk together using only nonsense words, or numbers, names of colours, or letters of the alphabet and allow the inflexions to express the meaning.

VERBAL MACHINES

Verbal machines are a good follow-up to *Machines* (see page 50). Choose a subject—school, for example—and ask someone to start off a School Machine. He comes out from his place and starts a repetitive verbal pattern

'What page, sir?' . . . 'What page, sir?' . . . 'What page, sir?', making the same movement each time, looking up at the imaginary teacher. He continues doing this without a break, while a second person is beckoned in to build up the next part of the machine, fitting in rhythmically with 'That's *my* pencil' . . . 'That's *my* pencil' . . . 'That's *my* pencil', and then a third chimes in, fitting his phrase in with the other two, 'I can't see the board' . . . 'I can't see the board' . . . 'I can't see the board'. The machine can be stopped by 'Freeze' and started again by 'Action'. Rhythm, timing and projection are three important points of technique here. The different machine parts can be spoken from different levels: standing, sitting, kneeling, or lying down. Three people working together is a good number to make up a verbal machine but more, indeed the whole class, can be used.

Other types of verbal machines include a Teacher Machine, a War Machine, a Food Machine, a Fashion Machine, a TV Machine, a Pop Machine, a Theatre Machine, a Hairdresser Machine, a New-born Baby Machine, and many more.

Other categories are verbal machines using different *emotions*: an Angry Machine, a Frightened Machine, a Love Machine, or a Mad Machine; or *Contrasting Machines*: the Insults Machine and the Compliments Machine, the Noisy Machine and the Quiet Machine. A Quiet Machine has a particularly calming effect.

SNEEZE, COUGH, LAUGH, CRY, ETC.

The boys and girls form a circle. Ask them all to start to sneeze, then cough, laugh, cry, yawn, hiccup, belch, stammer in a realistic way. Then, individually, one tells us something about himself, only he punctuates it with sneezing; someone else tells us something about himself punctuating his story with coughing, another laughing, crying, yawning, etc.

It is important to sustain the train of thought by thorough concentration, and of course each person must create for himself a reason for laughing, or crying, or whatever it is.

The most difficult one of sneeze, cough, laugh, cry, etc. to produce is laughing. Work can be done on different kinds of laughter: sniggering, uncontrollable laughter, mocking laughter, sarcastic laughter, laughter at a *risqué* joke, polite laughter, embarrassed laughter, belly-laughter, even laughing yourself to death.

This can be done with a whole class, in groups or individually.

ASIDES

Make reference to Shakespeare's use of the aside and the two voice pitches used — the straight one, which the actor uses to the character he is talking to, and the other, lower pitched, out front to the audience or to a third party. Comedian Frankie Howerd is a master of the aside.

For an exercise on asides, two people have a conversation on a given subject, e.g. husband talking to wife about mother-in-law coming to stay. He starts in a straight voice 'So your mother's coming to stay again?' and, in an aside, turning to the audience and dropping his voice a tone 'Interfering old busy-body'. Back to straight voice again: 'Why does she always have to come on a Sunday when I like to have a drink with the boys?' Then to the audience in an aside: 'She does it on purpose, I know, just to make trouble with me and the wife.'

A telephone can be useful in an exercise on asides, the actor talking straight to the person on the phone and, with hand over mouth piece and lowering the voice, making the asides to someone else in the room.

Asides can be done in a genuine way, or else with humorous intent.

STAGE FALLS

Without going far into the technicalities of stage fighting and stunt work, it might be a good idea to try some stage falls, which are popular with children.

In a stage fall the two requirements are to fall realistically but at the same time to avoid hurting yourself.

To avoid hurting yourself a number of things are required. You must fall on parts of the body which are well padded — notably the bottom — and avoid hitting sensitive places such as elbows, knees and head, or jarring your wrists. If possible, break your fall, instead of taking the full force of it in a single impact. You must make sure there are no hard objects, or people, in your way. If you wear spectacles, you should take them off when practising stage falls.

For realism, you must know the reason why you are making the fall as this, of course, will considerably affect the type of fall it is. Has someone shot you with a pistol? Were you knocked down in a brawl? Is it a faint? Have you dropped down dead with a sudden heart attack?

If it is a death fall, then the aftermath is important — concentrating on complete stillness.

When practising stage falls it is necessary to have plenty of room for each person and only three or four people working at the same time to avoid clashing of heads, etc. The signal, representing the gunshot or whatever, is given by the teacher, either to each person individually, or all at once.

Afterwards you can test for relaxation as in 'curl and stretch' (page 42).

EYE CONTACT

The class go into pairs. In an atmosphere of serious concentration, each pair looks into each other's eyes. Continue to hold this mood for fifteen or twenty seconds. Introduce different emotions in turn — hostility, fear, friendliness, boredom — the exercise is to maintain eye contact in that emotion, fearful eyes to fearful eyes, friendly eyes to friendly eyes, etc.

The eyes are a most important feature in drama and theatre, as they are such an expressive part of the body. Children can be encouraged not to be afraid or embarrassed when making eye contact, particularly between the sexes. This is important, not only for drama or a theatrical performance, but also when meeting people, in interviews and so on.

STANDING, WALKING AND SITTING

This is an advanced exercise in which everyone in the group takes part together. To work properly it depends on 100 per cent concentration from everybody.

The class sit on chairs in a large circle. The teacher selects a mood or character-state for all the group to adopt. For example, he may say 'You are good-humoured, cheerful people, on good terms with yourselves most of the time, and not easily depressed' and the group become good-humoured people, not by producing any obvious visible signs of good humour in a crude way, such as grinning all over their faces, but by creating the inner feeling of being a good-humoured person. In other words, the emphasis is on being rather than doing.

After allowing a few moments for the feeling to develop, the teacher says someone's name and that person gets up from his place, walks to a vacant chair in the circle, and sits down again, maintaining the same good-humoured mood throughout. Then someone else does the same thing, and someone else again. Keep it up for one to two minutes and then change the mood to something else.

Other moods or character-states that can be used are: self-confident, self-conscious, arrogant, depressed, successful, harassed, undisciplined and frivolous, fit and athletic, intense, relaxed, aggressive, dominant, preoccupied, narcissistic, indecisive.

Exaggeration must be avoided.

VOX POP

Vox populi (voice of the people) is a technique used in current affairs and magazine-type tv programmes, in which a series of interviews on a given subject are conducted with members of the public, and then short sections are edited out of each interview and shown as an uninterrupted sequence.

In a vox pop improvisation, five or six people are asked to stand in a line and produce the same effect as in vox pop on television. For example, you may tell them 'I want you to imagine that you (either being yourself or a different character) have been stopped in the street and interviewed about Crime, the rising crime rate, what should happen to criminals when they're caught, the effect of people's environments on whether they become criminals, and so on. Think about what you might have said. We're going to see just a sentence or two from each interview. Action.' Starting from one end of the line we hear a middle-aged housewife, 'I think it's disgraceful, the way things are going round here; you can't go outside your front door'; straightaway on to the next person, a youngish man, 'Mind you, I don't blame the kids for what they get up to. I'd do the same if I was their age'; another woman, more aggressive, 'I'd soon put a stop to

it, I can tell you. Lock them *all* up, that's what I'd do';
an older man, 'Next thing I knew I woke up in hospital.
Concussion and twenty-five stitches in my head'; an
impassive-faced man, 'I don't know anything about it,
mate'.

This demands quick thinking and concentration, and
also the ability to be economical with words and
condense as much as possible about a character into a
short space of time.

To introduce the technique, simple questions can be
used, like 'What's your favourite meal? What's your
favourite animal and why? What do you look for in a
holiday?' Other topics are politics and current affairs,
television, education and opportunities for young people,
moral questions such as sex before marriage, divorce, etc.

You can pick out one or two characters you find
interesting and ask them more questions about themselves
and the subject. Later on, you can make the exercise even
more testing by having only two people, each one doing
alternate characters, or even only one person doing five
or six characters one after the other.

Vox pop can be used as a lead-in to either discussion
or character work; it is also a useful device for performances.

DRAMA VOCABULARY

Just like any other specialized subject, drama has its
own vocabulary and this can be brought in to drama
lessons as the need arises.

The use of simple drama vocabulary not only helps
in expressing things briefly and precisely, but children
respond favourably and it helps to instil an outlook that
is professional, in the sense of being serious-minded and
aiming for high standards. (See over for list of
definitions.)

100+ Ideas for Drama

Improvisation	Making it up as you go along, using your own words.
Mime	Acting with actions but without words.
Props	Properties: the items, other than costumes and scenery, used in drama.
Freeze	Stop absolutely still like a statue.
Action	Begin the action of the drama.
Cut	Stop the action of the drama.
Dialect	Different accents; different ways of speaking English.
Applause	The clapping of an audience.
Encore	A French word meaning 'again', used when asking for a repeat performance.
Audience	The people who watch a performance.
Playwright	Someone who writes plays, e.g. William Shakespeare.
Script	A play, written down.
Dialogue	Conversation in a play.
Corpsing	Laughing when you shouldn't be.
Set	The set represents the place where a scene happens.
Costume	The clothes worn in a play.
Project	Speak loudly and clearly enough to be heard by everyone.
Concentrate	Keep your mind on the job in hand.
Director	The person in charge of a drama event.
Cue	Signal for next performer to being action.
Prompt	Reminder made to an actor if he forgets his words.
Wings	Sides of a stage.
Proscenium	A picture-frame stage.
Theatre-in-the-round	Theatre with the audience on all sides.
Tragedy/Comedy	A tragedy is a sad play, a comedy is a happy one.
Monologues/ duologues	A monologue is one person talking, a duologue is two people talking.
Professional/ amateur	Professional actors are those who are paid to act; it is their job. Amateurs do it for the love of it; as a hobby.

Another 100 + Ideas for Drama

Introduction

Another 100 + Ideas for Drama is the sequel to *100 + Ideas for Drama* and like its predecessor it is intended to be used as a source book by drama teachers, students, youth and community workers, members of theatre groups – in fact by anyone who is interested in drama for or by young people. Like the previous volume it can be described as a recipe book, containing hundreds of drama ideas in improvisation which can be used in a variety of ways; but, whereas in *100 + Ideas for Drama* the emphasis was on short drama workshop exercises, here there is a greater concentration on more developed ideas that require a longer time-span, or can be extended from session to session, or can provide the theme for a whole term's work, or make a production for performance to an audience.

There are chapters on 'Developed Work in Improvisation', 'Channelling Creativity', 'Umbrella Themes', 'Short Productions' and 'Full-Scale Productions'. In each chapter the introductory paragraphs are followed by a wealth of ideas presented in a way that makes them easy to follow, use and adapt to whatever your particular situation may be – from classroom to living-room, from youth club to theatre studio. In general we have used the words 'class' and 'teacher' to represent the group and the person leading it, but that does not mean that any of the work in the book need be limited to a school setting. Neither have we been specific about the age range with which particular ideas can be used. Many of them, with suitable variations in approach, can cover the whole range from infants to adults, or large parts of it. In this, common sense and trial and error are the best guides.

The last chapter, 'More Ideas', contains additional material in all the categories used in *100 + Ideas for Drama* that we have developed in the years since that book came out. Both short and snappy ideas and solid and developed ones are included alongside one another for you to adapt to your own individual way of working. There is also a short section on video work.

WHY IMPROVISATION?

Improvisation – making it up as you go along – is the most

immediate form of drama. In an improvisation, the participants become part of the action straight away, without any lengthy preparation or memorizing. It does not demand any skills of literacy. While keeping in touch with the everyday concerns of the participants, it enables them to express deeper feelings as well. The skills it does use and develop are articulacy and the ability to be aware of and draw on one's own emotions. Expressing and understanding one's own emotions *and* those of others is an important, and neglected, area of education. The experience of having to stand in someone else's shoes and feel as he or she feels will help the individual to think through the results of his or her actions in real life. This develops tolerance, understanding and appreciation. Practice in speaking articulately and having to express oneself clearly is particularly valuable in a system in which the stress is generally on written, rather than oral, education. Imagination, again, is stimulated and developed through being used.

Because of its immediacy, improvisation is a valuable teaching tool in itself; it enables a teacher to 'get round the class' and give the maximum number of people the maximum amount of time with the maximum level of involvement. Beyond the obvious applications to social and moral education, improvisation can be applied to help teach literature, history, Greek mythology, the Bible, and so on.

Despite its accessibility, improvisation is not just 'instant theatre'. An improvisation need not be just an isolated piece of work that is produced, used and then thrown away. It can be kept, developed and built on, and this book deals particularly with the processes involved in this — the creation of developed work that has its roots in improvisation.

One thing that is of paramount importance — and this is where the role of teacher or director comes in — is to provide a clear, positive brief. Only the most highly skilled, and confident, can spin improvisations out of thin air. Start with something specific, even though things may later change, for, as King Lear said to Cordelia, 'Nothing will come of nothing'.

HOW DOES IMPROVISATION RELATE TO WORK WITH WRITTEN PLAYS?

First, always remember that the text is not the play. Plays are live events that appear on a stage; the books they are written in are, if you like, a kind of storage device. But they are essential because, without them, the unique creations of individual playwrights would not survive.

So what does experience of improvisation equip your students with when they approach a script for the first time? They should be looking on the characters as live people, existing in all their dimensions of thought and feeling. They should be looking at the way each character relates to the other characters and particularly how this changes as time elapses and we pass turning-points in the plot. Even in plays where characters are personifications of abstract qualities, they must still have their special individual human characteristics.

Because of this, when working on a specific play, improvisation can provide a particularly important stepping-stone to the text. Working from improvisation to the text and vice versa helps give the character in the play his own unique persona, his own flesh and blood and understanding. How does he or she feel in relation to the others in the play? Does he or she know how they feel about him? Through improvisation an actor can find his character.

Specific methods that can be used in rehearsal are to improvise the content (action, conflicts and emotion) of particular scenes without using the words of the playwright, or to improvise round the characters, playing scenes between them that are not in the actual play but might have happened. Characters can be interviewed and describe themselves (in character), their life and what happens to them in the play.

All this will help to flesh out and realize the characters, but you must always respect the playwright, who has created them to speak and behave in a certain way. If, through improvisation, you find a different interpretation that is going to alter this, then there must be a dramatically valid reason — and you must not diminish the strength of the play as a whole.

CLASS CONTENT

How do you go about putting together the improvisational ideas in this book to make a useful drama session or class?

First, always remember your general educational aims: to increase your students' knowledge of themselves and others, to develop their talents and to supplement the rest of their education.

Certain ground rules must be laid down at the very start. The first is: 'When you talk — I listen to you; when I talk — you listen to me.' This is simple good manners and it works both ways. It's a case of 'Do unto others as you would have them do unto you'. Students need to be told that before they can learn to act they must learn to be a good audience. Theatre is an art-form and as in all art-forms there are skills to be learnt. This requires discipline, but discipline must not be imposed in a way that stifles creativity, so it must be tempered with humour – though not at the expense of members of the class who may be more sensitive than you realize.

· Suppose a newcomer is joining the class on his or her first day. After a warm welcome, allocate a special friend to look after him or her. Then firmly, but in a friendly way, establish that first ground rule of audience behaviour. Introduce the idea of improvisation, which may be a new one and, perhaps, extend this to the importance of believability, listening to one another and sharing with the audience. Sharing is an important keyword. Besides being a vital thing in itself, the use of drama ideas that involve sharing – problems, recommendations, recipes, ideas, friendships – helps students to become members of a cohesive, harmonious group. Another important way of doing this at the beginning of a session is for everyone, led by yourself, to find a space and take part in a really thorough warm-up. Follow a vigorous physical warm-up, done to music, with a verbal warm-up, such as some of the popular tongue-twisters you'll find later on in the book. After the warm-up everyone should be relaxed physically, concentrating mentally, and ready to get on with the session.

After this, use a carefully planned programme of drama workshop ideas, perhaps starting with some quickfire work that involves everybody. Then use some 'think on your feet' exercises such as 'talkabouts'. Continue with some developed work in characters, or more evolved improvisations or plays. End on a high note with an 'endgame' or something else that everyone takes part in together. After that, briefly summarize a key point that has been covered, give thanks or praise to anyone who specially merits it and remind the group when you will next be seeing them.

Always have more material prepared than you will need. That way you are covered. Be flexible; be ready to slip items into your programme or alter them as the situation demands. Be sensitive to the mood of the class so that, for example, you can put in a couple of minutes of something completely different as a light interlude to a heavy piece of work.

If you are following a theme, it can be brought in or referred to in several items in a lesson. The aim is to make an integrated, logical whole, but don't allow your sessions to become predictable. You must have an organized framework, but part of the appeal of drama should be its spontaneity. Not always knowing what is going to happen next helps to develop lively minds. So always be on the lookout for something new and, if you can at the same time build up a repertoire of old favourites that everyone likes doing, so much the better.

Every class is different, so trial and error is an essential part of the process. Be prepared to experiment, and carefully monitor the results, both as you work and afterwards. Keep a record of the ideas you use and review the situation regularly, looking back on your classroom comments on·what worked and what didn't work; keeping an eye on each individual's progress, particularly those who most need encouragement.

Set aside times, say once a term, when you discuss content with the class. What do they want more of, what do they want less of, what do they want that's different? Gauge the general feeling but don't make it a popularity poll; it's your own responsibility to make the final decisions.

Finally, don't be disappointed because you can't do the perfect job; no teacher ever can. If there are setbacks learn from them; if there are successes build on them.

METHODS AND INFLUENCES

It is not only prudent but also wise to be open to all kinds of influences rather than taking a blinkered view. Don't just follow one guru. Have a pluralistic outlook. There are many different theorists in theatre and educational drama and there is something to be learned from each of them.

Stanislavsky, co-founder of the Moscow Arts Theatre, said, 'One must love art and not oneself in art' and 'All acting is giving and receiving'. He believed in a simple, truthful interpretation, and that acting was a matter of *being*, rather than doing.

Bertolt Brecht spoke about the 'alienation effect' – which has nothing to do with alienating the audience but means that audience and actors should always retain a critical distance, remaining aware that the play is not real life and that a particular message is being put across. While Stanislavsky's approach is very much to do with emotion and empathy, Brecht's is about logic and reason. Technique is emphasized. The actors must never get so carried away in the part that they lose touch with the political or social implications.

Lee Strasberg, director of the New York Actors' Studio, was the principal exponent of the Method, an American adaptation of the work of Stanislavsky, in which the actor immerses himself completely in his role. The Method uses improvisation as a training tool. It is an approach which tends to regard actors as individuals rather than members of a team and has produced such stars as James Dean and Marlon Brando.

These are theorists of the public theatre, but their ideas apply equally to drama in general and we incorporate elements from each of them in our work at the Anna Scher Theatre.

We have three golden rules: believability, listening and sharing. We passionately believe in people's individuality – but individuals working within a team. Technique starts becoming important as soon as an audience is present; as soon as people are watching, include them rather than exclude them. Technique is needed to ensure that there is no obstruction between the actor and the audience he is trying to reach.

Consideration of purposes and messages is essential as soon as you are dealing with plays. Knowledge is required both about the subject of a play and about the way human beings behave in real life.

But drama is inescapably about people's feelings and it is also an activity in which people must work together and understand the feelings of others. Seeing a situation from another point of view from one's own not only makes one a better actor but also a more tolerant and understanding person. We have an exercise in which someone sounds off on a particular subject; then the same person does the exercise from a diametrically opposed point of view – using the best points of the opposing case, not the worst. This helps to develop an awareness of what it's like to step into someone else's shoes.

Talent thrives on training together, learning from every situation and sharing with each other.

Influences can come from anywhere – from religion, myths, proverbs, philosophy, folk stories, from other teachers and from the students you are working with. A friend of our own theatre, the actor David King, philosophizes about the importance of 'the three hums' – humanity, humility and humour. A good philosophy not just for any actor, but for any human being.

So what you bring to your teaching yourself is very important. No two teachers can be, or should be, alike. You will have things to offer that no one else has.

In life's perpetual see-saw of give and take, if you give a little more you'll usually get it back. Thus the children of today will be the good parents of tomorrow. Always encourage a generous spirit.

1

Developed Work in Improvisation

We have already discussed the value of improvisation. The requirement to use one's own words builds up articulacy and general competence in language. Both creating and producing a piece of drama, at the same time, is a powerful piece of self-expression which helps to build up self-confidence. The need to follow through consequences in a logical way is a good thinking exercise. The need to interact with other people in an improvisation develops the ability to co-operate. The need to think carefully about more than one character's thoughts and feelings in the context of the play makes a person more socially aware of those around him or her in the context of life.

This chapter is about how work in improvisation can be developed into something that is more than just 'instant theatre'.

All improvisations have to start from something. Hence the importance of a clear brief for a particular piece of work. The teacher must start off the class with instructions that are simple, concise and unambiguous. There should not be any mystique about drama; a straightforward, common-sense approach is much better. You can demystify theatre without taking away any of the magic.

Once the class have got the message, they're away. They can all work at once, and then you can spotlight particular individuals, pairs or groups for everyone to see, or you can see them one by one. With practice they'll very quickly feel the shape of an improvisation; but if a scene goes on and on the teacher can quietly interject 'Ten seconds to finish' (or twenty seconds or one minute, or whatever). This is a most useful stopping device. 'Action' and 'cut' are also useful words for beginning and ending an improvisation.

What if, having set up the 'rules of the game' for a piece of work, you find that the rules are being broken, in other words that someone is not following the brief? Generally, let it run. A good piece of work is a good piece of work even if it's not what you intended to happen. After it's over you can, if necessary, put things back on course with a comment like 'very good, but it's not what I asked for' and a reminder of the initial brief. Of course there is a difference between someone forgetting, or misunderstanding, the brief and someone who is being self-indulgent or won't accept the discipline that's necessary to work with other people; *that* you need to deal with straight away.

Sometimes an idea falls flat on its face. The class's imagination is not fired or they can't get the hang of what you mean. You have to decide then whether the brief you gave wasn't clear enough, or whether the idea is pitched at the wrong level for the class you are working with, or whether the idea itself does not provide good dramatic material, and act accordingly by altering the brief or discarding the idea altogether and moving on to something else. Generally, to stimulate good improvisation, an idea has to have the seeds of conflict, or dramatic tension, in it, whether the conflict is of an obvious or a subtle kind.

Your own preparation is important. Apart from having a programme worked out for the class, you need to have thought things through and have one or two alternatives ready in the back of your mind depending on what response you get. If you are doing work that requires a factual background, do the necessary research; it's worth re-reading things even if you already know them, just so as to have all the facts at your fingertips.

Don't flog an idea to death: no one wants to see twenty similar interpretations of the same thing, one after the other. If you want to show the class a few people's work, use your observation to spot the person who has got something good to contribute, or ask for a volunteer who's done something different. Be aware of who might benefit from an opportunity, and always be ready for people to catch your eye.

Usually, after you've given the brief, the class can start improvising straight away. For a more complex idea they may need to consult each other and decide what they're going to do before actually doing it. (During the discussion time you or your stage managers can set up for the improvisation.) At other times you may want to discuss an idea with the whole class.

While some discussion beforehand is good, don't take the steam out of an idea by discussing it for too long – leave something to the imagination. For 'Tonight We Improvise'.

Once the class has come to grips with improvising simple situations, character and plot development will gradually start to take place. Paying attention to detail – dotting the i's and crossing the t's – will begin to matter. The details of the way characters behave tell us so much about them. Technique plays an important part, as does emotion – but in the end believability is paramount. Did you really believe in the work or was it, perhaps, a shade unsubtle? Tell the class never to underestimate the intelligence of the audience. For example, elderly people are not necessarily decrepit. Encourage your class to develop more complex and interesting characters. Real people are not one-dimensional; they have their good and bad sides, their ambiguities and subtleties. And as real people change under the influences of real life, so it is one of the essentials of drama that characters should be changed by events.

Plot development progresses in the same way. At every point of an improvisation there are dozens of possibilities. Applaud a piece of work that doesn't follow the obvious path downhill but has an unexpected twist. By avoiding the predictable you can catch the audience with their guard down and make a piece more effective. Encourage your group to be sensitive to shape – beginnings, middles and ends. A circular construction, when the end is an echo of the beginning, is very satisfying. Foster an appreciation of pace – how fast things happen, pauses – the vital spaces between the words or actions – and timing – the speed of response to what the other person has said.

With a clear brief, sound groundwork, constant encouragement and constructive comment, work in improvisation will start developing well. Great oaks from little acorns grow.

ROLE REVERSAL

Role reversal is a useful and effective way of bringing the message home when it comes to seeing an opposite point of view. It is also a piece of character work in which students learn to put themselves inside the mind of someone quite different from themselves. Here are some ideas, as they might be introduced to a class. Your actors can first play the parts one way and then reverse the roles; this gives them the opportunity to experience the situation from both points of view.

Late Home from School

'Dionne, you are a single parent. Kelda is the daughter you are bringing up on your own. On this particular afternoon it's six o'clock, and Kelda is usually back from school at a quarter past four, give or take five minutes. You are worried. You've rung her best friend, Ann. You've rung the school but neither Ann nor the school know where Kelda is. You are actually on the point of ringing the police when

Kelda walks in. Your first line is "Where on earth have you been? I've been worried sick about you." What happens then? What reason is given for being late? Is it the truth? Action!'

No Application

'Tracey, you are Darren's teacher and he's been in your class for two months. Now the thing about Darren is that he has enormous talent – but he's not doing anything with it. He's just wasting time day in and day out. You say to him, "Darren, you've got talent – but no application." Action!'

Babysitter

'Dawn, you are babysitting for your sister Marcia's baby and you've done it countless times before and always done it well. On this particular occasion, however, your friend Zoe across the road asks you to come over and listen to her latest Spandau Ballet record. You'll only be two or three minutes and the baby's fast asleep anyway. You go, and just after you've gone Marcia returns and is devastated to find baby Wayne left on his own. Dawn re-enters. Marcia: "Have you gone out of your mind leaving an eight-month-old baby here on his own?" Action!'

Appearance Counts!

'Sadie, you are the manageress of a rather smart ladies' dress shop – not quite a trendy boutique but a rather upmarket place for the mature woman. Sally has been in your employment now for two weeks. You originally employed her as her references showed her to be punctual, reliable, conscientious and honest – though it has to be said that you were not impressed by her appearance, but she did make an effort on the interview. However, Sally's appearance has got steadily worse. The time has come for her to smarten up – or else. First line – "Sally, could I have a word with you?" Action!'

There are many monologue and duologue pieces in Chapter 6 that are suitable for role reversal and in the case of the monologue it's always interesting to hear the imaginary person's right of reply.

SOLILOQUIES

The soliloquy: one actor on his own speaking his thoughts to the audience. The soliloquy provides a good opportunity for an actor to get to grips with a character. By expressing his thoughts to us he is revealing the character's innermost self. We, the audience, share his thoughts and get to know him from the inside. It's an artificial device that can be made to seem entirely natural.

Take the characters from a duologue and straight after their scene tell the actors you now want to see soliloquies – at the point of time when the scene ends. So now both sides of the story are summed up clearly and without ambiguity. The soliloquy is a way of increasing self-knowledge, and it is a sharing experience.

THE IN-DEPTH INTERVIEW

Another way of finding out about characters is to ask them about themselves and have them reply *in character*. This was described in *100+ Ideas for Drama* as 'People Meet People', which is a television interview idea. To probe a little further, one can set up a situation in which a character is interviewed in depth by yourself as a psychiatrist or counsellor. This idea was inspired by Dr Anthony Clare's excellent radio series *In the Psychiatrist's Chair*, in which he interviewed a number of well-known people about the influences and relationships which had formed their lives.

Take a character from a play the class is working on, or from an improvisation, and set up a situation in which such an in-depth interview might credibly take place. For example, you could have a rebellious teenager in conversation with a friendly teacher. Help the person find his or her character by asking some routine questions such as name, age, occupation and hobbies, and then go on to ask about family background, early childhood, life history, and hopes and fears for the future. How does the subject get on with the other people in his life? How does he feel about the other characters? How does he think the other characters feel about him? What turning-points have there been?

Concentration and a sympathetic atmosphere are essential. Once in character the person has to react automatically. There's no time to think it out. Equally, the 'psychiatrist' must believe in the situation and use all his or her knowledge of human nature and psychology to draw out the key points.

Some sample questions:

> 'What is your earliest memory?'
> 'What sort of a child were you, when you were little?'

'Did you feel that one or other of your parents favoured you
over your brothers or sisters?'
'Have you ever had a serious illness? What was it like?'
'What was the happiest time of your life?'
'What sort of person did you think your husband or wife was
when you first met?'
'Was there ever a time when you began to think that life
might not turn out as well as you hoped it would?'

Not only is this an effective way of developing characters, but it will
also provide insights for both the class and yourself on the similarities
and differences in the way people think and feel. Encourage them to
observe people – how they sit, stand and walk, for example, and the
way all the parts contribute to the whole person.

RELATED IMPROVISATION (OR PLAYLETS)

The 'related impro' is like a mini-play and is very effective for a
school assembly piece. Each related impro is made up of three or four
(usually four) separate scenes with a *vox pop* ending in which each
character sums up in a line or two his or her feelings about what has
happened. The teacher casts it, gives an outline of the characters and
plot and uses either incidental music or maracas as a scene divider.

The Bully

> *Characters*   in order of appearance, Bully, Boy, Best Friend,
>   Teacher
> *Set*   school playground
> *Scene 1*   Bully and Boy
> *Scene 2*   Boy and Best Friend
> *Scene 3*   Boy and Teacher
> *Scene 4*   Boy, Teacher and Bully

'Nobody likes a bully and, casting completely against type, Darren
would you play the part of the bully, please? *Scene 1*: You are in the
playground and you start jibing at Bernard. Bernard, you can't stand
it. "Why are you always picking on me?" you say. And the scene
builds up to a climax. *Scene 2*: Bernard is very upset and his best
friend Mmoloki comes along. Mmoloki tries to console Bernard but
this time Bernard seems to have taken it really badly. Mmoloki
advises him to tell the teacher. *Scene 3*: We see the teacher, Miss

Hanson, and Bernard in conversation. Miss Hanson gives Bernard some sound advice. *Scene 4*: Bernard, Miss Hanson and Darren — are we going to see a grand reconciliation? That is up to you. As usual we end with the *vox pop*.'

No Smoking

> *Characters* in order of appearance, Mum, Child, Aunt
> *Set* home scene (settee, with chairs at either side, television with flowers and telephone on top)
> *Scene 1* Mum and Child
> *Scene 2* Child and Aunt
> *Scene 3* Mum, Aunt and Child

'They say that smoking can be bad for your health. Heather, you are very worried about your mum. Mrs Page is now up to forty a day — ever since Dad left home. It seems clear to you, Heather, that, as every advertisement says, "cigarettes can seriously damage your health", and you are concerned that your mum seems oblivious to these warnings. You've noticed that her smoker's cough has got a lot worse over the last couple of months. You decide on a heart to heart. *Scene 1*: Mum and daughter. First line from Heather — "Mum, why don't you give up smoking?" The duologue ends with Mum having to go to her evening class. *Scene 2*: Aunt Joanne pops round and Heather confides her anxiety to her aunt (her mum's sister). Heather really is very worried. Aunt Joanne promises to have a good talk with her sister when she returns from evening class. Heather is relieved. *Scene 3*: Mum returns and is somewhat surprised to see her sister Joanne there so late. "Is anything the matter?" she says. The conversation gets a bit heavy and Heather is told by her mother to go to bed. The two sisters have an argument about Mum's smoking, the effect on her health, and the effect on Heather. *Vox pop*.'

The Tubby Child

> *Characters* in order of appearance, School Doctor, Mum, Child, Dad
> *Set* medical room at school and home scene
> *Scene 1* School Doctor, Mum and Child
> *Scene 2* Mum and Child
> *Scene 3* Mum and Dad
> *Scene 4* Dad and Child

145

'*Scene 1* is set in the medical room at school. Behind the desk is Dr Saul. In front of the doctor's desk are Sylvia and her Mum – Mrs Lewis. The prognosis is that Sylvia will have to go on a diet. She's been eating far too many sweets, sticky buns and junk foods that are bad for her. First line from the doctor: "I'm afraid, Mrs Lewis, that Sylvia will have to go on a rather strict diet." *Scene 2*: We see Mrs Lewis and Sylvia in their sitting-room. First line from Sylvia: "I want something to eat." Second line from Mrs Lewis: "You heard what the doctor said." The two of you have quite a row which culminates in Sylvia going out and slamming the door. *Scene 3*: Enter Dad – "What's the matter with you, love? You've got a face as long as Oxford Street." Mum and Dad discuss the problem of their overweight child. They decide that Dad should have a word. *Scene 4*: Dad and Sylvia. Dad – "I'd like a word with you, love." At the end of *Scene 4* we see all four characters in a *vox pop*.'

A Child's Stay in Hospital

> *Characters*   in order of appearance, Child, Mum, Nurse
> *Set*   in hospital
> *Scene 1*   Child and Mum
> *Scene 2*   Mum and Nurse
> *Scene 3*   Nurse and Child
> *Scene 4*   Mum and Child

'Most of us at some point in our lives have a short or long stay in hospital. Mark, you are in hospital for the very first time – to have your tonsils out. More than likely, you're only going to be there for a few days. *Scene 1*: We see Mark sitting up in bed reading, and bang on two o'clock, the start of visiting time, in comes his mum. First line from Mum – "How are you today, son?" Now, Mark, in fact you are fine but you play up a bit to your mum. Which is very naughty! *Scene 2*: Mum is worried – though unnecessarily – and before she goes she has a word with the nurse. Mum says, "I'm rather worried about Mark." The nurse is a very considerate lady and tells Mark's mum she has nothing to be worried about. *Scene 3*: The nurse gives a jolly good telling off to Mark. She tells him to stop playing his mum up. *Scene 4*: The next day. Mark makes it up to his mum, admitting he was exaggerating how ill he was. He genuinely apologizes. We end, as usual, with the *vox pop*.'

Divided Loyalties

> *Characters*   in order of appearance, Mum, Child, Dad, Best
> Friend
> *Set*   home scene plus playground in school
> *Scene 1*   Mum and Child
> *Scene 2*   Mum and Dad
> *Scene 3*   Dad and Child
> *Scene 4*   Child and Best Friend

'I don't know if you've ever been in a situation where your loyalties
have been divided and you're left with very mixed feelings. This is
such a situation. Richard, your best friend is Billy Chatt (Sid, will you
be Billy Chatt?). Now Billy Chatt's reputation is notorious. He plays
knock-down-ginger on all the old ladies in Barnsbury Street – he
thinks it's very smart to knock on doors and run away. He bunks off
school. He gives cheek to his mum. But you, Richard, think that Billy
Chatt is the bee's knees. On the other hand, your parents cannot
tolerate him. They say, "Tell me who your friends are and I'll tell you
who you are," but you, Richard, hotly defend Billy Chatt. *Scene 1*:
Mum is just finishing a telephone call to Mrs Smithers, one of the old
ladies down Barnsbury Street. Apparently Richard and Billy Chatt
have been at it again – playing knock-down-ginger. Enter Richard as
Mum puts the phone down. Mum – "I've had it up to here with you.
Ever since you've been hanging round with that Billy Chatt." Mother
and son have an almighty row which culminates in Richard being sent
to his room. *Scene 2*: Dad gets back from work and both parents
discuss the problem. Mum tells Dad to deal with it. She feels there's
nothing more that she can do. *Scene 3*: Dad and Richard. Dad wants
Richard to drop Billy Chatt. Richard's loyalties are really tested
now. . . . *Scene 4*: The next day Richard has a heart-to-heart with Billy
Chatt. I'll leave it to you, Richard, as to how you want to handle
things. And we'll end with the *vox pop*.'

'When People Complain of Boredom
They Have Usually Done Nothing to Deserve It'

> *Characters*   in order of appearance, Mum, Child, Dad
> *Set*   home scene
> *Scene 1*   Mum and Child
> *Scene 2*   Mum and Dad
> *Scene 3*   Child, Mum and Dad

147

'I'd like this related impro to be topped and tailed with this saying —

> "When people complain of boredom
> they have usually done nothing to deserve it"

— so will you announce the title at the beginning *and* end, Martha, please? Three characters: Mum, Dad and Child. You be the child, Michael, and Dawn and Robert the mum and dad. *Scene 1*: Michael comes home from school and the first thing he does after switching on the television is say, "I'm bored." Mum, you say, "That word is not allowed in this house." *Scene 1* ends with Mum getting so exasperated with Michael that she sends him to his room. *Scene 2*: Dad returns from work. Mum and Dad have words about Michael and how he's always so bored with everything. Dad suddenly hits upon it. *He removes the television!* No more instant entertainment. Michael will have to make his own entertainment from now on. Exit Mum and Dad. *Scene 3*: Michael enters and goes to where the television would normally be. He gives a double take. Where is it? Re-enter the parents and we see what happens. I wonder if Michael has learnt any lessons! *Vox pop* — and Martha tails the scene with:

> "When people complain of boredom
> they have usually done *nothing* to deserve it."'

The Practical Joke that Misfired

> *Characters*   in order of appearance, Sister, Brother, Mum
> *Set*   home scene
> *Scene 1*   Sister and Brother
> *Scene 2*   Mum and Sister
> *Scene 3*   Mum and Brother
> *Scene 4*   Mum, Sister and Brother

'Being at the receiving end of a practical joke isn't always funny and it certainly isn't when it misfires. John and Kelda, you are brother and sister and on this particular occasion Kelda returns from school, takes off her coat and settles down to watch *Dramarama*. John, you creep up behind her wearing a grotesque mask; you put your hand on her shoulder. Kelda turns round and screams blue murder. It wasn't so much the mask that frightened her — though it is pretty grotesque — but it was all totally *unexpected*. Kelda says, "You frightened the living daylights out of me." And such is her state of shock that she proceeds to rant and rave at John. The scene ends with her in tears and you, John, cross with her for getting in such a state. You might tell her how cowardly she is. Anyway, you leave her to it and go to your room. That's *Scene 1*. *Scene 2*: Enter Mum, who is concerned to see Kelda in such distress. Kelda tells her what happened. Mum soothes her daughter and suggests that Kelda go to the kitchen (off) to make some tea. *Scene 3*: Mum calls John down and reprimands him. It transpires that no harm was meant but clearly an apology is in order. *Scene 4*: Mum with Kelda and John. John apologizes to Kelda magnanimously. He is sorry for what he has done. *Vox pop.*'

Mutton Dressed as Lamb

> *Characters*   in order of appearance, Daughter, Mum, Dad
> *Set*   home scene
> *Scene 1*   Daughter and Mother
> *Scene 2*   Mother and Father
> *Scene 3*   Mother and Daughter

'When the mature woman dresses very young some people might unkindly say: "Mutton dressed as lamb". That is our situation today. Sharon and Dionne are mother and daughter and, Sharon, you're ever so proud of your mum but you feel she's been dressing a bit *too* fashionably lately. You honestly think she's past wearing the clothes that people of your age wear. Sharon, your intentions are good. You really do mean well. You simply do not want your mum to be the laughing-stock of the estate. So, in *Scene 1*, daughter Sharon has a heart-to-heart with mother Dionne about it. As to how you take it, Dionne – well, I'll leave that up to you! Sharon has certainly given her mum something to think about. *Scene 2*: Later that evening – Sharon has gone to the pictures and Dionne is watching television with her husband, Tony. Dionne, you come straight to the point: "Tony, do you think I look like mutton dressed as lamb?" Tony, I trust you'll make *sensitivity* the keynote of this scene. I'd like you to play it extremely sympathetically, listening intently, but, Dionne, I want it to be *you* that reaches your own conclusions. *Scene 3*: The next day. Mother and daughter again. It will be interesting to see what has transpired. First line from Dionne: "Sharon, I've been thinking over what you were saying to me yesterday. . . ." After *Scene 3* we'll go straight into *vox pop*.'

149

Lies

> *Characters*　in order of appearance, Girl, Boy, Pick-Up Girl,
>   Jealous Friend
> *Set*　home scene and at the bus-stop
> *Scene 1*　Girl and Boy
> *Scene 2*　Boy and Pick-Up Girl
> *Scene 3*　Girl and Jealous Friend
> *Scene 4*　Boy and Girl

'They say it's a sin to tell a lie. Well, that may be, but as far as I'm concerned honesty is not just the best policy – it's the only policy. Lies – black or white or fibs or sins or whatever you call them – can only cause unhappiness. Bernard and Susan have been going out together for three months or so but things are getting a little shaky. It's not that Bernard isn't fond of Susan but there are other fish in the sea and he is only sixteen. Susan is getting a touch paranoid about Bernard and she's hearing half-truths here and there, and now from a so-called reliable source she hears he's been seeing someone else. Has he? We don't know. *Scene 1*: Bernard calls for Susan at her house to be greeted by Susan saying, "You lied to me!" Bernard soon flies into a rage himself and the scene ends with both of them flying off the handle. Bernard leaves Sue – in a stew. *Scene 2*: At the bus-stop. Bernard meets an old flame and proceeds to pick her up. They are being watched by someone (the jealous friend) whom we do not see. *Scene 3*: The jealous friend calls round to Susan and reports on what she has just seen. She starts by saying "I feel sorry for you" to poor unfortunate Sue. *Scene 4*: Bernard returns to Susan. Will they make up or finally break up?

> "O, what a tangled web we weave,
>   When first we practise to deceive!"

Certainly deceits and lies have no place in any relationship. I'll leave the ending up to you. And finally the *vox pop*.'

Temptation

> *Characters*　in order of appearance, Younger Sister, Boyfriend,
>   Older Sister
> *Set*　home scene
> *Scene 1*　Younger Sister and Older Sister's Boyfriend

Scene 2   Two Sisters
Scene 3   Older Sister and her Boyfriend

'Since time immemorial, when the serpent tempted Eve with the apple, temptation has reared its head again and again. Kerryann, you are Bernadette's younger sister. Costas is Bernadette's boyfriend. You're practically engaged – but not quite. *Scene 1*: Kerryann has just got back from boarding-school and Costas calls for Bernie. Bernie is at the hairdresser's. Costas can't quite conceal how grown-up and attractive Bernie's baby sister has become to him and can't resist making a pass at her. Whether things develop further is up to the two of you. Kerryann, do you find your sister's boyfriend attracrive? Are you horrified at his advances? Or flattered? And what about your loyalty to Bernie? First line from Costas: "Gosh you've changed since I last saw you!" *Scene 2*: Ten minutes later. Bernadette arrives home. Costas has gone now. We see the two sisters together. Kerryann: "Costas has just been. . . ." But something about her tone of voice makes Bernadette suspicious. How you play it largely depends on what has happened in *Scene 1*. *Scene 3*: Bernadette and Costas. I wonder if we'll see a show-down in the grand manner or not? An open scenario – it's up to you. Plus *vox pop* at the end.'

Variations

As in 'Temptation' above, you can suggest different plot alternatives to choose from, or else you can outline a related improvisation up to the point at which you give the participants a free choice of ending. You can always explore more than one variation by repeating an improvisation, directing the actors to keep as close as possible to the original until they come to the 'fork in the road', and then to take the other path. So, for example, in 'Temptation', if, the first time round, Kerryann has admitted her infatuation for Costas, the second time she can be asked to disguise it. Other variations can be created by throwing in an extra plot factor in the background – 'Costas had a terrible row with Bernie last night' – or some alteration in the personality of one of the characters – 'Kerryann is a compulsive liar'. The variations can be technical as well as in the plot or characters – 'the emotions are still there but I want you to underplay them' – or you can ask for a change of pace or style. These are not just acting exercises; they also teach something about human nature.

151

THE RULES OF THE GAME

This is an advanced and open-ended improvisation idea, in which an overall situation is laid down and the members of the group invent characters and perform an improvised play in which their entrances and exits are determined by a series of prearranged rules. For example:

The Mish

The Mish (short for Mission) is an inner-city youth project. The members of the group can choose any character that might appear there in an evening: teenagers of all ages and sorts – at school, at college, at work, unemployed – youth workers, voluntary helpers, teachers, neighbours, the police, and any of their family or friends. Suggest an outline in which one or more disturbed youths join the Mish and try to take it over. Float the idea that the various loyalties and emotional entanglements within the group will emerge in the story.

The rules of the game are that not more than three people can appear in the play at the same time. When one of them exits he or she unobtrusively touches someone else on the shoulder and this licenses that character to go on – though he doesn't have to go on straight away. Point out that the choice of who goes on next is vitally important as it often affects the plot and the shape of the piece. Each character is allowed to go on twice, and it is convenient if after their second exit the participants go and sit in another part of the audience, in order not to be chosen again.

Having introduced the idea and explained the rules, arrange a general-purpose set to represent a side-room at the Mish. Meanwhile the group has a chance to form their characters and find their relationships – boy- and girl-friends, sworn enemies, and so on. When they're ready, repeat the rules, and then ask the characters to introduce themselves individually, giving their name and role (for example, occupation, relationship to other characters). It's a good idea for people to retain their own names in this particular piece of work unless they need to change them for character reasons. Having heard these, designate the first three characters that are allowed to go on and, if all goes well, the play will then proceed from beginning to end.

At the first try you may need to intervene from time to time to keep things running smoothly. In your initial direction point out that the play must have a good ending and that it is up to the last three participants to find one. It is a demanding exercise, because you are asking your actors to create a coherent plot, as they go, within an arbitrary structure. Selfish acting will kill the whole thing, and too many high dramatic moments will make it farcical, but if the actors are sensitive to each other and pick up on references from within the story a satisfactory play will emerge.

The rules for 'The Mish' would suit a group of a dozen or so but there is room for any amount of variation to suit the number of people, the length of time and the storyline you have chosen. For example, you can allow more people on stage at once (though too large a number quickly get out of control); you can allow each character a normal ration of only one appearance, unless specially chosen to reappear by one of the other actors; you can make one character a 'wild card' who can come or go as he or she pleases; you can use music to dissolve a scene and signal the passage of time, in which case the next scene begins with a new set of characters; or you can say that there will be a series of scenes in different places and draw names out of a hat to determine who appears in each scene – some, of course, more than once.

Other suggested situations:

The Pop-Inn   A fast-food restaurant one lunch time. The characters are the staff (permanent and temporary) and the customers – people having their lunch break, shoppers, people who've arranged to meet or who meet by accident.

Neighbours   The Swears, a very coarse family, live between the Upneys, a social-climbing family, and the Priests, a narrow, religious family. It is a hot day and the action takes place in and out of their back gardens. Suggest some situations – for example, young Miss Upney is sunbathing and young Mr Priest decides to convert her; the Swears' dog is about to mate with the Upneys' pedigree poodle, etc.

Tourists Stranded   Flights home from Santa Paloma have been postponed indefinitely so a party of tourists is stranded. The set can be the hotel lobby, poolside and a bedroom (to represent anyone's bedroom). The characters are the tourists (all ages, some in families or couples), the Santa Paloman hotel staff, tourists from other countries, and so on.

Warren Drive   A prosperous suburb. Most of the husbands are out all day, but the wives are at home. Sometimes they visit their neighbours. There are some children and teenagers. There are milkmen, decorators, plumbers, meter-readers, and anyone who's on the end of a telephone. All manner of domestic dramas may take place.

Plato Park   A television soap opera that's been on for twenty years. There is the regular cast among whom many relationships, good and bad, have developed. There are the actors in the smaller parts, the producer who created the series, the new director and possibly some of the crew. It is the lunch break during filming. Perhaps the characters should be asked when introducing themselves to say what they *really* feel about the programme.

The Ark   A group of people live communally in a remote country house because they believe that civilization is about to end. They believe in the development of 'inner space' through meditation, etc., and in 'absolute truth' – unwelcome facts must not be concealed. Two of the group are designated as leaders, and two more as newcomers; the rest are members of the commune.

Linda and Perry   Each person has a relationship – love or friendship – with two other people, either concurrently or consecutively. The first scene is played between A and B; the surroundings can be whatever they like. After this scene A chooses C, who will be B's next partner in a different scene in fresh surroundings. And so the chain continues until A reappears in the last scene.

Heroes in Paradise   This is set in the place where heroes go when they die. They may be famous people, heroes of fiction, or invented heroes, but here they spend eternity remembering their past triumphs, discussing the meaning of existence, and living together in the everlasting present. The characters introduce themselves by announcing their name and showing us a 'clip' of their earthly existence, which typifies them. One or two may be new arrivals.

THREES, GROUPS AND CROWD SCENES

As soon as there are more than two actors working together an important rule is that they don't all talk at once. They need to act in a *giving* way; if they are too 'busy', you will get a spiral effect in which people will try to top one another in order to grab the audience's attention. Listening, as always, is of the essence. And of course the greater the number, the greater the importance of having a clear, specific brief.

The Eternal Triangle

'Gillian and Oona, you share a flat together. Oona's boy-friend is

Tony; you've been going out together for a year. Every Tuesday Oona goes to an evening class at the local arts centre, but on this particular evening it's been cancelled and she comes back early to find her boyfriend, Tony, in the arms of her flatmate, Gillian.

'Can we start inside the flat, at the point half a minute *before* Oona returns.'

The teacher might ask for a soliloquy from each of the characters after the scene.

Spoilt for Choice

Take three boys – Sid, John and Wayne. It's a Saturday afternoon. Sid wants to go to the Michael Sobell Sports Centre, John wants to go to the Arsenal and Wayne wants to go to the Screen on the Green to see the latest Eddie Murphy film. Maybe Sid uses a bit of friendly persuasion on the others. Maybe John and Wayne agree to go to the Arsenal and Sid goes off on his own. Or maybe you all three go your separate ways and meet up later. Can you reach a happy compromise?'

The Intermediary

'I want the whole class to go into threes. The threes can be made up of family, friends or acquaintances. They might be mum, dad and daughter. Or three girl friends. Or employer and two employees. Whatever. The point is that two of the three are in conflict and the other acts as the intermediary. Can the intermediary, or go-between, bring the conflicting pair to harmony? Or at least can we fall back on that good old British compromise? Or are they going to stay in conflict?'

Two's Company, Three's a Crowd

'The home scene, please. I want Tracey and her boy-friend Mark watching *Top of the Pops* cosily on the sofa. Tracey's parents have gone to Margate for the week. The only thing to mar Tracey's joy is that she has to mind Joanna, her younger sister, who is mischief personified. It's a definite case of "Two's company, three's a crowd".'

Here are some firm favourites for *group work*.

Locations and Incidents

Each group chooses a location – the launderette, school, court, heaven, hell, the hairdresser's, the dentist's waiting-room, adventure playground, gymnasium, prison cell – wherever. An incident occurs at the location: perhaps at the launderette the washing machine overflows; perhaps at the adventure playground someone finds a bag containing £2,000 in used fivers. Whatever it is, something happens! We see the lead–up, the incident and the aftermath.

Chain Argument

Person No. 1 is minding his own business. Enter Person No. 2, who picks an argument with No. 1 – 'Where's the £5 I lent you last week?' The argument develops and culminates in No. 1 leaving. Enter No. 3, who now picks a different argument with No. 2 until No. 2 exits. Enter No. 4 – and so on. Go on until the first person comes back again to complete the chain – No. 1 arguing with No. 8. Listening is of paramount importance as references from previous arguments can perhaps be brought into later ones. A variation is to have the chain argument in whispers.

The Rumour

The structure of this is similar to the 'Chain Argument' but with a touch of 'Chinese Whispers'. Two people start off a rumour. You can give them a first line – 'Did you hear that Jenny's been sacked from her Saturday job?' After that duologue, one of them exits and the other repeats the rumour to a new person, somewhat changing the facts. The third picks up with a fourth, the fourth with a fifth, and so on till the rumour grows out of all proportion. In the end it gets back to the first person again. Tell them not to make the changes too unsubtle – just a little exaggeration goes a long way!

Family Occasions

All families have their ups and downs. Take a family occasion – sister's twenty-first, cousin's wedding, grandma's seventieth birthday, Christmas dinner, a baby's christening, a great uncle's funeral. Whether it is a time for celebration or for commiseration, the object of the exercise is for something to happen which changes the flavour of the occasion. For example, as the turkey is being carved a daughter announces that she has turned vegetarian.

Divide the class into groups of from four to six, appoint leaders and give them a few minutes preparation time.

Group Gossips

Women are supposed to gossip much more than men. But do they? Have a group of women gossips, a group of men gossips and a mixed group. Choose a location – mothers waiting for their children outside the school gates, the men's changing room of a sports club, the bar of a social club. A good first line – 'Have you heard the latest?'

Table Talk

Group people round tables in a restaurant. Conversations start round each table. The teacher 'freezes' them, then spotlights each table in turn, in no particular order, 'actioning' and 'cutting' them. After each 'cut' the group freezes till the teacher 'actions' them again. To warm them up each member of the group can order a meal from the menu – in character, of course. The teacher can be the waitress or waiter taking the orders. Then the table talk commences.

You can add to the brief if you like by designating various characters, such as a four-year-old or an American cousin; or groups, such as a family party, a business meal, or a staff outing; or plot points – perhaps one person must be given a very bad piece of news. Warn them not to be too 'busy'.

In this, as in many other exercises, the teacher can have a director's role in shaping the idea as it progresses, by choosing which table to cut to next, and putting in a word about what may have been happening in the interim, so that the whole piece will have a beginning, a middle and an end.

Teacher and Pupils

This is an exercise which must *not* be sent up. Each group has a teacher and the rest of the group are pupils. The teacher takes a class in whatever subject he or she chooses, for example, a geography lesson on Ireland, how to make an omelette, a computer studies lesson on programming. The teacher delivers an introduction and takes it to the point where the pupils are set to work by themselves.

This is a very good exercise for characterization and teamwork but you must emphasize the importance of keeping the teacher characters realistic rather than stereotyped, and the pupils must resist the temptation to get out of control. Another believability point is that the content of the teachers' lessons has to be accurate – they can't get away with waffling any more than a real teacher can!

Winning and Losing

Perhaps you can learn more from losing than from winning. Have a discussion with the class on winning and losing. Throw out a few ideas yourself – a tug-of-war, exam results pinned to a noticeboard, the end of a race, a war, an election, the football pools. Discuss people's reactions to winning and losing – good and bad winners and losers. What about the reactions of the winners' and losers' families and friends? Don't discuss the subject to death, however – leave something to the imagination. Divide the class into groups of about six and ask them to prepare a piece on winning and losing.

Gangs

Each group is a gang with its own set of rules. In order to gain admittance to the gang the prospective member has to show initiative or carry out some feat acceptable to the rest.

The Imaginary Invention

Start by talking about different inventions – Thomas Edison's light bulb, the speak-your-weight machine, an imaginary electronic gadget. Divide the class into groups of about six and set them the brief of devising their very own imaginary invention. Each member of the group will be an integral part of the invention – apart from the spokesperson who will explain its use and demonstrate its workings to the rest of the class. All inventions must, of course, be named and explanations and demonstrations carried out thoroughly realistically.

Accident

A crowd gathers to watch the aftermath of an accident (the crowd can be anything from a group of six to the whole class). The teacher specifies the kind of accident that has taken place – it could be a road accident, a fall, a fire. The crowd reacts as the teacher relates what is happening. The teacher can further direct the group by freezing and spotlighting when necessary. Make sure that the crowd drifts in (and out) gradually and don't let them get too 'busy'.

A useful follow-up would be to discuss what you would really do in such circumstances. Perhaps you can bring in some first-aid tips as well as detailing the emergency procedure of dialling 999 for fire, police or ambulance.

2

Channelling Creativity

Everyone has talent in some field. It is a myth that it is only possessed by a small minority of gifted people. Every young individual has the.potential to do many different things, given the opportunities and education. Equally, early ability can be stifled by lack of opportunity and encouragement. It's like the parable of the talents – you need to work at your talent rather than bury it in the ground.

Talent is developed by broadening people's minds and by training to improve their skills, while at the same time providing a secure emotional base so they are not afraid of failure. The key to it is praise, encouragement and improvement by gradual degrees, so that people are always being stretched but not stretched so far that they are likely to fail. Even when a high level of achievement has been reached, you have to keep in training in the arts, just as you do in sport, or else your ability will dissipate through lack of exercise. As Thomas Edison said, 'Genius is one per cent inspiration and ninety-nine per cent perspiration'.

A whole mix of talents are required for drama. Improvisation draws upon creative ability, and creativity is something that can be enhanced through training just like any other talent. Everyone has an imagination. The way to develop it is to release people's own inhibitions on using it, while at the same time teaching the disciplines which enable it to be channelled effectively.

LEADERSHIP

One of the social benefits of drama is that it gives participants experience of leadership and responsibility. Again, there is a myth that leadership ability is found only in a small number of people and is to be developed – or discouraged – in them only. On the contrary, leadership skills are something that everyone can, and should, learn. Sooner or later everyone has to be a leader – at work, in recreation, as a parent, or in the once-in-a-lifetime emergency where quick thinking, self-reliance and thinking of other people can make the difference between life and death.

Good leadership means the ability to communicate goals clearly, to take responsibility and to care for others, and listen and respond to them. Dictatorships don't usually last very long. One of the problems for a teacher is that in any class the same few people tend to emerge as the natural leaders. Because they are the only ones with leadership experience no one else can take their place effectively. If you wish to give more people a chance, it's no good throwing them in at the deep end. You have to introduce people to responsibility gradually.

The Imaginary Journey

This is an imagination exercise which can be done either in question-and-answer form with an individual or with the whole group. Start with 'I want you to close your eyes. Now look down at your feet. I want you to notice the pair of shoes you are wearing. Remember exactly what they look like, any details or marks on them. Now what sort of surface are the shoes standing on; is it a floor, or path, or pavement, or grass, or what? Without opening your eyes, look around you. Now you are going to go for a walk, it's quite a long way. Notice all the different things you see as you pass them.'

Give a few moments for the walk to continue, then say: 'In a moment you will come to a particular building. When you get to it I want you to stop and look at the outside and remember as many details as you can about the building. There's a sign on the building. Read to yourself what it says. Now you're going to go to the door of the building and, one way or another, go inside.'

And so it goes on. Maybe you will ask them to see something unexpected, or someone who (in the story) they love or hate. Maybe the person will ask them a question. What answer will they give? What will happen next? Maybe they will see a book, open it at a given page, count down a certain number of lines and read what it says.

The possibilities are endless and you can go on indefinitely. Everyone's story will be different and, if recounted, some of them will be remarkable. The exercise shows that everyone has untapped powers of imagination; because you've started with something very ordinary – the shoes – the class are more likely to use their imagination unselfconsciously.

FOSTERING CREATIVITY

In any group doing improvisation work, some of the students will want to start devising their own plays, drawing on the resources of imagination that improvisation has revealed. It is at this point, when groups start forming to work on their own projects, often in their own time, that advice from a teacher can be particularly valuable. This will often come in the form of comments on work you are seeing. What you say to the group about one of their plays, whether in performance or rehearsal, should always be positive and encouraging, but never fail to say anything that needs to be said to improve the play. While being specific, always try to point the general application of any points you make so that people will take them on board for other occasions.

What are the ingredients of a good play? It must have a strong plot and believable characters, and it should say something, perhaps in an original way. A 'twist' is often very effective and humour is another good ingredient to include.

When dealing with the *writing* of a play (even if it's a devised play that has not actually been written down), start with the basic idea. Is it an original theme or a hackneyed one? Has it been handled in an unusual way? Are there any unexpected dramatic moments or is it all too predictable? Does the play have a good, satisfying shape, a beginning, a middle and an end, with strategically placed turning-points? Are the scenes developed enough and do we get to know the characters as much as we would like to? Or are some of the scenes 'milked' and in need of editing? Is there a good, strong ending? Does the play have something worthwhile to say? A play doesn't necessarily need to have a message, certainly not at the expense of having credible characters, but if it comments on a moral or social or political question, then that gives the audience something to think about.

Scenarios

This is an exercise in devising ideas for plays. Divide the class into groups of about six and appoint a spokesperson for each group. Allow a few minutes for each group to think of an idea, then one by one they will tell the rest of the class a scenario or 'treatment' for a play: the theme, the location, an outline of the plot, the main characters, any turning-points and how it would be staged — and of course they must give it a title. Comment on any good points in each one and allow a brief discussion so that members of the class can suggest any additions they may have. The object of the exercise is to give practice in developing and moulding ideas, and, as it's done

161

fairly quickly and they are 'throw-away' ideas that don't matter, the class should be able to work in an uninhibited way.

This can also be done as a solo idea, or with the scenarios being written down, but not more than half a page on each. Sometimes a scenario can be chosen, developed and acted out. Sometimes they may turn into full-scale plays.

DIRECTION

At this stage directing often goes hand in hand with writing, and you will often find collaborations with two people sharing both roles. Particular points to comment on in direction are a choice of a particular style for a play, the casting (in a group that has worked together for a while there's a tendency for individuals to drop into stock character roles), and whether the acting area has been used to good visual effect. Pace – simply the rate at which events happen – is vitally important. It needs to be varied in a way appropriate to the action. Dramatic tension needs to be maintained. Characters in a play need thinking time, and so does the audience. In particular, the opening of any play sets an audience a riddle. What is being represented? Who are the people? Where? When? How does each relate to the others? The audience has got to work all this out. Too many characters introduced at once or a muddled opening and you will lose its attention.

No play can be developed without a great deal of teamwork, and different individuals will develop in different roles within the team. It's not usually a good idea for writers or directors to appear in their own plays. The work load is too heavy and it is very difficult to see things from the points of view of both director and performer at the same time.

Comment on the work of the non-acting members of the team. If you have stage lighting it needs to be used to illuminate the actors effectively and, perhaps, to isolate one part of the acting area from its surroundings. Brightness, direction and colour effects need to be chosen to represent the place (indoors, outdoors) and time of day or night, and also, possibly, to represent the emotional atmosphere of the play. Lighting changes and effects usually need to be unobtrusive so that they do their work without the audience being too aware of them, and often the most economical use of stage lighting is the most effective. A simple piece of stage-lighting 'grammar' is that a fade tends to leave the audience expecting another scene to follow, while a black-out will normally cue their applause.

If it is a play with music, whether live or from records, similar principles apply. The music needs to be skilfully chosen for its associations and emotional effects without giving the game away about the plot. It is important to use enough of any incidental music; it takes time for an audience to tune into it and have its mood affected — just the odd line or two of a pop song is not sufficient. Records need to be cued accurately at the right moment so that the audience does not hear any unwanted 'funny noises'. If music is being used under speech in a play the level needs to be low enough for the words still to be heard. When music is faded out, it needs to be done musically, ending at the end of a musical phrase or a line of a song.

Other matters that need to be attended to are costume, props and the set. It is easy to think of productions where spectacular use of any of these has made an enormous contribution to the whole, but it is important to remember that they are there to serve the play and not to distract from it. So, unless something striking can be produced that will add to the overall impact of the play, it is better to aim for costume, props and set that are sufficient to create the effect required in the minds of the audience, rather than try to emulate lavishly budgeted West End productions.

PROFESSIONALISM

In all your comments on the group's work, show that you are looking for professionalism in everything they do, not because you are necessarily producing professional actors, but in order to encourage them to be *professional people*: people who do things the right way and as well as possible, are reliable and get on with those they are working with. A good concentration exercise is to have the members of a class all close their eyes and concentrate and prepare themselves by thinking of all the words beginning with the letter 'p' that go towards being professional people: punctuality, preparation, persistence, poise, practice, perfection, patience — we are sure there are many more!

CRITICISM

Criticism can be enormously helpful as a general teaching tool as well as to improve a particular piece of work, but it must always be constructive, never destructive. The teacher's praise rather than punishment produces better results on the whole, and when negative comments have to be made they should be framed as kindly as possible. Young people are usually very fair and often generous when commenting on the work of their peers. Encourage this and clamp down on anything destructive. It is up to you to create the right atmosphere, so that people can give of themselves in their work without the fear of being slapped in the face for their pains. Destructive criticism can be a great spectator sport, but, like all blood sports, it is better not to be the victim. Nevertheless, learning to take criticism, particularly if it is well justified, is an important lesson as well.

SHARING

One of the keys to groups working together cohesively is sharing. Learning to share is vitally important. Sharing and competitiveness are not at opposite poles. The essence of good sportsmanship is that people can compete with one another and be all the better friends for it. One of the essential steps in learning to share with people is getting to know them, and learning how to get to know them − sharing their experiences, enjoyment, ideas, problems, recommendations, and so forth. A good way of developing this in a group is, after starting the class with a physical and verbal warm-up, to do some quick 'sharing ideas', getting people to swap partners and so forth so that they will not be working with the people they are most familiar with.

Sharing Ideas

Here are some sharing ideas that can be used with the whole class working together, usually in pairs, and then some being individually 'spotlit'.

Recipes

'In twos share a recipe − it can be a main course or a pudding. I'll allow two minutes of "talking heads" than I'll either hear one person's own recipe or, more difficult, the new recipe he or she has just heard!'

Fact Finding

'In twos − two minutes only to find out as many facts about each other as you can. You *must* find out at least six facts each. It might be the colour of your toothbrush, your mum's first name, the number on your front door. Find out as many facts about each other in two minutes as you can. Then we'll test some of you. Starting from *now*!'

The Best and Worst Thing ...

'In twos, find out the best thing that ever happened to you and the worst thing that ever happened to you. I'll give you one minute to tell each other, then we'll all hear about it.'

Sundays

'In twos or threes, tell each other what you do on a Sunday from when you get up in the morning to when you go to bed at night. You are forbidden to use the word "boring".'

Hobbies

'In twos or threes, tell each other three hobbies you enjoy doing, *not* including watching television. Not that I've got anything against television as such – but there are other things and TV is so instant you don't have to *do* anything, just sit down and switch on. So – three hobbies, please, not including television.'

Pocket Money

'In twos or threes, tell each other how much pocket money you get and what you do with it. I'll be interested to hear if anyone puts theirs into savings.'

Rooms

'In twos, describe to each other either your bedroom or any other room in your house. Let's have some vivid descriptions, please. I'd like to be able to "see" the room in my mind's eye.'

Three Jobs

'In threes, I'd like you each to describe three jobs you'd seriously contemplate doing when you leave school, and the reasons why you'd like to do them.'

News

'In twos, I want you to exchange three pieces of news – a piece of family news, a piece of local news and a piece of worldwide news. Let's hear about something that has really captured your attention.'

Mum, Dad, Nan, Old Uncle Tom Cobbleigh ...

'In twos, I want you to describe in detail a member of your family, either your mum, dad, nan, brother, sister or anyone else. I'd like to hear about what they look like, their personality and character, any idiosyncrasies or peculiarities they might have, their hobbies, how you get on with them, and so on.'

Your Friend

'In twos, describe a friend of yours. Tell your partner all about him or her – looks, personality, hobbies, what you do together ... I'll give you two minutes and then we'll hear about some of them individually. Start with their name. It's not a guessing game.'

Recommendations

'I want to go round the room hearing your recommendations. You can recommend a book, a film, a television or radio programme, or a theatre production. I want each of you to suggest something that you got a lot of enjoyment out of and tell us why you liked it so much. If it's a book, give the title, author and a sentence or two to say what it's about.'

From arts recommendations, you could try other subjects such as shops, restaurants, places to go. ...

Resolutions

'I want to go round the room and hear each person give from one to three New Year resolutions. Now, some people feel that if you break a resolution once you might as well give up trying to keep it altogether; I'd call that defeatism. As the song says, you should "Pick yourself up, dust yourself down and start all over again". Let's hear them.' This can be developed by suggesting a New Year resolution for someone else.

Holiday Reading

'In twos, recommend two pieces of holiday reading to each other. Give the title, author and a line or two on the subject matter.'

Back to School

'In twos, tell each other about three specific things you did in the school holidays.'

Lost and Found

'In twos, tell each other of any experiences you've had when you lost something important (perhaps a contact lens or a gold ring) and if you ever found anything valuable – in which case, I wonder what you did with it. Did you take it to the police station or was it "finders keepers, losers weepers"? If you haven't lost or found anything, I'm sure you know someone who has.'

Presents

'In twos, swap ideas about presents. First, tell each other about a present you would like to receive; next, a present you'd like to give; and then three presents under £5 suitable for your mum or dad.'

A Pleasant Surprise, an Unpleasant Shock

'In twos, tell each other of a pleasant surprise you've had and of an unpleasant shock. If you can think of neither of these that you have experienced personally, you may tell us of ones that have happened to people you know.'

Discoveries

'In twos, tell each other of two discoveries, big or small, that you have made in the last year. It could be a household hint, a little-known fact, or an unusual place to visit – in other words, any piece of interesting knowledge or know-how. Then I'd like you to share them with all of us.'

The Real and the Imaginary Problem

'In twos, tell each other a real problem and an imaginary problem; your partner has to guess which is the real problem and which is the imaginary one. Later on the whole class will try and decipher which is true and which is false.'

Dreams

'In twos, tell each other about two dreams – one that you've really had and one you've made up. Can your partner guess which is which?'

Group Work

Sharing Ideas can be done with larger groups of people as well.

Favourite Things

Form groups of from six to eight who one at a time will tell one another a few of their favourite things – books, places, shops, dinners, pets, hobbies, sport, puddings, magazines, records, jokes, films, etc.

The Inner and the Outer Circle

This is a good ice-breaking exercise. Divide the class into pairs, and tell the pairs to form a circle facing each other, making an inner and an outer circle. The partners get to know one another or, if they already do so, catch up on each other's news. After a short while, the teacher either rings a bell, blows a whistle, or calls out 'All change'. Then the inner circle stays put, the outer circle moves one step to the right and the new partners start all over again, and so on.

This is an ideal exercise to warm up a new group or to welcome people back after the holidays.

Another way of working in groups is to split a class into sections who will prepare work on a given theme to show one another later in the session. Groups can be self-selecting but it is often a good idea to split people in an arbitrary way so that they get used to working with different people. Appoint group leaders who have a chairman's casting vote to resolve any differences. The art in this kind of group work lies in finding an initial brief that will inspire good drama.

Subjects

A subject of general interest may be chosen for discussion; improvisation can follow on from this. It is often a good idea to suggest a title – one that provides a stimulus but not a limitation. For example, a discussion on 'The Family (Conventional and Unconventional)' might be followed by improvisations with the title 'One Family'; a discussion on 'Mental Illness' might be followed by work on 'The Case of XYZ (a person's name)'; one on 'What Makes a Good Holiday' might be commented on by 'Two Weeks in ABC (the name of a resort)'. If the title is made optional, you have the best of both worlds: you have provided a suggestion but if the group has a better idea your suggestion can be overruled.

A similar format is to discuss a present-day issue and then use improvisations to project it into what may possibly, or even improbably, happen in the future, under the general title 'The Surprising Future of . . .'. Thus a discussion on entertainment, or a subject connected with it, could be followed by improvisations on 'The Surprising Future of Entertainment', and similarly with love, war, childhood, and so on.

Locations

Alternatively, you can simply give them a location. One that works particularly well is 'Kitchen Scenes'. Another is 'Office Scenes'. Another that works well for pairs rather than groups is 'Bedroom Scenes' – bedtime conversations between husband and wife, parent and child, or any others who share a bedroom.

Titles

Another way is to give a brief and a title with no obvious connection between the two. The brief might be that a chosen subject should be brought into the play in some way or other – old age, science, smoking, foreign languages. The title can be one of a series you have made up and written down on slips of paper, or a title hybridized from a couple of well-known television programmes. A fun variation on this is to choose, say, the titles of a current hit record, a top-rated TV programme, a big box-office film and a best-selling novel. Give one to each of the groups. They can do any improvisation they like that fits this title, but it must bear *no* resemblance to the original work that bears the same title.

Festivals

As group work develops it is often a good idea to have a target for everyone to work towards. We have found an end-of-term festival very successful – see the section on Festivals in Chapter 4.

TOTAL THEATRE

This is another form of group work in which the entire class works together (if there are too many, divide it in half). Give them the brief of what the overall situation is, then each of them chooses a character who could be in that situation and, without further preparation, improvisation begins, interrupted only if you want to freeze the action and spotlight a particular set of characters for a while, in the same way as in 'Table Talk' (Chapter 1).

Examples of settings that could be used are:

A Youth Club on an Ordinary Evening   Start with a show of hands to make sure you have the right proportion of youth workers to members. The action begins when the person with the keys opens up the doors and ends when the same person locks them again.

A School Playground at Break Time   From bell to bell. You can put in a few extra details such as a staff-room that overlooks the playground, or a wall that backs on to somebody's back garden.

The Staff Christmas Party of a Large Business   It is held at a big hotel and everybody is there, from the cleaners to the managing director, and from different areas — factories, offices, sales reps, and so on. The seating plan mixes people together so they can get to know one another, and there's plenty of drink flowing. Everyone is going to let their hair down. This scenario might be helped by having the characters introduce themselves, name and position, one by one. It could be tailed by asking for scenes involving selected characters in the hotel corridors afterwards.

A Marriage Guidance Group   The group is split into couples, who decide on an outline of their age, background, family, and the problems they may have. The group is led by a counsellor and we are going to see the characters arrive and discuss their own and other people's problems. Perhaps this one can finish with the couples being seen in turn on their way home together.

The Friends Circle   This is a bit like Alcoholics Anonymous or Weightwatchers. Each member has a personal problem or idiosyncrasy that makes his or her life difficult. They meet once a week and talk about how they've coped in the previous week. You might appoint a leader, or not. Alternatively, to make it more of an exercise, you might have them draw cards with the problems written on them: alcoholic, insomniac, overweight, paranoid.

For these improvisations to be successful, subtlety in characterization and generous, unassertive acting are essential. All the situations have potential for humour and they must be played straight and not sent up. This is particularly true when comedy is the intention. Often you can finish off the piece of work by interviewing some of the characters, in character, asking them to give their account of what happened, how they feel about some of the other people, and so on.

3

Umbrella Themes

To take an umbrella theme for the term is to choose a subject, be it literary or cultural, from which you can draw material for use throughout the term. For example, if your umbrella theme is Aesop's Fables you take a different fable each week which will provide a substantial part of the material for that session. After you have introduced the fable of the week you can explain the context and background and have a short discussion with the class on any points it raises. The fable can then be used as a starting-off point for improvisation, situation drama and plays.

As well as supplying good dramatic material, the subjects chosen are areas in which students can benefit from increasing their general knowledge. The umbrella theme provides an orderly way of working on them. This concise way of dealing with subjects gives a target, a shape and an identity to your term's work.

It is very useful to display your umbrella theme of the term on your notice board. For example:

FABLE OF THE WEEK

The Boy Who Called Wolf

SPOTLIGHT ON

Credibility

PROVERBS

Proverbs are old and wise sayings which make excellent material for discussion and improvisation. Take 'A friend in need is a friend indeed'. Start with a discussion on friendship. Talk about the qualities that make a good friendship – loyalty, confidentiality, humour, compatibility, or indeed the attraction of opposites. What is most important in a friendship? What makes friendship last? What is the best thing a friend ever did for you? What is the best thing you ever did for a friend? What is the worst?

Continue on these lines until you're ready to set up an improvisation on the week's proverb, possibly using an optional first line — 'Some friend you turned out to be', or 'I really appreciated what you did for me yesterday'. You can do an assortment of duologues on this theme, with or without a first line as starting-point. This can be developed further into a piece of situation drama or a related improvisation.

Here is a list of proverbs that work well:

> Practice makes perfect
> Never judge a book by its cover
> Don't bite the hand that feeds you
> The early bird catches the worm
> There are no roses without dung
> A leopard never changes its spots
> Self-praise is no praise
> Lend money, lose a friend
> Necessity is the mother of invention
> When the cat's away the mice will play
> Honesty is the best policy
> There's no accounting for taste
> One man's meat is another man's poison
> What the eye doesn't see the heart doesn't grieve over
> Actions speak louder than words
> Don't spoil the ship for a ha'p'orth o' tar
> Money is the root of all evil
> Forbidden fruit tastes twice as sweet
> Criticism is the only tool that works all the better for being blunt
> Once a man gets above himself he rarely rises any higher

MOTTOES

A motto, to quote the dictionary, is a 'saying adapted as rule of conduct: short inscribed sentence: word or sentence on heraldic crest'. Here are some ready-made for improvisation:

> 'Be prepared' (Guides, Scouts)
> 'Lend a hand' (Brownies)
> 'Who dares wins' (SAS)

'Rise and shine'
'Lente sed attente' — 'Slowly but carefully'
'Ambition sans envie' — 'Ambition without envy'
'Let them talk'
'Fortune favours the brave'
'A bonis ad meliora' — 'From good things to better'
'My word is my bond' (Stock Exchange)
'Nil desperandum' — 'Never despair'
'Manners Makyth Man' (William of Wykeham, 1324–1404)
'Nulla rosa sine spinis' — 'No rose without thorns'
'Audio sed taceo' — 'I hear but say nothing'
'Constantia in ardua' — 'Perseverance against difficulty'
'Respect faith, but doubt is what gives you an education'
'Love makes the world go round'
'Never put off till tomorrow what can be done today'
'Do as you would be done by'
'Reality before theatricality' (East 15 Acting School)

POEM OF THE WEEK

Compile a list of favourite poems — your own and the class's. From
the list, choose poems that have aspects that can be highlighted
through improvisation. For example, in 'Jim' by Hilaire Belloc you
could home in on *caution*, while in 'The Snare' by the Irish poet James
Stephens you could choose the subject of cruelty to animals.

Remember to put on your notice-board under 'POEM OF THE WEEK'
its title and the poet's name and dates. Of course, different
age-groups will appreciate different poems and, indeed, different
teachers will find different aspects to highlight in each poem. Some
poems won't work because they are too abstract, but here is a list of
ones that have worked well for us.

'Matilda', Hilaire Belloc (1870–1953)
'Lies', Yevgeni Yevtushenko (born 1933)
'If', Rudyard Kipling (1865–1936)
'When You Are Old', W. B. Yeats (1865–1939)
'For Anne Gregory', W. B. Yeats (1865–1939)
'Little Billee', William Makepeace Thackeray (1811–63)
'Lucy Gray', William Wordsworth (1770–1850)
'Lord Ullin's Daughter', Thomas Campbell (1777–1850)
'Death the Leveller', James Shirley (1596–1666)
'Not Waving But Drowning', Stevie Smith (1905–71)

'A Crabbit Old Woman', Anon.
'My Mother Said', Anon.
'The Donkey', G. K. Chesterton (1874–1936)
'Gus, The Theatre Cat', T. S. Eliot (1888–1965)

QUOTATION OF THE WEEK

The pithy quote is a very good source for interpretation through discussion and improvisation, in the same way as proverbs, mottoes and poems. Here is a list.

'Love thy neighbour as thyself' (Leviticus; St Matthew)

'A soft answer turneth away wrath; but grievous words stir up anger' (Book of Proverbs)

'Physician, heal thyself' (St Luke)

'Sed quis custodiet ipsos custodes' – 'But who will guard the guards themselves?' (Juvenal)

'Strange how potent cheap music is' (Noel Coward, 1899–1973)

'To be successful at anything you have to have the guts to be hated' (Bette Davis, twentieth-century film actress)

'Genius is one per cent inspiration, and ninety-nine per cent perspiration' (Thomas Edison, 1849–1931)

'A man, Sir, should keep his friendship in constant repair' (Dr Samuel Johnson, 1709–84)

'The struggle in my trapeze act is the same struggle that I feel in my life – the struggle for balance' (Wendy Parkman, The Pickles Family Circus, 1980s)

'To err is human, to forgive, divine' (Alexander Pope, 1688–1744)

'A little learning is a dangerous thing' (Alexander Pope, 1688–1744)

'Two things I can't stand – one is if actors are late, the second is if they cannot learn their lines' (Otto Preminger, twentieth-century film director)

'Liberty means responsibility and that's why most men dread it' (George Bernard Shaw, 1856–1950)

'One must love Art and not oneself in Art' (Konstantin Stanislavsky, 1865–1938)

'All acting is giving and receiving' (Konstantin Stanislavsky, 1865–1938)

'The buck stops here' (Harry S Truman, 1884–1972)

'If you can't stand the heat – stay out of the kitchen' (Harry S
    Truman, 1884–1972)
'There will always be people that don't go for your chemistry
    – make sure they go for your skill' (Orson Welles,
    1915–85, to Joan Plowright)
'There is only one thing worse than being talked about, and
    that is not being talked about' (Oscar Wilde, 1854–1900)

SHAKESPEAREAN QUOTATION OF THE WEEK

Shakespeare is another good source of quotations for improvisation.
We have chosen a list of popular ones, many of which are now part
of the language, such as 'What's in a name?' You may need to explain
some of the Elizabethan English. Also, you will need to describe
where the quotation comes from in the text – this will be helpful in
introducing the plays.

'My salad days,
When I was green in judgment' (*Antony and Cleopatra*)
'Though it be honest, it is never good
To bring bad news' (*Antony and Cleopatra*)
'Frailty, thy name is woman!' (*Hamlet*)
'The lady doth protest too much, methinks' (*Hamlet*)
    'All that live must die
Passing through nature to eternity' (*Hamlet*)
'Neither a borrower nor a lender be,
For loan oft loses both itself and friend' (*Hamlet*)
'The better part of valour is discretion' (*Henry IV, Part 1*)
'If all the year were playing holidays
To sport would be as tedious as to work
But when they seldom come they wished for come' (*Henry IV,
    Part 1*)
'Self-love, my liege, is not so vile a sin as Self-neglecting'
    (*Henry V*)
'The fault, dear Brutus, is not in our stars
But in ourselves, that we are underlings' (*Julius Caesar*)
'That was the most unkindest cut of all' (*Julius Caesar*)
'Ambition should be made of sterner stuff' (*Julius Caesar*)
'It is a wise father that knows his own child' (*Merchant of
    Venice*)
'The course of true love never did run smooth' (*A Midsummer
    Night's Dream*)

'Your play needs no excuse' (*A Midsummer Night's Dream*)
'O! beware, my lord, of jealousy,
It is the green-eyed monster which doth mock
The meat it feeds on' (*Othello*)
'What's in a name? That which we call a rose
By any other name would smell as sweet' (*Romeo and Juliet*)
'Parting is such sweet sorrow
That I shall say good-night till it be morrow' (*Romeo and Juliet*)
'Condemn the fault and not the actor of it?' (*Measure for Measure*)
'Nothing will come of nothing' (*King Lear*)
'All's well that ends well' (*All's Well that Ends Well*)

SHAKESPEAREAN PLAY OF THE WEEK

The unfamiliar Elizabethan language is often the stumbling-block
when it comes to understanding Shakespeare. Start by telling the
story of the plot in your own words, allowing the characters to come
through as real flesh-and-blood people. Discussion, improvisation and
text work follow in that order. Then, when the class see a
performance of the play, knowing the plot and dramatic content, they
are more likely to appreciate the language in which it is written.

But first some background notes.

William Shakespeare (1564–1616) was born in
Stratford-upon-Avon on 23 April, which is also St George's Day. He
attended the local grammar school – the King's New School of
Stratford-upon-Avon – but did not go to university. At eighteen he
married Anne Hathaway, who was eight years his senior, and they
had three children, Susanna, and twins, Hamnet and Judith. Hamnet
died at eleven. When he was in his twenties Shakespeare moved to
London and joined James Burbage's company of actors, the Lord
Chamberlain's Men. As actors in the sixteenth century were otherwise
classified as 'rogues and vagabonds', patronage from nobility was
necessary.

William Shakespeare started as an actor with James Burbage's son
Richard but soon wrote plays for the company. In all he wrote
thirty-eight plays – comedies, tragedies, and historical plays. He
wrote some poems, most notably *Venus and Adonis* and *The Rape of
Lucrece*. And he wrote one hundred and fifty-four sonnets
(fourteen-line poems), the most popular being 'Shall I Compare Thee

to a Summer's Day?' Shakespeare retired to Stratford-upon-Avon in 1611, a prosperous man, and died there on his fifty-second birthday.

Famous contemporaries of Shakespeare, apart from Queen Elizabeth I and James and Richard Burbage, were the playwright Christopher Marlowe, born in the same year, 1564, but tragically killed in a drunken brawl in Deptford, London, in 1593; the actor Edward Alleyn; the clowns Will Kempe, Richard Tarleton and Robert Armin; and the playwrights Ben Jonson, Richard Greene, Thomas Kyd and Beaumont and Fletcher.

The Elizabethan theatre was open to the sky with a raised apron stage which had a trapdoor in the middle. Behind the apron stage was a wall with curtained doorways giving access to an inner stage and the dressing-rooms. The wall supported a gallery for musicians or the actors themselves and a tower above housed machinery. The area above the stage was called 'the heavens' and the area below, 'the hell'. There was no scenery but rich costumes and plenty of stage properties. There were no women on the Elizabethan stage; their parts were played by males. As a member of the audience, where you sat (or stood) depended on your pocket. The 'groundlings' stood round the apron stage for one penny – the best part of a pound in today's money. People with more money would sit on seats looking down on the stage from one of the galleries. The richest people had private boxes, or stools round the edge of the stage itself. A trumpet call announced that the play was about to begin and a flag was flown during performances, which usually took place early in the afternoon. The theatres were built outside the city walls, and most of Shakespeare's plays were performed in the Globe, which Shakespeare refers to as the 'wooden O'.

Here are five of Shakespeare's Plays with storylines briefly summarized and 'spotlight' points detailed.

1 Hamlet, Prince of Denmark

Spotlight on 'Revenge'

The ghost of his father appears to Hamlet and tells him that he was poisoned by Hamlet's uncle, Claudius, who has since married Hamlet's mother, Queen Gertrude. The play tells how Hamlet seeks revenge for this. He appears to go mad and this, in turn, drives his lady Ophelia insane. Hamlet asks a company of players to perform a play with a plot similar to his father's murder and Claudius reacts in a way that proves his guilt. Ophelia drowns herself and her brother Laertes swears revenge. He fights a duel with Hamlet and both of them die, as do Gertrude and Claudius.

Mention other features of the play such as Hamlet's soliloquy 'To be or not to be . . .', or Polonius's words of wisdom 'Neither a borrower nor a lender be,/For loan oft loses both itself and friend.'

Discuss the spotlight subject 'revenge'. Do you believe in an eye for an eye or turning the other cheek? In soliloquy, monologue or duologue, set up improvisations with the first line

'I'm going to get my own back on her/him.'

Choose a piece of text to work from, for example, the Ophelia–Polonius duologue (Act II scene i), where Ophelia has been frightened by Hamlet's madness and seeks her father's help.

2 Romeo and Juliet

Spotlight on 'Forbidden Fruit'

The Montagues and the Capulets are rival families in Verona. Romeo, Montague's heir, falls in love with Juliet, Capulet's daughter, at a masked ball. They meet by night and Friar Lawrence marries them secretly the following afternoon. Tybalt, Juliet's cousin, challenges Romeo to a fight. Romeo refuses but his friend Mercutio, enraged, accepts the challenge and is fatally wounded. Romeo kills Tybalt in revenge. He is banished and Juliet is ordered to marry Paris, a nobleman. Friar Lawrence devises a plan by which Juliet, by taking a potion, can feign death, thus avoiding marriage to Paris. He sends word to Romeo to come and rescue Juliet from Capulet's tomb but before this can happen Romeo has received a message that Juliet is dead. Romeo hurries to the tomb, kills Paris and takes poison. Juliet awakens and, finding Romeo dead, kills herself. The Montagues and the Capulets are reconciled over the bodies of Romeo and Juliet.

No discussion of *Romeo and Juliet* would be complete without reference to the famous balcony scene between the 'star-crossed lovers'.

Discuss the spotlight subject 'forbidden fruit'. Do you think that Romeo and Juliet would have been so passionately attracted to one another had their parents approved of their relationship? Does forbidden fruit taste twice as sweet? If so, why? In twos, as parent and offspring, use the first and second lines:

'I forbid you to go out with that boy/girl'
'But why?'

An apt piece of text work would be the duologue between Juliet and the Nurse (Act II scene v), in which we see the Nurse teasing Juliet, holding back to the end the good news that Friar Lawrence will marry her to Romeo.

3 Julius Caesar

Spotlight on 'Conspiracy'

The conspirators, Cassius, Casca and Brutus, plot to murder Julius Caesar because they believe he is growing too powerful. A soothsayer warns Caesar to beware the Ides of March (15 March), but he goes to the Capitol where he is stabbed to death. His body is carried to the Forum, where Brutus justifies the assassination to the mob; then Mark Antony addresses them and turns them against the conspirators. Civil war breaks out between the triumvirate (Mark Antony, Octavius and Lepidus) and the conspirators. They will meet in battle at Philippi; Caesar's ghost appears to Brutus telling him that he will see him again at Philippi. The battle lost, Cassius orders a servant to stab him, and Brutus runs on his own sword. Mark Antony delivers his epitaph.

A scene that provides excellent discussion material is the one in which Cinna the poet is murdered by the mob just because he has the same name as Cinna the conspirator – an example of mob mentality, when a crowd will behave collectively in a way they would not do as individuals. Another discussion subject that comes up is that of ambition. Who was the more ambitious, Caesar or the conspirators? How far should one pursue ambition at the expense of others?

Discuss the spotlight subject 'conspiracy' – plotting, paranoia, bad-mouthing, slandering. In twos, use the first line:

'You've been plotting against, me, haven't you?'

A good piece of text work is Mark Antony's famous speech in the forum: 'Friends, Romans, countrymen . . .' (Act III scene ii). Brutus has made the mistake of allowing Mark Antony to speak after him. Without overtly speaking against the conspirators, Mark Antony skilfully manipulates the mob's feelings and turns it against them.

4 Othello

Spotlight on: 'The Green-Eyed Monster'

The three protagonists of the piece are Othello, the black Moor of Venice, his wife Desdemona and Iago, one of his officers. Iago is consumed by envy of Othello. Othello is sent to govern Cyprus, where his new lieutenant, Cassio, egged on by Iago, gets drunk and is disgraced. Iago, who has hinted to Othello that Desdemona is unfaithful to him, suggests to Cassio that he should ask Desdemona to intercede for him. Iago persuades his wife Emilia to steal Desdemona's handkerchief, which he plants on Cassio. Iago then points out to Othello that Cassio has given it to his mistress, Bianca. He inflames Othello to the point where Othello swears he will kill Desdemona. He smothers her in bed. Emilia comes in and, horrified by Desdemona's death, reveals what Iago has done. Iago stabs her. Othello kills himself and Iago is taken away to be tortured.

As with Shylock in *The Merchant of Venice*, some of the racial references to Othello are abusive. Nevertheless, Othello is a majestic character who transcends stereotypes. The subject of how black people are depicted in the media down to the present day is a very fertile one for discussion.

Discuss the subject 'the green-eyed monster' — jealousy:

> 'O! beware, my lord of jealousy,
> It is the green-eyed monster which doth mock
> The meat it feeds on.'

Take it from different points of view in turn as a monologue *en masse*. First from Othello's point of view:

> 'I have proof you were with Cassio.'

Next take it from Desdemona's point of view:

> 'Othello, you've got it all wrong!'

From Iago's point of view:

> 'Othello, not being horrible or anything . . .'

Now from your own point of view:

> 'Othello, you are blinded by jealousy . . .'

Simple modern day duologues can be set up using various first lines to depict the subject of jealousy, for example:

> 'Look here, everyone knows you're just madly jealous of
> Tony . . .'

For text work there is a very powerful duologue between Iago and Othello at the beginning of Act IV scene i, in which Iago, making great play with the handkerchief, is taunting and cruel to Othello's wretchedness and despair.

5 A Midsummer Night's Dream

Spotlight on 'Love at First Sight'

The play is set in an imaginary Athens. It has three parallel stories: the romantic story of two pairs of aristocratic lovers, the exploits of the immortals (the fairy folk), and the comical antics of the mechanicals (a group of tradesmen rehearsing a play). Hermia has been ordered to marry Demetrius but she refuses as she is in love with Lysander. They decide to elope together, meeting in a wood. Meanwhile, her friend Helena, who is in love with Demetrius, has told him about their plan, and he too goes to the wood, followed by Helena. The wood is the haunt of fairy folk and Oberon and Titania, king and queen of the fairies, have quarrelled over a changeling boy. Oberon orders Puck (also known as Robin Goodfellow) to fetch a flower, the juice of which, squeezed on the eyelids of Titania, will make her fall in love with whoever she first sees on awakening. He also orders him to squeeze it on Demetrius's eyes, but by mistake Puck anoints Lysander, who when he awakens falls in love with Helena. The mechanicals meet in the wood to rehearse their play and by magical means Puck puts an ass's head on Bottom the weaver. Titania wakes up and promptly falls in love with him. Finally, Oberon and Puck remove all the spells and Bottom awakes, as if from the strangest dream. The play 'Pyramus and Thisbe' is performed at the palace — farcically. Midnight strikes and all retire to bed, leaving the world to the fairies.

Point out that 'A Midsummer Night's Dream' is full of *dramatic irony*, which is when the audience know something that a character in the play is unaware of. A subject that can follow on from the play is 'dreams'. Both their content and meaning provide good material for discussion and improvisation.

The spotlight subject, 'love at first sight', makes a good talking-point. What first attracts you to someone? Looks? Personality? What makes for a good relationship? What makes a good partner for life? How do you feel about arranged marriages? Divide the class into pairs — they are best friends or girl-friend and boy-friend. Now, as Lysander says in the play, 'The course of true love never did run smooth' — the situation is that the friends or lovers have just had their very first quarrel. The first line is 'Well, what can I say?'

A suitable piece which demonstrates unrequited love is the

duologue between Demetrius and Helena in Act II scene i, starting
with Demetrius's 'I love thee not, therefore pursue me not', and
ending with Helena's 'I'll follow thee, and make a heaven of hell, To
die upon the hand I love so well.'

THEATRE THROUGH THE AGES

This umbrella theme can be helped enormously if you make your
own theatre time chart in advance. If you do so, it is well worth
adding the main figures in literature, music, art, history, science and
invention. Try not to see theatre in isolation, as it were, but in
conjunction with the other arts, social history and, indeed, sciences. If
that proves too academic then at least keep the literature section —
theatre and literature walk hand in hand. Obviously you cannot go
into the other subjects in any great depth; the idea is to form a
bridge to other school subjects, so that they are not being studied in
isolation.

Reference books, particularly on the history of British theatre, will
need to be looked into before you embark on this project — an
essential piece of homework.

Theatre through the ages can be conveniently divided into seven
stages, though you might start with an introduction and end with a
recapitulation.

On your notice-board, under the heading THEATRE THROUGH THE
AGES, write: *This Week* (to be followed by the title of the week's
stage), *Play of the Week* and then *Other Features*.

Stage 1

Stage 1 is 'Before 1000'. You might recommend the play *The Trojan
Women* by Euripides and talk about the Greek and Roman theatre.
Other Features might include Aesop's Fables and you might also
mention Homer, Virgil and the long narrative poem Beowulf.
Historically, Julius Caesar came to Britain in 55 BC, the Roman
invasion of Britain took place in AD 43, and the Revolt of Boadicea
was in AD 60. The emergence of Christianity was of immense
significance. For your improvisation work you might take the subject
of 'suffering' from *The Trojan Women* or read selected extracts from
the play. There is a mass of material to be improvised or mimed from
Aesop's Fables, so we have treated this as a separate theme.

Stage 2

Stage 2 is from the eleventh to the fifteenth century — medieval theatre. Liturgical or church drama in the shape of mystery plays (stories from the Bible), miracle plays (stories about the saints) and morality plays (about good versus evil) provides excellent material for improvisation and discussion. Recommend the play *Everyman*, anonymously written, about the struggle between Good and Evil and in which it is your good deeds that count in the end. *Other Features* might include Geoffrey Chaucer (*c.* 1340–1400) and *The Canterbury Tales*. Or you might like to home in on the Arthurian legends, Excalibur, the magic sword, the wizard Merlin, Lancelot and Queen Guinevere.

The great artists of the Renaissance such as Leonardo da Vinci (1452–1519) came at the end of this time and, historically, the Norman Conquest (1066), the Domesday Book (1086) and Magna Carta (1215) are of significance. Another dramatic figure of this period was Joan of Arc (1412–31), which might lead to some work on courage. (In fact, 'Heroes and Heroines' is another umbrella theme in its own right.) A good first line for an improvisation, using *Everyman* as your motivation, would be 'You know the difference between right and wrong.'

Stage 3

Stage 3 is the sixteenth century – Elizabethan theatre. William Shakespeare (1564–1616) is synonymous with the Elizabethan theatre and there are several of his plays you can recommend. *Romeo and Juliet* is particularly suitable for a teenage class. Christopher Marlowe was a direct contemporary of Shakespeare's, born in the same year, 1564, and tragically murdered in Deptford, south London in 1593. His three great plays, *Doctor Faustus*, *The Jew of Malta* and *Tamburlaine the Great*, all provide excellent dramatic material for readings or improvisations. The poet John Donne (1572–1631), who wrote the immortal line 'No man is an island', is also a good source for improvisation work.

Historically, there was the Reformation from 1517, Henry VIII, 1491–1547, and the Spanish Armada, 1588. Compare the Elizabethan theatre, which we have written about in the previous section, with the theatre today. In Elizabethan times theatres were disapproved of by the authorities, had to be built outside the city walls and were often closed because of the plague. Mention also the Italian *commedia dell'arte* - a marvellous combination of dancing, singing, mime, acrobatics, comedy and improvisation.

Stage 4

Stage 4 is the seventeenth century – Restoration theatre. You might recommend *The Way of the World* by William Congreve and talk about the 'comedy of manners' style, where wit and sometimes sarcasm is displayed while depicting people's manners and idiosyncrasies. Samuel Pepys is one of the century's most colourful figures. His diary, written in cipher, gives us vivid descriptions of the seventeenth-century theatre. He tells us that the seats of the theatre were not numbered or reserved but that servants could keep them for their masters. You might also talk about famous diaries, from Anne Frank's to Adrian Mole's. A good first line for duologue work might be 'How dare you read my diary', followed by soliloquies using the first line 'He/she's got a nerve . . .'. Historically the Gunpowder Plot, Guy Fawkes (1605), the Pilgrim Fathers (1620), Oliver Cromwell (1599–1658), the Plague (1665) and the Great Fire of London (1666) were some of the important events. The great scientists of the age were Galileo and Newton. Oliver Cromwell, the Lord Protector and a Puritan, was responsible for closing the theatres, and when Charles II came back to England the monarchy was restored. Thus this period is called Restoration theatre.

While in France, Charles II saw the early comedies of Molière and he was keen to see English theatres flourish again. The Theatre Royal, Drury Lane, was the most popular of the day. By now the theatres were roofed over so plays could be performed by artificial light, such as candles, torches and oil-lamps. Women appeared on the stage for the first time and Nell Gwyn, a former orange seller, was a well liked actress at Drury Lane. Inigo Jones introduced the proscenium, or picture-frame, stage. It had curtains and, because of the poor lighting, the stage was extended out into the audience – an apron stage.

Stage 5

And so, on to stage 5 – the eighteenth century. Recommend Richard Brinsley Sheridan's *The School for Scandal* or *The Rivals*. Sheridan, like William Congreve before him, and his contemporary, Oliver Goldsmith, wrote in the 'comedy of manners' style. Pantomime, a derivative of the Italian *commedia dell'arte*, with its spectacular elements, was popular. It was at this time that plays were put under the censorship of the Lord Chamberlain to ensure that nothing was being written against the government or the Crown. There is a lot of good improvisation and discussion work to be found in the subject of censorship. Take a duologue, parent and offspring, using the first line 'Don't you ever use that foul language in this house'.

Daniel Defoe and Jonathan Swift were great literary figures of the eighteenth century. This was known as the 'Age of Reason' and towards the end of the century came the beginning of the Industrial Revolution. Other points in the historical background include American Independence (1776), the French Revolution (1789) and Napoleon (1769–1821). This was the century of the great classical composers Bach (1685–1750), Handel (1685–1759) and Mozart (1756–91).

Stage 6

The nineteenth century is stage 6. Stage lighting made enormous improvements – first gaslight and then electric lighting, introduced at the Savoy Theatre in 1880. Machinery was used to make the stage sink or revolve. Scenery was lavish and the box set was popular. Music hall was a great success and Marie Lloyd ('A little of what you fancy does you good') a great favourite. Recommend *Pygmalion* by George Bernard Shaw, which has since become the musical *My Fair Lady*. The central characters – the cockney girl, Eliza Doolittle, and her mentor, Professor Henry Higgins, who teaches her to speak properly – should provide good material for improvisation and discussion.

Jane Austen was a great novelist of the nineteenth century. The life and works of Charles Dickens would be an excellent example for your *Other Features* category. The Romantic poets, Wordsworth, Coleridge, Byron, Keats and Shelley, will provide excellent material for poetry readings. Highly recommended is 'Lucy Grey' by Wordsworth, a poem about a little girl who gets lost in the snow, never to return. The century's leading composers include Beethoven and Brahms.

Historical events include the battles of Trafalgar (1805) and Waterloo (1815) and the Crimean War (1854–6). Many of the inventions which shape the modern world – the railways, the telephone, the car – first appeared in the nineteenth century and it was also an age of humanitarian and social advance; for example, slavery was abolished.

Stage 7

The seventh and last stage is the twentieth century – modern theatre.

185

You might recommend *Look Back in Anger* by John Osborne as your play of the week. The central character, Jimmy Porter, was the prototype of the 'angry young man'. He was angry about the class system in Britain. Ask the group what, if anything, makes them angry – a good first line for improvisation would be 'I'll tell you why I'm angry'. Give them a free rein to sound off on any subject. George Orwell, with his *Animal Farm* and *1984*, might be a candidate for the *Other Features* category. If you can lay your hands on any reproduction picture cards of Picasso's work they could be included in the project. The First World War (1914–18), the Russian Revolution (1917), the Second World War (1939–45) and Indian Independence (1947) are some of the more significant events. Elgar and Stravinsky were leading composers, though you might like to use the Beatles or other twentieth-century popular music. As we all know, this has been a time of immense technological development.

A simple and effective idea is to have an 'Enter/Exit Music' spot, illustrating a different composer for each century, with his details on your notice-board.

In common with all umbrella themes of the term, it is important to recapitulate as you go along, and most certainly at the end of the project.

DANCE OF THE WEEK

Dance of the week can be linked with other items in your class content. For example, if the Irish jig is the dance of one particular week, it could be linked with, say, dialect work contrasting the Irish brogue north and south of the border. There could be discussion work and situation drama on an Irish theme. Similarly, other dances will throw up important links to be used in the session.

Here is a list of popular dances that could be used:

> Zorba's Dance
> Irish jigs and reels
> The Hora (sometimes known as Hava Nagila, an Israeli folk
>   dance)
> Cha-cha-cha
> Rock 'n' Roll
> Ska
> Waltz
> Cancan
> The Polka

The Twist
Body popping
Break dancing
Disco dancing

Of course there are lots of folk and nationality dances you can add to your repertoire, such as the Gay Gordons and the Dashing White Sergeant. Dances through the ages, such as gavottes and minuets, could be an added dimension to your theme. The more specialized dances — such as tap, ballet, contemporary and modern — require years of discipline and training but, if you have someone in your class proficient in any of them, do have them demonstrate their skills. There is nothing to stop you, or the class, from choreographing your own dances.

Keep up with what's in vogue and remember the traditional dances too — and don't forget the Birdie Song!

AESOP'S FABLES

The sixth-century BC Greek slave Aesop told the most marvellously simple stories, mainly about animals. Each story has a moral and through discussion it is easy to find present-day parallels. The following ten have worked splendidly for us.

1 The Hare and the Tortoise

The hare is the faster runner but the tortoise wins the race because he is more persistent. Steady progress is better than a flash in the pan.

2 The Fox and the Crow

The fox flatters the crow about her voice; she opens her mouth to sing and drops the cheese. Never be taken in by flattery.

3 The Fox and the Grapes

The fox can't reach the bunch of grapes so he walks away in disgust saying, 'They were sour anyway.' It is 'sour grapes' to put down something you can't have.

4 The Lion and the Mouse

When the mighty lion is captured, it is the tiny mouse who gnaws through the ropes and releases him. Even the humblest creature is not beneath consideration.

5 The Town Mouse and the Country Mouse

The town mouse can't get used to the simple ways of the country and the country mouse is frightened of the busy town. A case of 'One man's meat is another man's poison'.

6 The Boy who Called Wolf

After the shepherd boy has raised several false alarms, no one believes him when the wolf really does attack his flock. People who tell lies lose their credibility.

7 The Dog and the Reflection

A dog with a bone, seeing his reflection in a pool, tries to steal that bone too, thus losing both. By being too greedy you can lose everything.

8 The Mice in Council

The mice decide that a bell should be put on the cat so that it won't be able to catch them; but who will bell the cat? It is easy to be an armchair critic.

9 The Dog in the Manger

Although the dog can't eat hay himself, he lies on top of it and makes sure the horse can't get any either. Don't deprive someone of something just because you can't have it yourself.

10 The Boys and the Frogs

Throwing stones at the frogs may be fun for the boys, but it is a matter of life and death for the frogs. Bullies should look at things from the point of view of their victims.

Aesop's Fables can be dealt with dramatically in a variety of ways. Divide the class into groups and allocate each group a different fable; they have to devise a playlet re-enacting the original fable in modern terms. An idea for individual work is for the class to hear one end of a telephone conversation; at the end of it they must guess which fable was being represented.

GREEK MYTHOLOGY

Greek mythology is important in all the arts. The myths have been preserved by the Greek poet Hesiod and by Homer in the *Iliad* and the *Odyssey*. The Greek dramatists of the fifth century BC – Aeschylus, Sophocles and Euripides – relied on myths and legends for most of their plots. Examples are *Medea* and *The Trojan Women* by Euripides. Throughout the ages playwrights have drawn on the Greek myths. Many of the terms have seeped into our language – *Achilles' heel*, your weak spot; *laurels*, the symbol of victory; *narcissistic*, intensely vain; *nectar*, the drink of the gods.

The Greek myths provide excellent material for storytelling, as well as improvisation and mime. Here are some that have proved very popular.

1 Pandora's Box

Pandora, the Eve of Greek mythology, was as beautiful as any goddess but she had a box which, when opened, loosed all the evils there are in the world, leaving behind only hope.

Thus woman gets the blame for all the evils in the world.

Spotlight Subject: 'Blame' Getting the blame, whether deserved or not.

2 Demeter and Persephone

Persephone, daughter of Demeter, goddess of nature, was kidnapped and taken to the underworld. Zeus, chief of the gods, agreed to get her back but, as she had eaten six pomegranate seeds in the underworld, a compromise had to be reached by which she spent part of the year there and the remainder with her mother.

This is supposed to be the origin of the seasons.

Spotlight Subject: 'Compromise' When two people disagree they can agree to differ or find a way of reaching a compromise.

3 King Midas and the Golden Touch

King Midas was granted a wish by the god Dionysus and he asked that everything he touched should turn to gold. Midas soon regretted his wish when even his food turned to gold. Dionysus bade Midas bathe in the River Pactolus, whereupon the golden touch passed into the waters, which flowed with gold ever after.

Today we talk of someone having the 'Midas touch', meaning that everything they turn their hand to is successful and makes money.

Spotlight Subject: 'Greed' There is a difference between having a

ANOTHER 100 + IDEAS FOR DRAMA

good appetite and being greedy. This applies to money as well as to food – and the greedy person always has to pay a price.

4   Daedalus and Icarus

Daedalus and his son Icarus were imprisoned in the labyrinth, a maze which he himself had built. They escaped by making wings from feathers held together by wax. Elated by the thrill of flying, Icarus ignored his father's advice and flew too near the sun. The wax melted and Icarus fell to his death.

Thus, Daedalus, the father of invention (he also devised the saw and the axe), saw his own son destroyed by his brainchild.

Spotlight Subject: 'Risk'   Nothing ventured, nothing gained – but beware the thrill of danger; risk-taking can become a compulsion.

5   The Stories of Perseus

Acrisius was warned by the oracle that his daughter Danae would have a son who would kill him, so he locked her up in a tower. But Zeus, chief of the gods, visited her there and fathered a son, Perseus, who grew up to have many adventures. Years later, when Acrisius was an old man, Perseus accidentally killed him when throwing the discus, so the prophecy came true.

Spotlight Subject: 'Fate'   Are certain things destined to happen or can people alter the inevitable course of events?

One of Perseus's adventures was when a king, Polydectes, wanted to marry Perseus's mother, Danae, against her will. Deceiving Perseus into thinking he was going to marry someone else, Polydectes sent him to cut off the head of the Gorgon Medusa as a wedding present. Medusa was so ugly that anyone looking at her turned to stone. Perseus cut off her head, but on his return he found Polydectes still pursuing Danae, so he showed him the head, turning him to stone.

Spotlight Subject: 'Deception'   If someone is deceived into doing something, the deceiver often gets his just deserts.

On his way home with the Gorgon's head, Perseus visited Ethiopia, where the queen, Cassiopeia, had claimed to be more beautiful than the sea nymphs, thus causing the land to be ravaged by a sea monster. The only solution was to sacrifice the king's daughter, Andromeda, to the monster by chaining her to a rock. Perseus killed the sea monster, rescued Andromeda and married her.

All the characters in this story are represented among the constellations of the autumn night sky.

190

Spotlight Subject: 'Sacrifice'   Few worthwhile things can be achieved without sacrifices, but the sacrifices can sometimes be too severe.

6   Orpheus and Eurydice

Orpheus, son of Apollo, was such a wonderful musician that even the animals listened to him. He was married to Eurydice, but one day she was bitten by a snake in the grass and her spirit went to the underworld. Orpheus descended to the underworld after her, playing his lyre and charming the three-headed dog, Cerberus. Hades and Persephone agreed to release her, on condition that Orpheus would not look back at her, but just as they arrived at the gates he did and she disappeared for ever.

Spotlight Subject: 'Regret'   It is no use trying to change the past but you can learn from it.

There are, of course, many more Greek myths and it is worthwhile to research them in both children's books and more academic ones. Improvisations can be built round the spotlight subjects and the myths lend themselves to re-enactment in modern terms.

BIBLE STORIES

The Bible is a great source of eminently suitable material for improvisation. Powerful storylines and themes of good versus evil make for strong dramatic content from which a moral can always be drawn.

Use 'This Week's Bible Story' as your umbrella theme in conjunction with 'Word of the Week' and 'First Lines'.

> Adam and Eve – 'temptation' – 'I told you not to do that'
> Cain and Abel – 'jealousy' – 'You're just jealous!'
> Noah's Ark – 'shelter' – 'You don't appreciate a thing I do'
> Tower of Babel – 'language' – 'No foul language in this house'
> Abraham – 'birth' – 'I'm pregnant'/'My girlfriend's pregnant'
> Isaac – 'sacrifice' – 'A little bit of self-sacrifice goes a long way'
> Jacob – 'deception' – 'How can you be so deceitful?'
> Joseph – 'dream' – 'Last night I had this incredible dream'
> Moses – 'rules' – 'You know the rules of this house'

And so on right through the Old and New Testaments.

BOOK OF THE WEEK

Theatre and literature walk hand in hand. There are all kinds of ways of bringing books into a drama class, from recommending favourite books or holiday reading suggestions to discussion work on books the class has read.

The book of the week can also be linked with a word of the week.

> *Gulliver's Travels* by Jonathan Swift (1667–1745) – 'travel'
> *The Happy Prince* by Oscar Wilde (1854–1900) – 'selfless'
> 'How the Whale got his Throat' from the *Just So Stories* by
>   Rudyard Kipling (1865–1936) – 'enterprise'
> *Treasure Island* by Robert Louis Stevenson (1850–94) – 'pirate'
> *The Three Musketeers* by Alexandre Dumas (1802–70) – 'three'
> *The Hound of the Baskervilles* by Sir Arthur Conan Doyle
>   (1859–1930) – 'eerie'
> *Around the World in Eighty Days* by Jules Verne (1828–1905)
>   – 'time'
> *The Wind in the Willows* by Kenneth Grahame (1859–1932) –
>   'conceit'
> *Peter Pan* by J. M. Barrie (1860–1937) – 'age'
> *The Ugly Duckling* by Hans Christian Andersen (1805–75) –
>   'prejudice'

The word of the week need not be taken too literally. For example, when doing *Treasure Island*, the word 'pirate' could be connected with the pirating of ideas, video piracy, and so on. A simple word like 'three' (*The Three Musketeers*) can lead to such diverse topics as the eternal triangle; two's company, three's a crowd; St Patrick's illustration of the Holy Trinity using a shamrock; the three Rs; the three wise monkeys; and all the words beginning with tri–.

You can give the flavour of a book by reading apt extracts from it. It is very useful, particularly with juniors, to have your own fund of stories that you can tell in your own way. Plenty of raw material can be found in fables and fairy tales, let alone making up your own – however tall. A delightful tale to tell in your own words is the story of the Willow Pattern from ancient Chinese folklore – of course you must use the picture for illustration.

PERSON OF THE WEEK

'Person of the Week' can include all manner of prominent people –

artists, writers, composers, scientists, people in history, people in the news. Your choice of person can tie in with their date of birth or death or a centenary or a connection with something topical or newsworthy. Again, 'Person of the Week' works well with 'Word of the Week'.

> Thomas Hardy (1840–1928) – 'fate'
> George Orwell (1903–50) – 'satire'
> Mozart (1756–91) – 'talent'
> Mendelssohn (1809–47) – 'wedding'
> Charles Dickens (1812–70) – 'debt'
> Captain Cook (1728–79) – 'discoveries'
> Vincent Van Gogh (1853–90) – 'destructive'
> Sir Alexander Fleming (1881–1955) – 'health'
> St Patrick (c. 389–461) – 'confessions'
> Henrik Ibsen (1828–1906) – 'isolation'
> Queen Elizabeth I (1533–1603) – 'suspicion'

Obviously, we are not summing up a person's whole life in one word but rather homing in on one aspect and using it for dramatic purposes. Take Thomas Hardy. You would tell the class about his life and his works, perhaps read one of his poems, and describe Wessex and the typical names he uses for his characters. You could describe the role played by fate in his novels (you might, of course, have chosen a different word). Are members of the class fatalists or not? How much are people in control of their own destiny?

HEROES AND HEROINES

First introduce the topic by discussing the characteristics of heroism. What makes a hero or heroine? Perhaps they are the kind of people worthy of our admiration. What would you regard as heroic qualities? Courage? Daring? Great deeds? Contrast heroism and hype. Invite individuals to nominate a person they admire and say why.

Draw up a list of heroes and heroines from the past and present and choose a 'spotlight' word to home in on with a first line to follow.

The following list proved an effective one for us:

> Thomas à Becket (c. 1118–70) – 'resolute'
> 'No way. There is no way I'm going to change my mind.'
> Joan of Arc (1412–31) – 'messenger'
> 'Didn't you get my message?'
> 'What message?'

Horatio Nelson (1758–1845) – 'duty'
　　'Don't you have a sense of duty?'
Elizabeth Fry (1780–1845) – 'reform'
　　'You'd better buck up your ideas.'
Mary Seacole (1807–81) – 'prejudice'
　　'I'm sick to death of your prejudiced remarks.'
Martin Luther King (1929–68) – 'dream'
　　'Last night I had this really strange dream.'
Mahatma Gandhi (1869–1948) – 'truth'
　　'That was a bare-faced lie.'
Bob Marley (1945–81) – 'emancipation'
　　'Why do you allow yourself to be treated like that?'
Bob Geldof (born 1954) – 'generous spirit'
　　'Why can't you be more supportive?'
The Unknown Warrior (buried 1920 Westminster Abbey) –
　　'remembrance'
　　'You've got a short memory, haven't you?'
Mother Teresa of Calcutta (born 1910) – 'selflessness'
　　'Self, self, self. That's all you ever think of.'
Nelson Mandela (born 1918) – 'perseverance'
　　'I'll tell you something – you give in far too easily.'

The first-liners can be conveniently used in duologue form with or without soliloquy – as you will.

Much mileage can also be gained from 'talkabout' duologues. For example, with Elizabeth Fry and 'reform' the pairs cold talk about areas of improvement personally and professionally. Or with Mahatma Gandhi and 'truth' the class could play the game 'Tall Tales or True'. The subject tells a tall tale and a true tale; the class has to guess which was the tall one and which was the truth. This can also be done in pairs.

Clearly some research will need to be done on the individual heroes and heroines, but you will find that quite a few of the class will gladly do some of this, so encourage optional homework!

A good ender on this topic is to pose the question to every member of the group, 'Which hero/heroine meant the most to you and why?'

A Heroes/Heroines Quiz might be another fun finish.

PLAYWRIGHT OF THE WEEK

This umbrella theme provides a useful 'in' to a writer's work. On your notice-board have three headings:

```
PLAYWRIGHT OF THE WEEK

RECOMMENDED READING

THIS WEEK'S SUBJECT
```

Underneath these headings put your selections for the week. Hold a short discussion on the writer's life and work and the subject you have selected for improvisation. The following have worked well for us:

> George Bernard Shaw (1856–1950), *Pygmalion*, 'hypocrisy'
> Oscar Wilde (1854–1900), *The Importance of Being Earnest*, 'wit'
> John Osborne (born 1929), *Look Back in Anger*, 'grievance'
> Christopher Marlowe (1564–93), *Doctor Faustus*, 'debt'
> Arnold Wesker (born 1932), *Roots*, 'desertion'
> Harold Pinter (born 1930), *The Birthday Party*, 'unprovoked attack'
> Nigel Williams (born 1948), *Class Enemy*, 'language'
> Brian Clark (born 1932), *Whose Life Is It Anyway?*, 'choice'
> Tennessee Williams (1914–83), *A Streetcar Named Desire*, 'suffering'

The format for 'Playwright of the Week' is similar to 'Person of the Week'. Use of the subject need not be confined to its original meaning in the play – the group can branch out in any direction. For example, *Class Enemy* is a play with a great deal of swearing in it. You might mention that plays in the British theatre were censored by the Lord Chamberlain until 1968. How far is it justifiable to use bad language in a play or an improvisation? When does it become gratuitous and undermine the believability of the piece? You can then extend into foreign languages, dialects, accents and snobbery, sign language, malapropisms, slang, and so on.

OTHER THEMES

With older groups there is literally no limit to the themes that can be chosen for discussion and improvisation. Here are some suggestions taken from a series we did on contemporary topics: 'Snobbery', 'War', 'Religion', 'Sport', 'Power', 'Love', 'Animals', 'Alcohol', 'Defeat' and 'Rumour'. For example, 'Rumour' – stories that spread from person to person, but on a larger scale than gossip. It is hard to determine how rumours start but they can only spread if people, in some sense, want to believe them. Discuss how rumours start, spread and change. Why do certain people repeat (and embellish) rumours of particular kinds? Rumours tend to concern charismatic figures, fatal incidents, the supernatural, and high technology, and they are particularly common in wartime and other times of stress. See how many examples people can think of and then follow up with group work with the optional title 'The truth about . . .'.

It is a pity that the arts and sciences are so polarized. If you have some knowledge of science or a scientific colleague who is interested in theatre it is a field rich with possibilities. Just as we don't teach drama only to create actors and theatre audiences, similarly we don't teach science just to produce scientists, but to produce people with open minds who are willing to test theories by finding out the facts. Ground that can be covered includes opinions and attitudes to science, the dramatization of scientific ideas and the effects of scientific and technological developments. Science need not be confined to things that are done in a laboratory and a good 'talkabout' subject is 'One thing you've found out about, whether in a science lesson or not'. Another is 'One thing you wonder about – how something works, or why something is'. Improvisations can be based round situations where, for example, one invention is cancelled (for example, televisions either don't work or have never been invented) or one scientific law changes. Or, again, two people are given the responsibility of creating a new universe: what differences will they make from the one we have already got. A good topic for group plays is life fifty or a hundred years in the future. Start by looking back the same length of time and pointing out all that has changed.

Sometimes topics can be connected with particular styles of theatre. For example, a session on 'dreams' might connect with the Theatre of the Absurd, and perhaps you could go on to the Theatre of Cruelty, Surrealism and nonsense literature. One on 'journalism' or 'the media' might be linked with biographical theatre. Going back to playwrights, another way of working with older groups is to concentrate on the style and atmosphere of each writer's plays. Often a good 'way in' is to find a phrase that characterizes the writer, for example:

Samuel Beckett	Life and death in the wasteland.
Noel Coward	Exquisite wit. The characters often combine intensity and flippancy.
Mike Leigh	Caricatures of normality.
Joe Orton	Hilarious terror.
Harold Pinter	Extreme ordinariness – but with undercurrents of aggression and nothing completely explained.
Sheridan	Polished society comedy.
Tom Stoppard	Brilliant absurdity – confusions, parodies and jokes.
Oscar Wilde	Elegant high comedy.
Tennessee Williams	Decayed gentility – set in the Southern states of the USA.

Groups can even try to improvise in the style of a playwright they are studying, but, to be anything more than pastiche, such improvisations must be played very straight.

4

Short Productions and Drama Workshop Entertainments

It is always fascinating to be a 'fly on the wall' watching a good drama class in action, so it is not surprising that a drama workshop, presented to an audience, makes such a good form of entertainment. This requires a group who are technically proficient and confident enough to appear in front of an audience, and selection of the right material for the situation is important too. Professional improvisation groups have used a drama workshop format to good effect, and, particularly with unscripted intervention from the audience, this can be the liveliest form of live performance. You do have to be careful, though, to protect your performers to some extent: in a class you are used to producing an atmosphere in which people can experiment without the fear of failure; any failure in front of an audience is more likely to knock their confidence, so you cannot be so experimental.

THE TEN-MINUTE ASSEMBLY

A school class's first venture into drama workshop entertainment is likely to be a 'ten-minute assembly'. More than likely this will be tied to a topical subject or a date in the calendar – we've listed some later on – but our 'Umbrella Themes of the Term' (Chapter 3) should provide another fund of ideas to be narrated, mimed or improvised, such as Aesop's Fables, Greek mythology, the Bible, and so on.

Building up your own record and/or tape library is invaluable not only for mood and movement purposes but also because some musical narratives – for example, 'Tubby the Tuba' and Prokofiev's 'Peter and the Wolf' – lend themselves particularly well to a short entertainment.

Improvisations on topics currently being taught in class in such subjects as history and geography provide a good opportunity for a presentation to the rest of the school, and for sharing valuable information at the same time.

Take a history project, 'People Through the Ages'. There would be an endless list of people to choose from: St Patrick, Alfred the Great, Robert the Bruce, Sir Thomas More, Sir Walter Ralegh, Captain

Cook, Clive of India, Elizabeth Fry, David Livingstone, Florence Nightingale, Captain Scott, Lawrence of Arabia, Sir Alexander Fleming.

The narrator tells the story, possibly with mood music of the period topping and tailing his words. The main body of the piece can be mimed or improvised. Any extras such as costume, pictures or other material would be a bonus.

Children love a good story and assembly time is a good time to tell one. The story of Robert the Bruce and the Spider is a good example.

Robert the Bruce of Scotland was fighting a battle against King Edward of England. But Robert was feeling very downhearted as he was losing the battle. So he went down into a cave underneath the battlefield and laid himself down. As he lay there pondering he saw a spider weaving its web in a corner of the roof of the cave. But, every time the spider tried to weave the web, the web broke – again and again and again. But the spider did not give up hope, it went on trying again and again and again, until finally it succeeded in weaving the most beautiful web right across the roof of the cave. Robert the Bruce thought to himself, 'If at first you don't succeed, try, try, try again.' So he got himself up and on to the battlefield, fought the battle of his life – and became King of Scotland.

Another example is the story of St Patrick teaching the Irish people about the Holy Trinity. 'What do you mean, Patrick, by three in one? Do you mean three gods or one god?' Patrick bent down and plucked a shamrock from the Irish soil. 'Look,' he said, 'look at this shamrock. It's got three leaves but only one stem, three in one. God the Father, God the Son and God the Holy Ghost – three in one.' A large cardboard cut-out of an emerald-green shamrock would be a necessary visual aid to illustrate this.

A lot of material can be had from a project on 'Different Countries of the World'. Living in the multiracial society that we have today, we can find great pleasure and joy in sharing each other's cultures, from food to folk stories, from dialect to dance – in short, the way we live. For example, comparing a day in the life of an Israeli boy or girl with a day in the life of a Jamaican boy or girl – right down to eating matzos and roti – would be great fun.

In all these ideas, whether you're illustrating another school subject or not, it is vital to have strong dramatic content that will stand up in its own right, and even in a short production like this a good shape with a strong beginning and ending is essential. Do not over-rehearse the action – it is improvisation and you don't want to kill the spontaneity; but do give some attention to the practicalities — how are people going to get on and off the stage, where is an imaginary doorway going to be, which way are people going to be facing, etc? That way the actors are working in a secure framework. Audiences notice all the small details; one thing to try to avoid is a mixture of real and imaginary props, which looks false. Advise your actors, if they make a mistake, to stay in character and carry on as if nothing has gone wrong. It is not the mistakes that the audience notice so much as the actors' reaction to them.

OUTSIDE PERFORMANCES

The next step a class or club might take would be to perform a drama-workshop show in a children's library or a hospital or a pensioners' club. About a dozen is a good number. All the equipment you need can be put in one box or basket — some records, masks, a couple of telephones and a bell, a football rattle, a scarf, maybe two or three other special props or costumes you know you will need. Always make sure in advance that a record-player will be available and check what furniture you will be able to use and that the acting area and seating plan are all right.

Here is an example of a *Drama Workshop Entertainment* suitable for a library or adventure playground audience. The format could be made to work with any age-group from five to fifteen, but it is useful if you can find out the expected age range from the organizer in advance. It is also a good idea not to allow admission for under-fives. If the venue is one that you need to attract people to — a youth club, say — you can visit it a few evenings before to do some pre-publicity with its members (at the same time you can check the technical requirements are in order) and you can leave behind a poster:

DRAMA WORKSHOP ENTERTAINMENT

Come and watch — or, better still, join in!

Once the show begins you will be in charge of controlling the audience and bringing them into it as required. You will have some set pieces for your own performers and some items in which you will invite the audience to join in. It is usually easy to spot who is ready to come forward and you can gradually build up the amount and degree of audience participation.

The following programme may serve as a guide.

1

The masked dance is a good opener. Each member of your team wears a different mask. They come in one by one and freeze in appropriate postures. When they are all in, the tableau can be restarted and then frozen again for dramatic effect.

2

Mask characters provide another good set piece to follow. Take two popular mask characters – perhaps the baby and the ghost, or the boy and the gorilla, or the sailor and the blonde – and have two other people's disembodied voices talking for the two masked characters. Maybe the baby is frightened of the ghost – who happens to be the ghost of the library (or whatever) where you are working.

3

Hands improvisation – get your best talker to welcome the audience and introduce you as the leader of the group. While he (or she) is chatting away another of your team is standing right behind him with his arms through the speaker's armpits providing his 'hands' – with all the gestures (the speaker's arms go round behind both of them).

4

Enter yourself to welcome the audience and introduce the team.

5

The team members introduce themselves by giving their names plus, perhaps, the food they love to eat and the food they hate to eat.

6

You start the physical warm-up with the team plus members of the audience, if they are willing to join in. Some may prefer to watch – don't force them.

7

Voice warm-up, using tongue-twisters, four times after a count of two – 'good blood, bad blood', 'unique New York', 'red lolly, yellow lorry', 'bed spreaders spread beds but bread spreaders spread bread'.

8

The Inner and the Outer Circle (see Chapter 2), the team working with the audience.

9

Fact-finding – each member of the team has a partner from the

audience and each has to find out at least five facts about the other in
two minutes. Hear some of them.

10
Duologues – parents and children. The team play the parents. First
line – 'You know the rules of this house.'

11
A mini-play (the audience go back to their places) – 'Divided
Loyalties' (see Chapter 1), topped and tailed with music and with a
vox pop from each character at the end.

12
Mime and music – the instruments of the orchestra. To suitable music
the team and the audience together mime different musical
instruments from the string, woodwind, brass and percussion families
– not forgetting the conductor with his baton.

13
Story time – three props on a box. Select three props – say, a
hairdryer, a vase of flowers and a pair of scissors (they can be
virtually anything you happen to have). One of the team tells a story
including all three props. Perhaps one of the audience is ready to tell
a story too.

14
Bell stories. Your best storyteller sits on a stool and starts to tell a
story. Every time you ring the bell he starts a new story (about four
in all).

15
One-word stories. Each member of the team chooses someone from
the audience and they act out a story as they tell it, each of them
supplying alternate words starting with 'we' – 'were'. . . . Give an
example or two from the team first.

16
Marching. One of the team leads the march, follow-my-leader style,
and picks, one at a time, anyone who wants to join in.

17
Endgame – Adam and Eve. The students form a circle sitting
cross-legged. Two of them are selected to be Adam and Eve and go
into the middle. Adam is blindfolded and has to try to catch Eve,
who has to stay within the circle. He calls out, as many times as he
likes, 'Where are you, Eve?', and she must reply straight away, 'Here I

am, Adam.' Thirty seconds to catch her in and then, of course, Eve can chase Adam too.

18
The masked dance can be your finale, so that you finish as you started.

The above programme will take between 45 minutes and an hour, but always have spare material at hand and be prepared to cut when necessary.

As always, check your props list and record-player before and after the show. It is also advisable to appoint two stage managers from within the team.

THEME SHOWS

The next step is to put on a show for the rest of the school, or for parents and friends. A good idea is to build a show round a particular theme. If you have been using an umbrella theme, items for the show will spring naturally out of the class's work, and you will have something to aim towards throughout the term. Themes such as we have suggested in Chapter 3 – mottoes, proverbs, poems, quotations, nationality or period dances, Greek mythology, Bible stories, books – would all lend themselves readily to a theme show.

Another approach is to be topical. Throughout the year many ideas will present themselves to you simply by being seasonal. Here are some well known and not so well known dates that might provide a jumping-off point:

January	New Year Resolutions
February	Chinese New Year
14 February	Valentine's Day
March	Mothering Sunday
17 March	St Patrick's Day
Easter	The Jewish Passover
23 April	St George's Day and Shakespeare's birthday
1 May	May Day
24 June	Midsummer Day
15 July	St Swithin's Day (which is supposed to determine the weather for the next forty days)
6 August	Hiroshima Day

15 September	Battle of Britain Day
September	Harvest home
24 October	United Nations Day
31 October	Halloween
11 November	Armistice Day
30 November	St Andrew's Day
6 December	St Nicholas's Day (the patron saint of children)
25 December	Christmas Day

There are many more you could choose and there are reference books that list famous days, saints' days, centenaries, and so on. And of course you can do a show on 'The Four Seasons' at any time of the year, possibly using Vivaldi's music.

Other ideas we have used in the past have included:

Pop Dreams A series of dreams in which pop records came to life.

Pictures of You Slices of life — a children's eyes' view of parents, families and neighbours.

Mystery and Imagination All manner of suspense and spookiness.

The Food Show All about food from diets to cannibalism.

British Allsorts About the many different kinds of people that make up the local community — West Indian, Irish, Greek, Turkish, African, cockney, etc.

Dear Aesop Modern-day equivalents of Aesop's fables, alternating with the stories being told in their original form.

Children of the Rainbow The rainbow and the colours that make it up.

The Rockney Rabbit A tribute to the cockney singers Chas 'n' Dave, using their songs as a springboard for plot and characterization.

Tribute shows often work well and the class's taste buds might be whetted by anyone from Beethoven to Bowie.

Hallelujah! A choir of forty plus singing gospel songs and all individually dressed in black and white.

Often the subject-matter will surface from whatever the class is currently into, be it comics or cosmetics, but, if you are stuck for a theme, open up a discussion or a talkabout and you are sure to get plenty of suggestions. If you're not sure how much mileage there is in an idea, you can make it the subject of a lesson in which the class divides into groups to devise improvisations connected with the subject that has been chosen. What you will be looking for is variety in content and mood and ideas with scope for development.

One way of organizing your theme show is to delegate specific research groups to work under various headings. So 'Children of the Rainbow' would have different groups finding out about the seven colours of the rainbow – red, orange, yellow, green, blue, indigo and violet. (You can remember the colours of the rainbow by the line 'Richard of York gave battle in vain'.) The red group would find out everything to do with red, from red London buses to red for danger, and the other six groups would each find out as much as they could about their colour, in the shape of bits of information, associations, improvisation, poems, songs and dances. Indigo could include the colour purple; violet has the flower and the girl's name. It is for the teacher to sew all the pieces together. The idea of God putting a rainbow in the sky as a promise to Noah and his family that he would never destroy the world again might top or tail the rainbow show.

Whatever method you use, you will have a period during which you are gathering and developing material. After a while you will be in a position to select the best of what you have, with an eye on the length of show required, and to construct a running order. The first thing to do is to find a beginning and an ending – something at the beginning that will gain the audience's attention and be an introduction to the whole theme of the show, and something at the end which will be a summation of all that has gone before. Then you need to find linking material – incidental music that can be used all the way through, or a narration or a motif or a storyline that can link all your different items. The items themselves must run in a logical order so that one thing leads to the next. If there can be a variation of light and shade so that a fast item follows a slow one, a comic one is set against a serious one, or a solo piece is followed by having the stage full of people, so much the better. Often practicalities such as set and costume changes will have to be taken into account.

At the devising stage, one of the advantages of a theme show is that you don't need to have the entire cast present at every rehearsal, as you can rehearse different items separately. Once you have a running order, though, the show will begin to knit together much better when you have all the cast together and are rehearsing 'from the top'. At this stage you can still make amendments and alterations, fit in extra sections and cut out items that aren't working. But in every show there comes a 'point of no return' where, however good the new idea may be, it is too late to implement it, and you will have to insist on 'no more changes'. Changes between the last dress rehearsal and the first performance are not advisable.

COMPILATION SHOWS

What if you want to have a show to work towards but don't have a ready-made theme, or have material you want to use that doesn't conform to any particular theme? Here you can use a looser structure – a compilation show. The only criterion then for including material is that the audience may find it enjoyable or meaningful. Nevertheless, you can still shape the whole show so that it becomes coherent: it could be 'A Day in the Life of the Drama Club', or a celebration of its anniversary. By adjusting the material a bit, you may be able to produce some sort of storyline out of seemingly unrelated items. It could be a 'Canterbury Tales' type of structure, in which a group of people each have their own story to tell, so each story becomes a 'play within the play'; or an 'Odyssey' type, in which the sections are a series of adventures happening to one or more characters; or it could have a chain structure, in which one character from each story connects to the next story, perhaps going round in a circle and back to the beginning. Or you can present the show like a variety show with your best stand-up comic as the MC.

FESTIVALS

Another idea is to hold a competitive festival. Our own Festival of Plays is held three times a year, at the end of each term, and unfailingly provides a most popular occasion to round off the term's work.

Throughout the term the members (from the age of eleven) put on their own improvised plays. They are given a virtual *carte blanche* as regards subject matter, casting, lighting, sound, music, and so on. Each director/writer/deviser (often a partnership) will have done some preparatory work in their own time on plot and characterization. On the day assigned for them to put on their play, they take out their cast plus sound and lighting people at the beginning of the lesson (after the warm-up) and take them to another area, where they rehearse for half an hour. They then put the play on for the rest of the class, after which we comment and mark the play, its direction and acting standard. There is a panel of four from the rest of the class who also comment and mark. The six plays with the highest marks are the entries for the end-of-term festival. Maximum length is about twenty minutes.

An adjudicator (usually a writer, director or producer) is invited to come along and give his comments and award the prizes. We supply four book tokens for the winning categories, normally 'Best Play', 'Most Original Play', 'Best Actor', 'Best Actress' — though sometimes the adjudicator suggests a different category such as 'Best Choice of Music'. The element of competition adds spice to the occasion but, as in the Olympics, the important thing is 'not winning but taking part'.

DRAMA IDEAS FROM OTHER SCHOOL SUBJECTS

Drama lends itself to use in a school in collaboration with teachers of other subjects, and not only the obvious ones, such as history, religious education and social studies. As mentioned in Chapter 3, science could be a fruitful area of co-operation, and we are also sure that the teaching of foreign languages could be helped by elements of dramatization.

The role of drama in this is illustrative: it 'brings things to life' as nothing else can. It is not a substitute but a supplement for other forms of teaching. It does not convey a great deal of factual information or explain complex causes and effects. And it is unlikely to give a balanced argument on a subject. What it can do is involve both participants and audience emotionally so that they can feel an experience intensely. For example, drama can do little to explain the causes of the First World War, but it can do something to help one to appreciate what it must have been like for the people who had to fight in it. Its ability to make us experience things as if at first hand, rather than at second hand, is what makes drama such a powerful teaching tool for other subjects.

5

Full-Scale Productions: The End-of-Term Play

The next thing you will want to do is to mount a full-scale production of a play. In some schools doing the end-of-term play is one of the duties that comes with the job. If it can be a focus of activity in the school so that, for example, everyone in one year is involved in the production in one role or another, so much the better. All are used to the best of their ability; it is a fine way of giving students a taste of responsibility and everyone will get a sense of achievement from the finished product.

There are not many plays in the repertoire suitable for a first production by children or young people – particularly if you want to do something in modern English with a large cast. So usually, by choice or necessity, you will have to create your own material. Here is a step-by-step guide to devising your own plays.

Starting-Point

First of all you have to find a point to work from. You may choose a theme such as those we have discussed in Chapter 4 – in fact a theme show can sometimes turn into a play, if all the parts of the show connect together. We once did one, 'Love Fifteen', with the theme of first love, which developed a single storyline which turned it into a play. Or you might choose a theatrical idea, a 'What if . . .?', such as Peter Shaffer uses in *Black Comedy*. What if the characters are in darkness when to the audience the stage is lit, and vice versa? Or you might pick on a promising improvisation and say: 'What happened before? What might happen afterwards? Who else might come into the story?' Each of these gives you a starting-point. The final play may bear little relation to what you start with – you can diverge as much as you like – but unless you start with something you will never get anywhere.

Devising

The next stage is to set your cast to gather ideas and produce raw material. Divide them into groups to work from the starting-point in different ways. Try out different things. Ask the 'what if' questions and be receptive to just the same sort of suggestions when they come from the cast. Improvise your way through a rough plot and discuss how it can be developed. One way to help build a consensus about the play is to improvise round the story – improvise scenes that wouldn't be in the play but help fill in the background. This is a collective creative process but the director must ultimately be the arbiter and editor.

Groundwork

At about this stage you will need to get some research done. Depending on the subject of the play, you may need either some factual information, or historical details or technical background. Even if the play is set in the future, you will need to decide what year it is set in, what has happened between now and then, and all about how the robots behave!

Getting a firm framework of this kind of detail helps everyone to believe in the reality of the play. Actors, especially professional actors, have to be magpies for information. They never know what part they may be going to play, so the more they know about the whole world from computers to cookery the better.

Characters

Now you need to know a bit more about your characters. An in-depth interview (see Chapter 1) with each of the main ones is a good idea, the whole cast being present. There has to be a certain amount of give and take on characters; they cannot be developed in isolation any more than real-life people develop in isolation. Once the background of a character has been developed, the key area to look at is how they react under stress.

Relationships

Characters do not exist in isolation so it is worth looking at each character in turn and their relationships with all the other characters they come across in the course of the play. In particular, how do the relationships develop and change and therefore how do the characters change?

Shape

As the plot begins to fall into place, the play develops its shape. You need a strong beginning and a satisfactory ending that is not anticlimactic. The turning-points must be well placed. Each character must be introduced to the audience. When the audience leaves, have all the questions that need answering been answered? Some scenes will need developing; others will need cutting. You may want to try out different things such as incidental music – something that will create the mood without describing the plot too literally.

Outline Script

At about this time you will be able to write down an outline script giving the scenes, the key lines, the plot points and the action, which you can give out to the cast. How much you continue scripting beyond this point is a matter of choice. If you do so, you may need to warn your cast that the scripted play is exactly the same play that they have been freely improvising up till then, otherwise the existence of the script can throw them and make them start reciting the lines woodenly. In a long and complicated play you probably do need to have a pretty full script for reference, and anyway it is good to keep a record. A word processor, if you have access to one, makes the job of continually redrafting much easier.

Planning

Of course, you must have had some kind of outline plan from the beginning, but now is the time to firm up all your arrangements. How many performances will there be? Fix the dates and times. How many rehearsals will you need? Err on the generous side and distribute a schedule. Be strict on punctuality; thirty people waiting ten minutes for a latecomer means that five hours of their time is wasted. Appoint stage managers early on: they need to be patient, intelligent, reliable and hard-working. Insist that everyone helps them by keeping props and costume tidy and putting things back in the right place.

If you haven't already got one, choose a title. If you've been using a working title, see if you can think of a better one for the show itself. If a set is going to be built, or anything else is to be made for you, this needs to be started early, so that there will be time to rehearse with it and make any alterations that prove necessary. Anything that you need to hire, buy or borrow must be obtained as early as possible as well. If you have a flexible seating plan work out the best arrangement and rehearse using the acting area which that gives you. You cannot of course sell more tickets than the number of seats you will have. If you're using copyright material, make sure that any fees have been paid (approach the publisher for plays, the Performing Right Society for music).

Rehearsals

The important thing when rehearsing now is to let the play run, in as large sections as practical, so that it develops a life of its own. After each run you can give notes and dissect any tricky points. For example, you may often have to change a move to produce a better visual effect or give the audience a better view of the action and it's as well to 'walk through' something like this a couple of times to make the change stick. It is a good idea to use costumes and props as early as possible, so they become a natural part of the play; if they are brought in at the last minute they are liable to cause problems. As rehearsals go on one of the things that can happen is that the play can lose its freshness; you need to make an effort to maintain the moods and emotions of the play, just as if what is being enacted is happening for the very first time.

There is so much to do in any production that the technical people tend to get neglected. It is worth having a technical run – a rehearsal that concentrates on lighting, sound and stage management – to sort out any problems they may have. If there are set changes you can nearly always speed them up by allocating individual tasks to different people and making sure that the new stage furniture is brought on before the old is taken off, which gives you your new set much more quickly. Another tip for stage managers is never to carry one thing balanced on top of another – particularly if it's a glass vase! Don't forget to rehearse the bows which are, of course, part of the show. Try to have your last dress rehearsal at the same time of day as the performance and make every single detail of what people do backstage, etc., exactly the same as what they will do on the first night. That way they will be completely prepared. Then, twenty-four hours rest and – you're on!

Production

Mounting a theatrical production is a bit like going to war – fortunately, without the bombs and bullets. As the producer, it is your responsibility to maintain morale, encourage the faint-hearted and control the impetuous, to make sure communications are good, to delegate responsibility but still ensure that the jobs get done, to keep order when chaos threatens and to cope with a situation where there never seems to be enough time to do all the things that need to be done. The shared pressures and comradeship help build lasting respect and friendship and all in all it is a good training for life.

One of the keys to making things run smoothly is to write things down. Have your own job list of things to be done, add to it as new ones crop up, and check off the items as they are done. On production nights have on a clipboard your own check list of what you are going to do in the order in which you're going to do it, and make sure that everyone else with responsibility has one too. Otherwise, when you're under pressure things are bound to be forgotten and you'll have the additional pressure of trying to remember if you have forgotten anything. If you've got a good team your main tasks will be to check that everything is going smoothly and to help with any unexpected problems. It is worth having a cast list (with telephone numbers in case of non-arrivals) and checking it off as people arrive, making a point of having an individual word with everyone, which is very heartening for them.

It is also a good idea to have separate lists of 'borrowings' — anything that has been borrowed or hired which must go back to the owner after the show — and 'consumables' — any food eaten in the play and anything that has to be damaged and must therefore be brought in or made up anew for each performance. Lighting and sound will have their cue sheets and stage management (and wardrobe if you have a separate person looking after this) will have a list of props and costumes so that they can check that everything is in the right place. Immediately after the show, they must re-run the list to get everything back in place before people leave the building having forgotten that they've got vital hand props in their pockets.

Some people like to have understudies. It is certainly a good idea to have a designated understudy for a very large part but, somehow, Dr Theatre is a great physician and, touch wood, it is rare for people to be taken so ill at the last minute that they cannot go on. Having understudies all round is liable to make people confused so it is probably best just to have an idea in the back of your mind of what you would do for each possible combination of absences. Of course, having a cast of actors well used to improvisation makes replacements that much easier. The theatrical tradition is for everyone to be in the theatre by the 'half', 35 minutes before the curtain goes up; with youngsters it is probably better to make it an hour.

If you want photographs taken, it is best to do this at a dress rehearsal or even to have a special photocall. Everyone likes to have something to keep as a memento of a show and it is a nice professional touch to have pictures on display as the audience comes in. It also reduces the interruptions caused during a performance by flashbulbs. A nicely designed programme always adds something, and if you are working in a school the art department may help with this. Do not forget to acknowledge all the people who have helped in any way.

You may or may not be responsible for the front-of-house arrangements. In either case, you need to run through the exact sequences of events and signals to get the show started at the beginning or after an interval, and how it is going to end. Make sure that front-of-house helpers know your requirements about discouraging eating, drinking, smoking and photography in the audience and the admission of babies – not to mention pets.

Text Work

Much of the above applies equally if you are working from an already written text. As outlined in the Introduction, it pays to get the feel of the play through improvisation before learning the words and you can flesh out the characters through discussing and improvising round the story. If the play is written in a type of language unfamiliar to the cast, you need to do quite a lot of groundwork on the vocabulary, the figures of speech, and so on, so that they can begin to 'think in the language' – making it seem to become a natural mode of expression. Do not be afraid to cut or alter a play if you believe that by doing so the playwright's intentions will be better carried out in the circumstances.

Musicals

If you are putting on a musical, or any play with songs in it, the main problem is to avoid the music and the acting coexisting unhappily as two separate areas of the show. Right from the start people need to see their singing as an extension of their acting performance; they sing in character and believe every word of the song just as they mean every line of the script. If you are lucky enough to have the music specially written for you, or are writing it yourself, one problem you have to cope with is the 'unfamiliarity factor'. That is, a song does not have as great an effect on an audience if they are hearing it for the first time as it does if they are already familiar with it. Don't forget that you can use some songs that already exist, possibly with changes of lyrics, and always look for ways in which you can reprise a number or use the same melody more than once.

Production Notes: Do's and Don'ts

Half an hour before each performance, give the cast your notes, last-minute advice and encouragement and any comments arising from the previous performance. Here are some standard reminders:

Believability   Believe in what you're doing and make it seem to the audience that what they are watching is real life happening for the very first time.

The Second Night   Beware of second-night blasé-ness. Keep first-night freshness throughout each performance. Don't forget that it's a new audience who have not seen the show before.

Beware of second-night disappointment. On the first night the adrenalin is running and it seems almost a miracle that you get through the show at all; by the second night everyone's level of expectation has been raised and some of the excitement has gone; everyone is liable to think that the play hasn't gone so well.

Audiences   Audiences vary. Keep the standard up in front of an apparently unresponsive audience. They may just be enjoying themselves quietly. Be prepared for people's laughter; keep concentration and don't laugh along with them. Don't try to go on speaking through a laugh; wait till it is dying down before continuing. Equally, never wait for a laugh if you are expecting one; it may never come.

Projection and clarity   The back row should not have to strain to hear. The audience has a blanketing effect on the sound in a room so you have to speak more loudly than in rehearsal.

Mistakes   If something goes wrong, improvise your way out of it and act as if it was intended to be that way all the time. The audience isn't to know that it wasn't. Never point out in any way that a mistake has happened.

Concentration   Do not think about who is in the audience. Concentrate all the way through even when not speaking; listening is very important.

Quiet   Insist on quiet backstage both before and during the performance. It's easy for this to be forgotten when people are excited and, apart from disturbing the audience and the other actors, it is a sure sign that people are not applying themselves to the job in hand.

Consideration   Put props and costumes back neatly in the correct place. Help the stage managers.

No Surprises   Do not try anything new in a performance without consulting the director. It might throw the other actors.

Last-Night Jokes   Don't. They are liable to spoil the show and it's cheating the audience.

GETTING IDEAS

Here are some lines of approach to finding ideas for plays.

1   *Find a Story that Already Exists*

We have already written about the possibilities of making modern-day equivalents of myths and fables. There is a wealth of material in fairy tales, literature, the Bible, Classical plays, novels and pantomime that you can borrow from, taking greater or lesser liberties with the plot. You can either follow the original story religiously, translating every detail into equivalent terms, or you can just preserve the core of the story and alter everything else round it, or you can use the original story as a jumping-off point and spin a new play entirely out of it. For example, *Romeo and Juliet* was much later reinterpreted in a musical version, *West Side Story*, but *Romeo and Juliet* itself, like practically all Shakespeare's plays, was based on an already existing story.

2   *Start with a Subject*

As when developing a theme show, you can start with any subject under the sun and work characters and a story out of it. One idea is to have a dramatized-documentary approach and choose either a subject from history – the slave trade, the building of the railways, or what happened in the locality in the Second World War – or a subject of contemporary interest, possibly one inspired by a television programme or newspaper article. Get your cast to research the subject, if possible by eyewitness interviews. In order to make the thing live you need to see it through the experience of one family or set of people and you want a play that is a work of imagination rather than just a dry retelling of facts. You could do a complete local pageant seen through the eyes of one family in succeeding generations. After the past and the present, another rich field is the future. What social and technological changes will there be and what will be their effects on people's lives? Again, the important thing is to create believable characters and an involving story set against the futuristic background.

3 Choose a Crisis

Sudden death, a racial attack, a factory threatened with closure, people held hostage by terrorists, someone reaching breaking-point and being struck dumb – these events all provide suitable situations. The play consists of what leads up to the crisis, the crisis itself and the aftermath. A good example is *Gotcha* by Barrie Keeffe.

4 Take a Familiar Situation and Add an Extra Ingredient to It

The situation is one the audience will know and recognize – perhaps a school journey, or a wedding day, a school assembly, a funeral, or a teenage party. Everything builds up and we see all the everyday details we are expecting. Then ... something happens.

An apt illustration is *Barmitzvah Boy* by Jack Rosenthal: all preparations are busily made for the grand occasion, but then, at the crucial moment of the service, the hero turns on his heel and walks out. The 'something happens' factor should be an unexpected turning-point which catches the audience unawares.

5 Put some Characters in a Stressful Situation and See What Happens to Them

Start with a set of characters each with their faults and virtues; perhaps they are based on characters already developed by some of the cast. Build a play round what happens when they are put in a difficult situation. It could be an extreme one, such as the threat of nuclear war, or a more everyday one, such as a couple getting married very young, a divorce, disability, teenage rebellion.

William Golding's *Lord of the Flies* is an example – a story about a group of boys who are thrown together on an island: how they cope, who becomes leader of the pecking order and what happens to the standards of the civilization they have left behind.

6 Dream Up a Theatrical Device

What if all the characters are animals? Or creatures from outer space? The device could be something that makes the world of the play different from the real world, as in Lewis Carroll's *Alice Through the Looking Glass*, or something to do with the staging, such as having the cast on roller-skates in *Starlight Express*, or giving a character additional powers, like the Inspector in J. B. Priestley's *An Inspector Calls*, who knows the guilty secrets of all the members of a family.

7 Find an Allegory

Choose an ordinary situation which can represent something much bigger. A man lives for his garden but it is a perpetual battle against the weeds, while a succession of strange people wander in and out of it. The garden could represent the whole world. A journey could represent the journey through life. There are plenty of examples, from the parables to *Gulliver's Travels*.

8 Make More of a Pastiche

Many young people are expert at adopting the styles of films and television programmes, be it *Dallas*, *EastEnders* or *Frankenstein*. Take one of these genres and develop characters and a storyline faithful to the style of the original but separate from it. Make it more than just a send-up, played for laughs.

9 Find a Location

A location – the ladies' room, a kitchen, a library, a betting shop, a doctor's surgery, a beach, Moscow, Marseilles, heaven, hell, the Cairngorms, a launderette, a bank, a supermarket – anywhere in the world may provide a setting for a play. What characters would there be there? What happens to them?

10 Build on a Character

Take a character, or perhaps a pair of characters, either ones that have already been created by people in your cast or an idea you have for a character that one of them could portray. Develop the characters as far as you can so that you and the actors know them inside out. Then put them on the starting-line and let the story begin. If the characters are strong you will find them, as it were, spinning out their own story.

6

More Ideas

In the years since *100+ Ideas for Drama* appeared we have developed
many more drama ideas. Here are some of them.

GAMES

Endgame is the title of one of Samuel Beckett's plays, the last moves
in the game of chess and often the last item of an Anna Scher Theatre
session. Physical games, mental games, old and new, traditional ones
passed on with bits and pieces added or subtracted. A game brings
people together at the end of a class and helps you to end on a
positive high note. Games are also useful as icebreakers and as an
interlude between more serious items.

Air Traffic Control

Lay out a 'landscape' of mountains, represented by chairs and blocks,
and in the middle chalk a 'runway' about a metre wide. The 'air traffic
controller' has to guide the 'pilot', who is blindfolded and has his
arms outstretched as 'wings', on a designated route round various
turning-points to land on the runway. He can only use the words
'left' (meaning 'start turning left'), 'right' ('start turning right') and
'straight' (meaning 'stop turning and go straight on'). The pilot goes
at a slow walking pace and may not stop. Have two teams divided
into pairs of 'controller' and 'pilot'. Each pair that lands safely without
stopping or hitting a mountain scores a point.

Alternate Bumps and Statues

A variation on 'Musical Bumps' and 'Statues' in which the first time
the music stops it's 'Bumps' and everyone has to go down on the
ground – last one is out. The next time the music stops it's 'Statues'
and everyone has to freeze – anyone moving is out. Anyone doing
'Bumps' when it should be 'Statues' and vice versa is out too.

Key on a String

You have two groups of six. Person no. 1 in each team is given a key which has a very long string tied to it. He puts the key down his clothes at his neck and out at his ankles and then passes it to no. 2. While no. 1 is still feeding the string through his own clothes, no. 2 has put the key down his or her clothes, and on to number three. The first team to get the key and string right through are the winners.

Thumper

The group sits cross-legged in a circle. Each person chooses a simple two-second mime to represent a different animal. For example, a rabbit is done by putting up your fingers behind your head to represent the rabbit's ears and wriggling your nose; for a goldfish you just open and close your mouth several times; and for an elephant you move your arm to represent the trunk. Go round the circle and have everyone announce his or her mime and demonstrate it. To start the game, everyone thunders their fists on their knees and shouts 'Thumper!' Then the first person performs his or her own mime, immediately following it with someone else's. The person whose mime has been done then has to repeat it, following it with someone else's mime again, and so on until someone hesitates, or makes a mistake, or does a mime incorrectly, or laughs while doing it, in which case he is out and names the person to restart the game.

As in all elimination games, either elimination can be by 'sudden death' or else contestants can be allowed two or three 'lives'.

President, President

Everyone sits cross-legged in a circle. The first person is 'President', the next 'Vice President', then 'Secretary', 'Treasurer', 'One', 'Two', 'Three', and so on. Teach them a rhythm of four claps: 'Together, knees, together, to the side'. When everyone can do this in time together the game starts, with the President saying to an eight-beat rhythm: 'President, President (clap, clap) Three, Three (clap, clap).' Three has to respond straight away: 'Three, Three (clap, clap), Secretary, Secretary (clap, clap).' The game continues until someone makes a mistake, breaks the rhythm or stops clapping. This player must then go down to the last number and everyone in between moves up one space and gets a new name or number. The object is to work your way up to President.

The Name Brain Game

Send two people out of the room. The rest of the class forms a circle and when the first person re-enters the teacher starts the class off calling out their *second* names, once round the circle, the first person repeating it back to them, which is a useful aid to memory. (If anyone hasn't got a second name, one can be invented.) The first person attempts to remember as many of the names as possible on one hearing. Then the second competitor is brought in and pitted against the first one. In a group whose members don't know each other, you can of course use first names. Variations: the class call out their favourite fruit, or door number, or what have you. A particularly funny version is 'The Pets' Name Brain Game', in which they give the kind of animal and the name of an imaginary pet – 'A goldfish called Rover', 'A hamster called Marilyn', and so on.

Survivor Word Tennis

This is a variation on 'Word Tennis' in which two people have to name items in a given category – colours, drinks, diseases, television programmes past and present, in fact any subject you like – until one of them cannot think of a new one within three seconds. In 'Survivor Word Tennis', all form a circle and are given the subject, which remains the same throughout the game. Start round the circle, and when people can't think of a new word they will be eliminated one by one. However long the game goes on, no repetitions are allowed. Last survivor is the winner. This is a particularly good way of sharing general knowledge of the theatre by using subjects such as 'Playwrights', 'Titles of Plays', 'Titles of Films', and so on. 'Playwrights' might start: 'Shakespeare', 'Sheridan', 'Shaw', 'Tom Stoppard', which is easy enough – but it quite soon gets difficult!

Deliberate Mistakes

Read out a news item or tell a story and from time to time make a deliberate mistake. The first person to raise a hand gets a chance to correct the mistake and score a point for his or her team.

Incidentally, if you want a class to concentrate on the details of something you are telling them, it is quite a good trick to warn them that you are going to slip in a deliberate mistake you want them to spot.

Christmas Presents

Everyone sits in a circle. You start by saying: 'I'm giving Sally a sausage – she'd like that.' Sally must continue: 'I'm giving Martin a video.' 'No,' you cut in, 'he wouldn't like that.' Martin continues: 'I'm giving Chris a car.' 'Yes, he'd like that.' The presents they would like are the ones beginning with the same letters as their names. You have not told them this but as soon as they work it out for themselves they know what presents to give other people and can join in the chorus of 'He'd like that' or 'She wouldn't like that' until everyone has worked out the rule. The more comical the presents are the better. Every time you play the game you can use a different rule: they will only like the present if it begins with the *last* letter of the person's name, or the first letter of the name of the person sitting on their left, or it must be something they're wearing, or maybe they'll only like the present if the person giving it is sitting with legs crossed, or hands clasped, or touches his or her face before speaking.

Five Question Quiz

This is a useful mental recap game for revising the content of your previous lessons. It can take the form of, say, a Shakespearian quiz or a drama vocabulary quiz. Quickfire on-the-spot questions asked in sets of five to individuals dotted round the room provide a nice five-minute ender to the class. For example:

> Name William Shakespeare's wife.
> What date was he born?
> Who were the star-crossed lovers?
> What was the name of the most famous Elizabethan theatre?
> Where was Shakespeare born and where did he die?
> (Answers: Anne Hathaway; 23 April; *Romeo and Juliet*; the
>   Globe; Stratford-upon-Avon.)

Demonstrate a Game

This is a group-work idea that is also a useful way of building up your repertoire of games. Divide the class into groups, who each choose a game they want to demonstrate and rehearse how they're going to show it. Then each group shows the class in turn, the leader announcing the name of the game and explaining the object and the rules. Finally, the whole group demonstrates how it's played.

SPEAKEASY/TALKING POINT/TALKABOUT

Three names for the same basic idea. Put a seat centre stage as the 'hot seat', announce the subject, and one by one people come up and talk about it. Here are some topics:

What gives me confidence
Choose a name for a baby girl and boy and explain your choice
One thing I regret and why . . .
My ideal holiday
Manners. Start off with 'I think it's good/bad manners to . . .'
April Fool's Day
Qualities in a friend
Who I trust and why
The best piece of advice I've ever had . . .
The good/bad thing about being old
New experiences in the last year; talk about the first time you did something
Something I'll never forget
What I'd do on a free day without money
Who I'd like to be with on a desert island and why
Saturday jobs
Jobs I do around the house
My idea of luxury . . .
What I like to eat and drink in hot weather
All the food I eat in an average day
If I were my own parent . . .
My idea of heaven on earth; my idea of hell on earth
A place I'd like to revisit
My Walter Mitty existence
What frightens you
My personal protest
What I do to lift my spirits when I'm down in the dumps
Superstition
Dreams and nightmares
My most treasured possession
The book I'd recommend and why
Fancy-dress ideas
My weekend
My bedroom
Nicknames
A club I belong to
My experience in hospital
What I'd do if I were unemployed

A tip for well-being – something that makes me feel good
The best/worst thing about the twentieth century
I'm an optimist/pessimist because . . .
At the end of your life, what would you like to have
   achieved?

DISCUSSION

Here are some ideas for your class to discuss. You are the one to
control the proceedings by using hand signals and keeping it 'in the
middle'. Top and tail it with your preparatory work.

Phobias
Problems and solving them
Insults and compliments
Success and failure
How we treat old people
Accents and dialects
Afterlife
Home truths
Neighbours
Guilt
Bad language
Spring cleaning
Mob mentality
Prejudice
Secrets
Crazes, catchwords, catchphrases
Health
Temptation
Appreciation
Sacrifice
Deception
Rules
Choice

MORE TALKING HEADS

Divide the class into twos and threes. Set them a talking-piece and
the room becomes a sea of talking heads. After a minute stop them
and select people to summarize to the class what they've been saying.
Here's some examples.

Likes and dislikes in your family
On the subject of breakfasts . . .
Full names of you and all the family
Favourite and unfavourite shops
Favourite things (pudding, member of the royal family, flower,
TV personality, magazine or comic, etc.)
Describe how to prepare a TV snack.
Your 'moan of the moment'
Be your own critic — comment on a recent book you have
read, or film or play you have seen
All about you (name, family, school, including best and worst
subjects, hobbies and the job you'd like to do when you
leave school)

STORIES

Bean Bag Stories

This is a storytelling game in which everyone stands in a circle. You
start a story, holding a bean bag. After a couple of sentences you
stop in mid-flow and throw the bean bag to someone else, who must
continue the story from where you left off. Anyone who hesitates,
can't continue, drops the bean bag or throws it unfairly is eliminated,
or else perhaps loses a life and has to catch one-handed. The next
person starts a new story.

Five-Minute Stories

A good ender, before the bell, for junior classes especially, is the
five-minute story. Some people are natural storytellers and telling a
story probably is preferable to reading it, but either way keep a
record of those that work well. Your stock of stories will be very
much a personal matter but bring in as much variety as you can. The
local library is generally very helpful in selecting popular choices from
the different categories. Firm favourites such as 'Perseus and the
Gorgon Medusa' and the story of Icarus from the world of Greek
mythology, 'The Boy who Called Wolf' and 'The Town Mouse and
the Country Mouse' from Aesop's Fables, 'Fin McCoul' and 'Cucullin
and the Children of Lir' from Irish folk tales, 'The Emperor's New
Clothes' and 'The Little Match Girl' by Hans Christian Andersen, and
One Hundred and One Dalmatians by Dodie Smith can hardly fail to

go down well but a lot will depend on whether they are told expressively and with good characterization. Apart from general categories – adventure, fairy, folk, Bible, history – the teacher can always make up his or her own. A good ghost story will almost always go down a treat.

At the same time, keep a collection of favourite poems. Hilaire Belloc's *Cautionary Tales* would make an excellent starter.

MIME AND MOVEMENT

Hand-Sign Duologues

See how many hand signs the class can think of. Thumbs up, fingers crossed, waving, beckoning, blowing a kiss – there are dozens of them. Does anyone know any gestures used in different cultures and what they mean? Ask the class to divide into pairs and work out some hand sign duologues together – that is, whole conversations in hand signs only, including rude ones if necessary. Then see them all, two by two.

Silent Action

This is not strictly a mime idea but rather an exercise in acting without words. Two people are to act a duologue, the characters and situation being up to them (give them a moment or two to consult), but the keynote of the scene is given by you, and it must start with at least thirty seconds of silent action in that vein before the first word is spoken. For example, you could say that the scene should start with thirty seconds of silent fancying by one of the two people, or thirty seconds of silent mutual antagonism. Other possibilities are:

> Pleading for forgiveness
> Irritation
> Gloating
> Imagining the other in a different situation from the one he or she is in
> Thinking about something miles away from what the other person thinks you should be thinking about
> Thinking about something you've planned but the other person doesn't know about
> Eating.

This is a good exercise in the use of body language and

appreciation of the spaces between words. It is interesting how silent action always holds an audience's attention.

Tableaux

This is a piece of group work that is especially good for juniors. A tableau is an abstract picture formed by the bodies of a group of people, standing, sitting, kneeling or lying in any position. To suitable background music each group makes its own individual tableau, both dramatic and acrobatic. Symmetry can be added to the brief as an optional extra. After preparation time see them one by one, giving marks out of ten for originality and presentation, if you wish.

Improvised Dance Circle

This is a good warm-up idea. The class forms a circle and to some suitable music you start a repetitive dance step which they have to follow. Then call someone into the middle of the circle who has to start a new step, which everyone picks up and follows. Then someone else takes the lead and on the changeover the class keeps up a simple step or clapping pattern to maintain the rhythm.

A variation on this is for everyone to work in pairs and devise a simple routine in which one follows in mirror image steps devised by the other and vice versa. Each of the pairs can then demonstrate in the dance circle. This simple choreography can be a good shared experience. A further development is for one of each pair to improvise a 'question step' and the other to do an 'answer step' in response to it. These can then be picked up in pairs round the circle.

CHARACTERS AND PROPS

Here are some more simple ideas which help to develop the ability to adopt and hold a character.

Complaints

Everyone has to complain from time to time about something. Some people positively enjoy doing so. In 'Complaints' we have one side of a complaint to an imaginary person in which the complainer adopts whatever character he or she wishes. The setting can be a shop, a restaurant, an office, or anywhere else. The complaint can be about anything at all, whether it's important or trivial, and the person can be polite or rude, vague or precise, personal or impersonal, depending on the kind of character chosen. You will get plenty of material for discussion about the most effective way of getting your point across without putting the other person's back up, whether you're complaining or being complained to. A variation is the 'Chain complaint', like the 'Chain argument' in Chapter 1.

Parent, Neighbour and Teacher

This is another idea that combines character work with seeing things from other people's point of view. Ask the class to think of an imaginary parent, an imaginary neighbour and an imaginary teacher. What do each of them think of you, the child? Ask them to try to sum it up in a sentence or two. Then hear some of them. 'The parent?' you ask, and the parent's point of view is heard. 'The neighbour?', and we hear it from the neighbour's point of view. 'And the teacher?', and the teacher's point of view is heard.

Bell Characters

This is like 'bell stories', in which every time the bell rings the storyteller has to start a new story. Someone sits in the hot seat and every time the bell rings he or she has to adopt a new character and give us a snatch of his conversation, either talking to himself or to an imaginary other person, continuing until, after about half a minute, the bell rings again. Four or five characters is a good number for one person, and the object is to make them both varied and believable. You can try it out with the class working *en masse* first of all, before putting anyone on the spot.

Compelling Conversations

If you have a stock of telephones you'll need them all for this; otherwise they can be mimed. Have half a dozen people working together, each of them talking to an imaginary person on the phone. The brief is that they must be *compelling conversations*, the sort that, if you got a crossed line and overheard them, would mean you just couldn't put the receiver down before the end. Everyone does it together and then you hear them one by one.

Status Scenes

Because of their personality or position (for example, officers and men in the Army) some people adopt high-status, and some people low-status behaviour. Some of the indicators of high status are obvious – standing up straight, holding eye contact as opposed to furtive glances – but some are more subtle. The brief for this piece of work is that one character should be of high status, the other of low status. High-status always asserts himself and low-status defers, but in a subtle way. Then you can have two high-status people trying to outdo each other, or two people trying to play lower than each other. Try the latter with a couple chosen for each other by computer dating. As they each try to abase themselves to the other they become more and more lovable.

SITUATION DRAMA

Windows

This is a quick situation drama idea in which the whole class works at the same time. Give them a broad brief: they are in family situations, or a situation where someone is worried, or giving or receiving good or bad news. They are to work individually, talking to an imaginary person. After everybody has worked together you can hear a brief excerpt of some of them, just as if you were opening a window, overhearing some of the conversation going on inside, and then closing it again. Use 'action' and 'cut' to direct them. This is a good 'acting warm-up' idea to follow the warm-up at the start of a session and can be done in duologue form as well as monologue.

Rescue from the Railway Line

This is a high-energy piece. Someone has fallen on to a railway line. He may be trapped or unconscious. A train may come at any moment. Two other people see what has happened. They have to climb down to the track, avoid the live rails, and pull the person clear before the train comes. Maybe they will succeed, maybe they won't.

Monologue *en masse*

The boys and girls sit on the ground while you give them the brief. Then the class does a monologue *en masse* – that it, the whole group works individually but at the same time. After about half a minute to a minute you call out 'Cut'; all sit down where they are and you spotlight various members of the group in turn.

Letters

'You receive a letter which either contains good news or bad news. It could be from your aunt who's just had a baby. It could be from a friend inviting you to go on holiday with him or her. Your cousin has had an accident. You have won a prize in a competition. Your grandad has died. Your library books are overdue. Good news or bad news. Start the letter with "Dear . . ." and your name. Stand up everybody and – Action!'

Locked in a Room

'You are in your bedroom reading. You happen to go to the door only to find that it is locked. You're puzzled. Is your brother playing a trick? Or is there something the matter with the lock? Or is there some more sinister explanation? Whichever, your slight annoyance builds up to a climax. You might even be a little bit claustrophobic. Let's start with you reading on your bed – Action!'

This idea could also take place in a lift.

Shock

'Who's good at screaming? Now's your chance! I'd like to start this improvisation with a little bit of mime. You are ironing a shirt. Or you might be changing the plug on an electric kettle. Or someone has unexpectedly slapped you on the back rather too hard. Whatever – you get a nasty shock. I'll give you a countdown of ten seconds – and then you scream. We see your reaction to the nasty shock – and then the aftermath. Are you shaken, angry, calm, tearful? Are you injured? How soon do you recover your composure? Ten, nine, eight . . .'

Problems – Psychosomatic or Otherwise

The class can find a space with their chairs for this piece.

'You are at the doctor's. You've got a problem. It might be an emotional one – your mum is very depressed. It might be purely physical – you have an ingrowing toe-nail. It might be that you want to tell the doctor something that you feel is highly confidential. I shall start off as the voice of the doctor and then you, the patient, carry on talking to the imaginary doctor. "What seems to be the problem?"'

Lost and Found

'You've lost something very important to you – it could be a signet ring, a £5 note, an exercise book. You're hunting everywhere for it. I want to see a growing frustration as the tension mounts, until you find it. We'll start with the realization that the such-and-such object isn't where you thought you'd find it. You might start with "Where have I put my exercise book?" Think for a moment, and – Action!'

You can preface this with preliminary discussion on 'things you've lost and things you've found'. There will be much room for development work in twos and threes, and plays to follow on from the monologue.

The Eavesdropper

'Nobody likes being talked about behind his back – though Oscar Wilde said, "There's only one thing worse than being talked about – not being talked about." That may be so, but most of us are pretty sensitive about what is said about us. You overhear a so-called friend of yours backbiting about you like nobody's business. You *eavesdrop* and, while you know eavesdroppers never hear well of themselves, you are transfixed. You get angrier and angrier till you let rip on your imaginary friend. Let's hear you give him his come-uppance. Maybe a good first line might be "How dare you talk about me behind my back!" And action!'

Caution

'Never talk down to people – whether to under-fives or over-fives. Let's see you do this exercise in two different ways – two interpretations – once in anger, and the second time affectionately. You are warning a child about road safety. An optional first line is "Always stop, look and listen when you cross the road". The first time you are angry – perhaps the child ran into the road after a ball, without heeding the Green Cross Code. Action!'

Jealousy

'Shakespeare calls jealousy "the green-eyed monster". It is a horrible feeling. Your boyfriend or girlfriend has been seeing someone else without your knowledge. You are being two-timed. You feel betrayed. You have it out with them. . . .'

This is an interesting exercise to see from the other point of view.

Everyone has the right of reply. What has the 'betrayer' got to say? The follow-up can provide some good strong stuff.

Showdown

'What is your "moan of the moment"? Maybe it's the neighbour's saxophone which for some reason he seems to prefer to practise after eleven at night. Maybe it's a pneumatic drill in the street outside. Maybe it's a friend of yours who's always on about the Arsenal — and you can't stand them. Maybe it's your brother always wanting to watch *Top of the Pops* when you want to watch the other side. Whatever the cause of your displeasure, now is your chance to get it off your chest. Here's your chance of a grand showdown. First line — "I've had it up to here with you." Action!'

Bee in Your Bonnet

Another monologue *en masse*. Everybody has something they're a little bit obsessive about — some people have more than one. It may be smoke from other people's cigarettes, dogs that foul the pavements, having to queue to buy a train ticket, food with artificial preservatives in it. Whatever it is, it's something that causes annoyance out of all proportion to its importance. Hear people sounding off about a pet hate — it could be their own real life pet hate, or someone else's.

Political Point of View

'You hold a political point of view that you want to air. It can be big politics or small politics or some moral issue. You sound off about something that you feel strongly about. It might be vegetarianism. It might be vivisection, troops in or out of Northern Ireland, the monarchy — for or against, socialism, Thatcherism, homosexuality, school dinners, school uniforms — whatever. You sound off about it from *your* viewpoint. First line — "Listen to me for a minute will you?" Action!

Immediately after this exercise follow it up with the same person arguing the case from the opposite point of view. This is much harder. If the player would convince an outsider that he holds the opposite point of view to the one he really does hold, then he has succeeded.

Opposite Point of View

'We've heard your views on various social issues. Now I want you to put the case forward from an opposite point of view to your own.

This is much more difficult. Marshal your facts carefully. Fight with reason as well as emotion. You don't want to be high on emotion and low on logic. Keep it balanced; don't send it up. First line – "Now you listen to me!" Action!'

First Thing in the Morning

'It's 7 a.m. and it's time to get up for school. You are very reluctant to leave the shelter of the warm blankets. "Only five minutes more," you plead. I want to see it from your mum's point of view first and then from yours. First we'll hear your mum, and her first line is "Get up out of that bed, *immediately!*" Action!

'. . . cut! And now we'll see it from your point of view, in prostrate position. Lie down everyone. "Only five minutes more." Action!'

Urgent Message

'You've got to deliver an urgent message. Your mother has just been admitted to hospital, your little brother has just swallowed some tablets, or your friend has fallen and fractured her arm. You quickly pass the message on – "I've got an urgent message for you." Action!'

This exercise is most effective when you spotlight people individually, giving them the further direction of, say, ten seconds of running from point A to point B before delivering the message. The physical action heightens the urgency.

Shoot First and Ask Questions Afterwards

'Shoot first and ask questions afterwards. Have you ever had a real go at someone only to find that they were completely blameless? We all do it occasionally and often feel bad because of it. You make a verbal attack on someone. Maybe you accuse your best friend of trying to steal your boyfriend when in fact there's a perfectly innocent explanation for their being seen together. I leave the reason up to you, but, whatever it is, you're barking up the wrong tree. Off you go!'

This is a good piece to see from the other point of view as well.

The Apology

'Saying sorry isn't always easy. But a genuine sincere apology can often make the world of difference to a relationship when someone has been in the wrong. And, equally, it's important for the other person to forgive. OK. An apology is in order. And smirks or sniggers are not counted as a *sincere* apology. "I really am very sorry about last night." Action!'

Emotions

Another monologue *en masse* piece. The monologue must have a controlling emotion — anger, fear, hate, love, envy, depression, elation. It is interesting how the vocal tone of the whole class varies with the emotion.

Duologues

A Problem Shared is a Problem Halved

'You've heard the saying "a problem shared is a problem halved". Well, one of you has got a highly confidential problem — your parents are getting divorced and you don't know how to handle it; or you've failed an important exam; or you've put on a stone in the last month. You are rather desperate. You tell your best friend. The first line is "I've got a problem." Action!'

This is a good exercise for listening and also for giving advice. Discussion on problems and how to solve them is useful either before or after the duologues.

Something Personal

'You are very fond of your best friend — and rather protective towards him or her. But there is something he ought to know, something he is not aware of. And, though it's a bit embarrassing to say it, you'd rather that it came from you than have him the laughing-stock of the class. Maybe he smells. Maybe he's overweight, or spotty. You start by using his name — "John, there's something I've got to tell you." Action!'

Confessions

'Confessions are something Catholics will be familiar with; they confess to the priest something they have done which was wrong. You have done something wrong and are feeling rather guilty about it. You decide to come clean and say it right away to your friend. "Mary (or whatever name), I've got a confession to make to you." Action!'

Insults and Compliments

'In pairs, I want you to do two short and separate pieces – one in which one of you insults the other, and one in which you pay him or her a compliment. You will find that *dramatically* the one on "insults" will be a lot easier to do because of the element of conflict – and drama is conflict. Make the compliments genuine, not sarcastic ones. Don't forget to be gracious in your thank-yous on receiving a compliment – but let's start with the insults. Off you go!'

Whispers in the Library

'You are best friends and you have your first row. But it takes place in a library! So you conduct your row in whispers. There is an imaginary librarian present at a desk at the front. Here's an optional first line – "May I have the £5 I lent you back?" Second line – "I'm very sorry but ..." In whispers – action!'

Parental Displeasure

'Let's have a parent and a child. The child has incurred the parent's displeasure in some way – and now you've got to face the music. Nobody particularly likes criticism but the onslaught that you are going to get from your mum or dad is certainly something to dread. What the situation is, is up to you. Maybe you've had some tattoos done on your arm. Maybe your parents can't stand your punk boyfriend. Maybe you've gone a brassy shade of blonde. Whatever, Mum – or Dad – is raging. Action!'

Ending a Relationship

'"Parting is such sweet sorrow," says Shakespeare – but, let's face it, none of us likes to be packed in! Michael, you've been going out with Sarah for three months now. She's a nice girl but there are plenty of other fish in the sea. You do the proper thing and say it to her face – not by phone or by note. I want no cowards in my class! Here's an optional first line – "Sarah, I'm sorry, it's over." Now, that could be said kindly or harshly, and Sarah's reaction could be shocked or heartbroken, or she may try to hold on to the relationship, or she may lash out angrily. That is up to you. Action!'

It could be any relationship – boy and girl, homosexual, mother and son, partners in business. Put the class in pairs to work out a relationship and why and how it might be ended.

Private

'You are either two sisters, two brothers or a brother and a sister. And while you obviously share lots of things there are some things which are private. Your diary is one of them. On this occasion one of you comes into your bedroom and sees the other doing the unforgivable – reading your diary. Let's first see your reaction – the one reading the diary is oblivious to your presence. First line, delivered in a quiet tone – "You have no business reading *my* diary." Action!'

This works particularly well if one of the pair has the diary – or letter, or photograph, or whatever – physically in his or her hand and the other tries to snatch it away.

The Sack

'Nobody ever likes to get the sack. The humiliation is often too much to bear for the person being sacked but it's none too pleasant to be the bringer of bad news either. The situation may be that you are employer and employee, or axing someone from a band, sending someone down from college, or telling someone he is no longer required for the team. Do not be afraid to grasp the nettle. An optional first line might be "Sit down! I'm afraid I've got some bad news for you." Action!'

Accident

'Have you ever accidentally broken one of the family's treasured pieces – Mum's priceless Waterford glass vase, say, or Dad's ship-in-a-bottle? The guilt can be crippling. How can you make it up to them? You are doing your Saturday morning chores when the unforeseen occurs – the wretched thing slips to the ground and is shattered into smithereens. Come clean straight away. The first line is "Mum, I'm afraid I've just broken your Waterford glass vase," or "Dad, I'm afraid I've just broken your ship-in-a-bottle." Good luck! And action!'

The Borrowed Book

'When you borrow things you simply must return them in as good a condition as when you borrowed them. It's unforgivable to do otherwise. Sylvia, you've borrowed Marcia's book, *The Secret Diary of Adrian Mole (Aged 13¾)* by Sue Townsend. Sylvia, you return the book to Marcia – *in a deplorable condition*. The cover is torn, you've used chewing gum as a bookmark – it's quite disgusting. And to top it all you are quite unaware of the state the book is now in. Start with "Thanks for lending me your book, Marcia." Action!'

Requests

'There's a right way and a wrong way of doing everything, and if you're asking for something, whether it's a favour or something you have a right to, there's a world of difference between asking for it politely and asking for it rudely. There is also a world of difference in the response you're likely to get. Choosing the right moment is important as well. So I want two versions of the same duologue. Each time the same thing is being requested, but in version one it's being asked for in the wrong way, and in version two in the right way. Of course, politeness should not be confused with timidity, and it's possible to assert yourself without being rude. Action!'

The Last Straw

'In twos – you may be two friends, two sisters, mother and daughter, father and son, whatever. We see you at the climax of some sort of trauma: things have got worse and worse and now you are at breaking-point. You have one minute to either make it up or break it up! First line – "Look, this really is the last straw!" Action!'

Coping with a Temper Tantrum

'It's one thing to get angry; it's another thing to lose your temper. In a temper tantrum the person has lost his or her temper and is right out of control. In this duologue, just such a temper tantrum is bursting out and the other person has to do his best to cope with it, calm the person down and not provoke him to fresh anger. Or perhaps the second person argues back, or winds up the first even further – in which case the quarrel may escalate to who knows where.'

Unrequited Love

'It's awful when you love someone but they do not love you in return. Bernadette, you have fancied Robert for I don't know how long and now here's your chance. You're in the launderette watching the washing go round and round when who should come in with his washing but the man himself. He puts his washing into the machine but does not know how to work it. Bernadette, you're a dab hand at working the washing-machines in the launderette – you've done it every week since you were nine! Robert, you like this helpful girl but you are very much in love with your own girlfriend, Dulice. Bernadette makes her attraction to Robert pretty obvious. What is Robert's reaction? Is it "I like you but . . ." or is it a direct put-down? And what is Bernadette's reaction to that? Her first line is "Can I give you a hand?" Action!'

The Last Bus Gone

Two people have gone out for the evening. They have to catch the last bus in order to get home. They have stayed a little late. It's cutting it a bit fine, but the bus will probably not be on time. They hurry round the corner to the bus-stop, only to see the back of the bus disappearing into the distance. What on earth are they going to do now? They only have the money for their bus fare. What is the safest thing to do? What will get them home most quickly? What are their parents going to say?

Schadenfreude

Schadenfreude – German for delight in someone else's downfall. Not a very pleasant reaction. Gail and Sanna, you've got my full permission to go as far as you like with this improvisation! Sabrina, the class snob, has just failed to get into drama school – or so you've heard through the grapevine. Sanna, we'll give you the first line – "Have you heard, Sabrina didn't get into drama school?" Action!'

Squeamishness

'If you can't stand the sight of blood this is a good one for you! It's about being squeamish. One of you is in some kind of pain – perhaps you've cut your finger with the carving knife, got a speck of dust in your eye, got really bad stomach ache. You go to your friend for help, but unfortunately your friend is unbelievably squeamish. Action!'

Real and Imaginary Ailments

One person asks 'Hello, how are you?' Instead of just replying 'Very well, thank you' or 'Not too bad', the other launches into a complete description of his or her medical condition. The twist is that they may either be describing the ailments they really have, or have recently had, or else they may be wholly imaginary ailments, and the rest of the group have to guess which. A good test of believability.

Suspicion

'If you've ever read Shakespeare's *Othello* you'll have been frustrated by all the unnecessary suspicion – through lack of trust. We, the audience, know what's going on but the characters don't – that's what's known as "dramatic irony".

'It's dreadful when someone feels betrayed. One of you feels very suspicious of the other's behaviour – nothing concrete, nothing you can quite put your finger on, but none the less your suspicions are aroused, especially since a mutual friend whispered something in your ear recently. First line – "What was that remark you made to Sandra on Friday?" Action!'

Marriage Scenes

A lot of duologues can be built round the lives of marriage partners or other couples who live together. Here are some examples:

> Breakfast time on the first day back at work after the honeymoon.
> She tells him she's going to have a baby.
> He comes home to tell her he's been made redundant.
> She's cooked his favourite dinner.
> He's cooked her favourite dinner.
> She hasn't cooked his dinner.
> He's been out late at the pub.
> She shouted at him that morning because the kids were under her feet. He's had a terrible day and is home late.
> He or she is having an affair and doesn't know if the other one suspects. The other doesn't.
> He or she is having an affair and this time the other one does suspect.
> They might have the mother of one of them living with them.

The Head

'The head' is an exercise in which each participant talks to an imaginary person represented by a head. Simply stand a wig block at head height on a plinth and give each participant a first line to start off in conversation with the head. The pieces are usually approximately a minute in length, but you can always put in the 'ten seconds to finish' signal from the sidelines. Remember, as well as talking to the head, each participant must listen, and react, to it as well.

First Lines

The first line provides an immediate way into a piece. The more open-ended the first line is, the better; and of course, you can sometimes make it optional. Here are some that have worked well for us:

'Promise you won't tell anyone.'
'Right! I've caught you now.'
'I've got an apology to make.'
'Please don't do that to me.'
'I've got a dreadful pain in my stomach.'
'Excuse me, I hope you don't think I'm being nosey.'
'I don't expect you had much chance to meet girls when you were at boarding school . . .'
'Trust you to spoil everything!'
'Is it the measles?'
'Look, snap out of it!'
'I don't believe it.'
'I beg your pardon.'
'It's disgusting!'
'Will you lend me . . .?'
'Don't you dare bring my mother into this!'
'Guess what happened to Mandy.'
'Chicken!'
'I'll give you three guesses what happened.'
'I've just lost Mum's purse.'
'What has your mum got against me?'
'I've told you before – the answer is *no*.'
'Stop that at once!'
'Johnny's been fired – did you know?'
'Can you keep a secret?'
'Don't you ever bring up that subject again!'
'Would you mind repeating that remark?'
'What on earth is the matter with you today?'
'Why can't you be punctual just for once?'
'Don't bite the hand that feeds you.'
'Why are you always picking on me?'
'What are you? A man or a mouse?'

'Money, money, money . . .'
'It's just not fair!'
'Why don't you ever listen to me?'
'My dog's just died . . .'
'What's the big idea, then?'
'Go on! Amaze me . . .'
'You've been talking about me behind my back, haven't you?'
'I saw you hit my little brother.'
'Don't go on and on and on about it.'
'Please don't tell her I told you.'
'What ever possessed you to do it?'
'You jealous or something?'
'He's/She's packed me in.'
'Why do you tell so many lies?'
'That's an excellent piece of work, but there's just one
    thing . . .'
'You've been chosen for a mission from which you are very
    unlikely to return . . .'
'I don't want to go to school today.'
'How can I tell him/her that it's over?'
'Do you know something? You really get up my nose.'
'Why are you always in such a bad temper?'
'Why did you tell Mum on me?'
'Dad's mad with you.'
'Don't be such a greedy-guts.'
'Stop pretending to be something you are not!'
'Don't be a dog in the manger!'
'Why can't you ever see it from my point of view?'
'Why did you hurt Mum's feelings like that?'
'You've got things out of all proportion.'
'Mum said, "Never accept lifts from strangers."'
'What a waste of money!'
'How dare you treat your pet like that?'
'I told you before, you must *not* bunk off school.'
'You're all mouth and no trousers.'
'It's easy to be an armchair critic – don't just sit there, *do*
    something.'
'Why do you give up so easily?'
'Why can't you take any criticism?'
'Haven't you got any manners?'
'Get up out of that bed immediately!'
'If you don't mind me saying so, you need to go on a diet.'

'I hate to say this, but I think you've got anorexia nervosa.'
'Look, I'm only giving you a warning.'
'Haven't you got any ambition in life?'
'Let them talk – who cares?'
'Shouting about it won't help.'
'This is absolutely the last straw.'
'You are so gullible.'
'I'm going to give you a piece of my mind.'
'You're getting a bit above yourself.'
'You haven't been very discreet, have you?'
'What do you mean by that sexist rubbish?'
'You're always making excuses! What is it this time?'
'Mum, I want to go abroad this year.'
'You really are very, very selfish.'
Scream! followed by 'You frightened the living daylights out
    of me.'
'I've had it up to here with you.'
'Grow up, will you? Act your age!'
'You're not old enough.'
'You are under my authority until you are eighteen.'
'You don't own me.'
'I'm sick to death of your prejudiced remarks.'
'Thanks for ruining my reputation.'
'You've let the cat out of the bag – that was supposed to be
    top secret.'
'Don't be a Scrooge.'
'Why are you always so nasty? Why can't you ever be nice?'
'Sarcasm is the lowest form of wit, didn't you know?'
'Look, Miss, you've got a grudge against me, haven't you?'
'What am I going to do? I'm heavily in debt.'
'Mum/Dad, can I have some more pocket money?' (Second
    line: 'More?')
'You're going to ruin your health.'
'I am not going to Nan's eightieth birthday.'
'Mum, I'm not coming home for Christmas this year.'
'You don't appreciate a thing I do.'
'No foul language in this house!'
'Sorry's just a word.'
'Don't be so pessimistic – look on the bright side.'
'Good grief! How petty can you be?'
'But, please, Mum . . .' (persuasion against will)
'How can you be so deceitful?'

'I feel sorry for you.'
'Look, I've got to get something off my chest.'

First lines can be used to start off monologues, duologues, soliloquies, or improvised plays. Sometimes you can give both the first and the second line, or even the second line only — in which case participants have a free choice of first line as long as it fits with the second. Try this with the second line 'You've just let the cat out of the bag.'

TECHNIQUE

Tongue-Twisters

Tongue-twisters provide an ideal verbal warm-up (after a vigorous physical one), being an aid to concentration, projection and diction. Four repetitions is enough for the one-liners; two or three for the longer ones. Start by saying, 'After two. One, two . . .'

Red leather, yellow leather

Red lolly, yellow lorry

Mixed biscuits

Unique New York

Richard gave Robin a rap in the ribs for roasting his rabbit so rare.

Sly Sam sips Sally's soup.

Betty bought a bit of butter,
But the butter Betty bought was bitter,
So Betty bought a better bit of butter
Than the butter Betty bought before.

Six sleek swans swam swiftly southwards.

If a gumboil could boil oil,
How much oil could a gumboil boil
If a gumboil could boil oil?

Three grey geese in a green field grazing,
Grey were the geese and green was the grazing.

How much wood would a woodchuck chuck
If a woodchuck could chuck wood?

Five flies flew round the farmyard
Frightening the farmer's friend.

Lazy Lenny licks Lucy's lolly.

Pack a copper kettle.

Round and round the rugged rocks
The ragged rascal ran.

Elly's elegant elephant

Harry from Hampstead hangs his hat on a hanger,
Hannah hangs hers on a hook in the hall.

If a good cook could cook cuckoos
How many cuckoos could a good cook cook
If a good cook could cook cuckoos?

Three fiddling pigs sit in a pit and fiddle,
Fiddle piggy, fiddle piggy, fiddle piggy.

A pleasant place to place a plaice
Is a place where a plaice
Is pleased to be placed.

I can think of thin things,
Six thin things, can you?
Yes I can think of six thin things
And of six thick things too.

Selfish shellfish.

Double bubble gum bubbles double.

Bed spreaders spread beds.
But bread spreaders spread bread.

Good blood, bad blood.

Can you imagine an imaginary menagerie manager
Imagining managing an imaginary menagerie?

Really rural.

This thistle seems like that thistle.

Sally's selfish selling shellfish
So Sally's shellfish seldom sell.

The sun shines on shop signs.

Which is the witch that wished the wicked wish?

Miss Smith dismisseth us.

Silver thimbles.

Peggy Babcock.

Tuesday is stewday, stewday is Tuesday.

For sheep soup — shoot sheep.

Super thick sticky tape.

This slim spider slid slowly sideways.

If you notice this notice you'll notice this notice is not worth noticing.

Pink pomegranate, purple pomegranate.

Once you start collecting tongue twisters your list will grow and grow. Once word gets round, the children will be forever adding to it. But, as with all ideas, do keep a record.

Stage Presence

Some people talk about stage presence as if it is a gift that one either does or does not have. Although some people do indisputably have it naturally, it is possible for anyone to improve their stage presence by developing their technique. What people need to do is to overcome and disguise their natural feelings of shyness. Some of the secrets of stage presence are:

Stillness   Avoiding body fidgeting, small hand and head movements, face-touching.

Energy   Both in movement and use of the voice. Fitness is the key to this.

Controlled Aggression   To be successful any performer must be prepared to give it everything and 'go for it'.

Crispness of Persona
Eye Contact
Total Concentration

The following exercises can be used to develop these aspects of stage presence.

Eye Contact   A group of people stroll down a beach and each of them fixes his eyes on something that interests him in the water. The 'something' is in the same position as the eyes of someone in the audience.

Dominance   Two science-fiction creatures confront each other. After a while one prevails and the other backs down without a fight. Freeze in the positions of dominance and submission.

Mastermind Plus   The 'victims' are spotlit in a chair and are grilled with harder and harder questions. If they don't know the answers they are made to work them out. Through all this they have to maintain a calm appearance. They are 'out' if they touch their face, fidget their hands, body or feet, shrug or laugh.

Energy Contest   Two people try to race each other round parallel courses of equal length. Anyone giving maximum energy, win or lose, passes the test and is allowed to have a rest. Those who fail have to race again against someone else.

Addressing the Rally   On the eve of an election, a political candidate in a country where democracy is threatened addresses a rally in a football stadium. He must make a final emotional appeal to the people to save the country. He must offer the last drop of his blood to them and give them a vision of the future they can still have. Nothing less than total commitment will be enough.

Script-Reading

If you're doing mainly improvisation-based drama, it makes a change occasionally to do script-reading. Apart from being practice at the generally useful skill of reading at sight, it is a good way of extending your students' knowledge of plays.

In any typical group of youngsters, you will find many who are either dyslexic or else poor sight-readers for one reason or another. Often the memory of past humiliations will add to their nervousness and make things worse. It is worth reassuring them that many people have reading difficulties – for example, the actress Susan Hampshire – and it is best to start with something as easy to read as you can find. If possible give them some time to read over and prepare what they are going to do. One useful tip is to encourage them to read at a slow pace; not only will this help them read more accurately, but it will also help them to read with good expression and intonation. Encourage them to read with natural pauses and not at one pace like a dictation exercise. Tell them to 'read the punctuation': a comma is a short pause, a full stop a longer one. Believability is still essential; they must imagine themselves right inside the part, even though they are reading it off the page. If someone makes a mistake, the natural tendency is to hurry up, as if to make up for lost time, and this often leads to more mistakes, so a good piece of advice is: 'If you make a mistake, slow down.'

VIDEO WORK

Many schools and clubs now have access to video equipment, so here are some suggestions for effective ways of using it. The first problem to overcome is the embarrassment barrier of seeing and hearing oneself on the screen for the first time. Everyone, particularly adolescents, seems to find that no one else looks and sounds as peculiar as they do. Anything that makes people self-conscious in their acting is not going to be helpful, so it is a good idea to start with students who are already well used to improvising and to have a first familiarization session purely so that they can be in front of the camera and see what they look and sound like on the screen.

Recording a lesson as it happens and then pointing out things and commenting on playback is a useful way of using video as a general teaching tool. Remember that playback takes just as long as recording, so if you are going to record a whole session and then watch it that will halve the amount of time you can use on the session. Then you can start to work on some of the elements of screen acting. The audience sees the actors from much nearer, particularly in close-up, so all effects are magnified and it is necessary to underplay relative to what one would do with a theatre audience. The actor must avoid exaggerated facial expressions and sudden movements that would take him out of camera shot. Talking to camera, a television technique, requires the subject to look directly at the lens and speak to it, imagining it to be a person he or she is talking to. Any look away from camera needs to be positive or it will look oddly surreptitious.

Video opens out possibilities of exploring subtlety in performances, particularly in work involving emotional reactions where you can use the direction 'The emotion is still there, but the character's not showing it.' It is particularly useful for character work and ideas such as the 'in-depth interview', which, being an imaginary television interview, works every bit as well when videoed, whether in preparation for a production or not.

If you do a production, it is nice to have a video recording as a permanent record. Doing this at a dress rehearsal rather than at a performance gives you more freedom of choice of camera positions, and also gives you the option of rerunning a scene if necessary. The next step is to mount your own video productions and, depending on the technical resources you have available, the sky's the limit.